Franz Zach / Rene Gromes

DURCHSTARTEN IN ENGLISCH

ENGLISCH
FÜR DIE 8. SCHULSTUFE

LÖSUNGSHEFT

KERLE
LERNHILFEN
MÜNCHEN
WIEN

DER ARTIKEL *(THE ARTICLE)*

DER BESTIMMTE ARTIKEL *(THE DEFINITE ARTICLE)*

Übung 1 (Seite 12)
1 Girls like wearing/to wear jeans. 2 I like butter and cheese. 3 Jam is made from fruits. 4 Brazil exports a lot of (very much) coffee. 5 There is (You have got) sand in your hair. 6 We need air to breathe. 7 Look at page 7. 8 Gold is heavier than iron.

Übung 2 (Seite 12)
1 I often ride my bike to school. 2 Jets (Jetplanes) can fly higher than helicopters. 3 Most children enjoy summer. 4 To many children TV (television) is very important. 5 The stranger had black hair and brown eyes. 6 Mary likes to go shopping to town. 7 I'd like to go to bed now. 8 Many jungle animals are in great danger.

Übung 3 (Seite 13)
1 The Masters have got a house on the Scilly Isles. 2 Vienna is situated on the Danube. 3 Charles Lindbergh was the first man that crossed the Atlantic. 4 Mr Fredericks works only in the morning and in the evening. 5 He usually sleeps in the afternoon. 6 The Tower of London is famous all over the world. 7 The autumn of (the year) 1991 was cool and wet. 8 My little brother was born on the evening of May 5 (the fifth of May).

Übung 4 (Seite 14)
1 My Dad always told me stories in the evening. 2 The air is cool today. 3 Sally goes to (attends) the same school as her Mum. 4 It was love at first sight. 5 The girl by the window doesn't feel good. 6 Most girls don't like violent (brutal) films. 7 Peter would like to have a house in the country. 8 The coffee is very hot; you have to put in (some) milk.

Übung 5 (Seite 14)
1 In winter the days are shorter and the nights are longer than in summer. 2 I bought my new bike with the money I got from Grandma. 3 All the boys of the "4a" have to go and see the doctor now. 4 I'm sorry I'm late. I'll try to be on time next time. 5 I saw Julia for the first time in the summer of 1992. 6 The Lake District is in the north of England. 7 Pepper and salt are not on the table. 8 It was love at first sight.

Flagge 1 (Seite 15)
1 In the evening the air is usually cooler than during the day. 2 Air and water are necessary to survive. 3 Love and friendship can help us a lot. 4 "The Life of Brian" is one of the funniest films I have ever seen. 5 Cheese is made from milk. 6 How did you like the cheese we had for supper last night? 7 There were dark clouds in the sky when we left the village. 8 Fish live in water and birds fly through the air. 9 I love music very much, especially the music of Kurt Ostbahn. 10 Television is a serious problem for many families. 11 It takes time and money to collect diamonds. 12 Tennis is a very popular sport among (the) young and (the) old. 13 The tennis that Thomas Muster plays is really fantastic sometimes. 14 There is dirt on the back of your shirt.

DER UNBESTIMMTE ARTIKEL *(THE INDEFINITE ARTICLE)*

Übung 6 (Seite 16)
1 A cat can be a good friend. 2 A koala bear is not an ordinary animal. 3 A horse can easily jump over a bush. 4 A cow gives us milk, a bull doesn't. 5 A supermarket is a boring place for a young person. 6 A TV-set and a telephone can be found in nearly every household. 7 An honest person is respected by everybody. 8 A banana and an orange a day give your body enough vitamins.

Übung 7 (Seite 18)
1 Mr Wilson was made headmaster of the new school. 2 He has been a teacher for 21 years. 3 Last year Aunt Lisa turned Protestant after being (a) Catholic for 45 years. 4 My Dad was elected chairman of the conference. 5 Knives are made of metal and plastic or wood. 6 Animals must have food and water to survive. 7 I eat an apple every evening before I go to bed. 8 I think Mac will be a lawyer when he grows up.

Übung 8 (Seite 19)
1 I've got half a litre of milk here. 2 What a sad story! 3 It was quite a good film, but not a great one. 4 That's too dangerous a development. 5 Frank has such a good voice that he always . . . . 6 The train arrived half an hour later than usual. 7 It was such a bad car crash that the passengers were taken to hospital. 8 It was too cold a night for camping.

Übung 9 (Seite 19)
1 What a nice girl Betty is! 2 That was quite a nice party at Ulla's (place). 3 What a silly mistake! 4 In 1994 we had such a cold winter that many animals froze to death. 5 That was too easy a question for Jim. He is our genius. 6 Today was (has been) such a hot day! 7 What a nice surprise! Peggy and Sue are here. 8 Mary was too clever an opponent for me. 9 You have half a week to think it over (to think about it). 10 Conny is quite/rather a pretty girl.

Flagge 2 (Seite 20)
1 There is an ugly insect in my beer. I hate beer with insects! 2 The video tape on the shelf is about a (the) woman who walked all the way to the North Pole and back. 3 It is nice to play a game of chess in a café. 4 Most people love

nature. 5 I like the grapes you brought us yesterday. 6 Look, there are clouds in the sky. You'd better take an umbrella. 7 The clouds over the lake are lovely. What a beautiful day!
8 Mother is a teacher at the school she used to attend when she was young. 9 The first day of school was too exciting a day for Steven.
10 Life is hard, but the life of my dog isn't! The dog has an easy life! 11 F.D.R. was President of the United States from 1932 to 1945. He was the President with the longest term of office.
12 Mac and Charlie are fond of grapes with cheese.

DAS ZEITWORT *(THE VERB)*

SIMPLE FORM UND *PROGRESSIVE FORM*

Übung 1 (Seite 26)
1 We are discussing the problem at the moment. Please . . . 2 Bob, what are you doing at the moment? – I'm having a cup of tea, you know.
3 Wait a moment! I'm trying to get my things into my bag. 4 Look, the ambulance is coming down the street! 5 Now I'm writing, but you can . . . 6 Look, the cat is sleeping. Let's not . . . 7 Listen, I am talking to you! 8 Dad is cooking lunch today, but don't go into the kitchen! You know . . .

Übung 2 (Seite 27)
1 Look, your mother is doing a step-dance! – I know. She often does that. 2 The sun shines by day, the stars shine at night. 3 Bad teachers never do good work. 4 Herman usually plays chess, but at the moment he is playing dominoes.
5 Listen, it is raining! – That's strange. It never rains here in August. 6 Dad is . . . . He is repairing my bike. I need it to get to school.
7 He always tries to repair things that do not work. 8 Listen, "Satan" is barking! – Yes! Something is making a noise outside.

Übung 3 (Seite 28)
1 While Sue was playing the piano, Jessie and I were talking about the holidays. 2 It was just beginning to snow when we arrived at the airport.
3 Tom and Steve were watching TV when the phone rang. 4 Sally was painting her fingernails while Tony was drying his hair. 5 Yesterday at 4 p.m. we were having our afternoon tea.
6 The baby was trying to sleep while Mum was hoovering the floor. 7 I was thinking of going to bed when Paul arrived with a new video tape.
8 Mac and Charlie were lying in the sun when a strong wind suddenly carried . . .

Übung 4 (Seite 28)
1 While we were watching TV last night we heard a strange noise outside. 2 I was trying to concentrate while Hilary was telling me about her boyfriend. 3 Teddy was looking for his glasses when the telephone rang. 4 Sheila was walking across the street when her hat blew off. 5 It was raining heavily when Frank got up in the morning. 6 The sun was shining when I came back home. 7 At 10 in the morning the lights were still burning. 8 I cut my finger while I was peeling apples.

Übung 5 (Seite 30)
1 Olivia has liked Sebastian since their schooldays.
2 Have you heard from Tim? We have not seen each other for some time. 3 I have not had enough time to finish reading the book . . . .
4 Uncle Rick and Aunt Annie have not eaten any meat for years. 5 They have been vegetarians since their holiday in India. 6 How . . .? She has not called me since my birthday. 7 Dad's old trousers are very dirty. He has been wearing them for over a week. 8 It has not rained in some parts of Africa for more than ten years.

Übung 6 (Seite 31)
1 I am really tired. I have been doing the same things for hours now. 2 Look at Wendy! She has been sleeping like this since three o'clock.
3 I'm at the station at the moment. I've been waiting for Judy for half an hour. 4 I've been trying to read this story for weeks. I wonder . . . .
5 What have you been doing with yourself since I last saw you? – Well, I finished school and I found a job. I've been training as an electrician for two years now, and I have two more years to go.
6 I know this town well. I have lived/have been living here since 1989. 7 My grandmother is ill. She has been lying in bed for two weeks now, and she is slowly getting better. 8 Maxwell has been playing computer games since six o'clock. He really ought to stop now.

Übung 7 (Seite 31)
1 I have been standing here since 6 o'clock; where have you been? 2 Fred has not visited Spain yet, but he has been learning Spanish for a whole year. 3 How long have you known Ellie? – Oh, for . . . . 4 I've been waiting for a taxi for a quarter of an hour, but it hasn't come yet.
5 Mr Schmidt has been talking about *present perfect tense* for a week, and now I think I under-stand. 6 Regina has been working in Paris since last February. She has not been back since then.
7 . . ., and we have not spoken to each other for weeks. 8 Our cat has been sleeping in her basket since this morning. I hope . . . .

Flagge 1 (Seite 32)
1 The little lady who is passing by our house right now lives next door. 2 Valentina is not at home. She is spending this weekend at her grand-mother's. She visits her once or twice every month. 3 Why are you doing your homework now and not at home, Walter? – I usually do it at home, sir, but I forgot. I'm sorry! 4 What are you looking at? – These pictures. They are great. I like good pictures. 5 Listen to those girls! They are making a lot of noise. – Yes! I always have to tell them to be quiet. 6 Fritz is flying to

Houston, Texas, today. He often goes to America on business trips. 7 On my way to the sports club I often meet Jim and Laura. They are in the same club as I. 8 Now I know the answer to question 3! – Don't tell me! I'm still thinking, and I want to answer the question by myself.

Flagge 2 (Seite 32)
1 I was looking out of the window when I saw Martin riding my bike. 2 Ted was having a cup of coffee when the toaster fell from the shelf. 3 Clarissa was singing while Francis was playing the piano. 4 We drank tea and ate cucumber sandwiches every day when we were in London. 5 When I met Veronica in town yesterday, she was wearing a miniskirt. 6 Dad was laying the table for dinner while the guests were having a drink at the bar. 7 What were you doing at 5:30 on Friday morning? – I think I was driving to work. 8 I was thinking about Monica when I had an idea. I rang her up and asked her if she wanted to go to the concert with me on Saturday. She said yes! I was the happiest man on earth!

Flagge 3 (Seite 33)
1 Tell me what you have been doing since I last saw you. 2 These photos have been lying on the desk for days. Has everybody looked at them? – No, I have not seen them yet. 3 I haven't been here for ten years, so I wonder what has changed in the village. 4 Dad hasn't had a day off this month. He has been working for three weeks now without a break. 5 I've been trying to call you since eight o'clock. Where have you been? 6 We have been working hard all week to finish our tree house; I think we'll be able to use it in a week or two. 7 Little Mary has been running around in the rain without shoes for hours. I wonder if she has caught a cold already. 8 Mr Ross has been teaching us music for half a year now, but we haven't heard a single record or CD so far.

Übung 8 (Seite 34 und 35)
1 I haven't seen Anita for more than a month. – That's no surprise. She was in Australia until last Sunday. 2 Hans gave me this book a week ago, but I have not read it yet. 3. When I came home last night, you were sleeping like a log. 4 I haven't seen this film for over a year, but I remember that we went to the cinema together then. 5 It was raining when we came home last night, and it hasn't stopped since then. 6 Ben has called you three times already, but you were (have been) gone all the time. 7 We bought the tickets two months ago. 8 My brother, who is in Australia at the moment, has not written to us for more than a month. We got his latest letter five weeks ago. 9 Look, Mum has made a cake! – Yes, she baked it while you were playing tennis. 10 Have you seen Dennis today? – No, not today, but I spoke with him yesterday. 11 Have you ever been to Monaco for the Grand Prix? – Yes, once. Dad and I drove there last year, and we enjoyed it very much. 12 While we were watching the race, somebody broke into our car and stole the radio.

Flagge 4 (Seite 35)
1 Where's Kevin? – I've no idea. I haven't seen him in the last twenty minutes. The last time I saw him he was talking to Lucy. 2 How was the "Rolling Stones" concert? – Fantastic! I've never seen such a great show before. 3 You ought to go to bed now, Ernie. You have worked/have been working long enough. – I know, but Mr Kane called this morning. He said . . . . 4 Arnold Schwarzenegger left Austria when he was 21. He has made more than 15 films since then. 5 Look, the new uniforms have arrived! We have waited/have been waiting long enough. 6 I sent a letter to "Greenpeace" last week, and now they have answered. 7 Dad caught a big fish yesterday. We have just eaten it. 8 Alina wrote a long essay last weekend, but she forgot to bring it today.

Übung 9 (Seite 36)
1 . . . he will be sleeping soundly. 2 You will still be repairing that clock in the middle of the night . . . . 3 I tell you, you will be doing your homework today and not tomorrow! 4 . . . with me. I will be waiting for you here in an hour. 5 Gloria is your sister, so you'll be helping her, if . . . . 6 This time tomorrow you will be playing your first big match. 7 . . . goes well, you will be crossing the Channel this time next week. 8 It will still be raining when you come back in the evening.

Übung 10 (Seite 37)
1 . . . came home, I had not done any of my tasks. 2 After the guests had left, we went to bed and . . . . 3 . . . after we had finished our work in the garden. 4 After I had taken a shower, I put on . . . . 5 James thanked me for what I had done for him. 6 We had lost our way before we got to the hotel. 7 Eve left the hospital after she had been there for two days. 8 Gertrude went to the doctor after she had fallen and hurt her elbow. (Nicht *had hurt*; das wäre eine Wortwiederholung.)

Übung 11 (Seite 38)
1 Martin told me that he had been sleeping all afternoon. 2 Doris said on the phone that she had been waiting for me for hours. 3 I heard that Frank had been studying for the test for three weeks. 4 Mum was angry because the lights had been burning all night. 5 I found out that Birgit had been practicing tennis since she was a little girl. 6 Dad informed his boss that he had been trying to find a better job for weeks. 7 I knew that Vanessa had been living in London since 1986. 8 . . . his holiday, he realized that somebody had been taking his mail out of the mailbox while he was gone. 9 Joe realized that Monica had been crying while he was gone. 10 We had been dancing for some time when

Julia and Robert arrived. 11 Mr Olson was angry when he saw that we had been playing in his driveway during his absence. 12 The car had been standing in front of our house for two weeks before they removed it.

Übung 12 (Seite 38)
1 I went home after I had finished my work.
2 Our guests told us that they had already seen the Tower of London. 3 Kurt told me that he had been waiting for me for several hours.
4 Harry said that he had been sleeping at home when I tried to ring him up. 5 In the paper I read that a terrible fire had broken out in my home town. 6 Our geography teacher asked us which European capitals we had visited. 7 We were surprised to hear that Tanja had been able to read and write at the age of four. 8 I wanted to tell you that the old man had been living in that house for more than forty years.

Übung 13 (Seite 39)
1 The Fords went to the theatre last week. They usually try to go once or twice every month. 2 I normally write with a pen, but today I am using my Dad's ballpoint. 3 After all her friends had arrived, Mary began to play the violin. 4 Quick, hurry! Mum is coming home in a minute and we haven't tidied the kitchen yet. 5 Fritz told me that he has been collecting stamps for five years. It is still . . . . 6 I had never seen a volcano before we went on holiday to Sicily. There we climbed up Mt. Aetna, which had broken out the year before.
7 Julius has been staying at the same campground for fifteen years. He has never gone to a different place. 8 Grass grows best in a mild and wet climate, such as in England.

Flagge 5 (Seite 39)
1 I have been working day and night since last week, but I haven't finished the book. 2 After I had written my first short story, I noticed that I had a lot of talent. 3 When I saw Harry two days ago, he was just getting off a bus./. . ., he had just got off a bus. 4 I threw away my old "Swatch" yesterday because Grandma had bought me a new one. 5 Have you heard?/Did you hear? Gertie won/has won the first prize in the lottery. This time next month she will be lying on a sunny beach somewhere in the Caribbean.
6 Uncle Edward said that he was sorry that he had forgotten my Christmas present again.
7 Michelle told me that she had been studying Russian for the last three years. This time next year she will be attending the University of Moscow.
8 I have not heard from Linda for some time. I wonder what she is doing at the moment.

DIE NENNFORM *(THE INFINITIVE)*

Übung 14 (Seite 43)
1 . . . your visit. We hope to see you again very soon. 2 . . ., but they promised to find it as soon as possible. 3 Do you want to eat now or later? – Later . . . 4 You must study . . ., Alan. You can't afford to get another bad mark. 5 . . . very friendly. He offered to show us around the castle himself. 6 Don't shout at me! I refuse to talk to you if you shout at me! 7 If you happen to hear from Sandra, tell her that . . . . 8 What's the matter, Dominic? You seem to be angry at someone. 9 What do you expect to do in Washington? – Well, we want to visit all the important sights. 10 . . . a new bike, and he agreed to lend me half of the money.
11 . . . works very fast. He always manages to return our tests in the next lesson. 12 Charlie decided to call Susi. He asked her to go to the cinema with him.

Übung 15 (Seite 44)
1 Congratulations! You have managed to convince me. 2 You must promise not to tell this story to anybody. 3 Look at Benny! He seems to enjoy the walk. 4 Can we afford to go on winterholiday this year? 5 More and more people refuse to eat meat. 6 I happened to notice that I had no petrol left. 7 Mr Brown agreed to give the opening address. 8 We decided to ask Brian for advice. 9 We hope to see you again next year. 10 I expect to have no problems in school this year. 11 We are planning to stay here till Sunday. 12 Susi: "Charlie, where did you learn to dance?" ("Where have you learned/learnt to dance?")

Übung 16 (Seite 45)
1 . . . in the house. I didn't see them come out.
2 They did not let us use our dictionaries, so I don't know . . . . 3 Look at the clock! We'd better leave at once or we'll be late again.
4 Shall I put the books on the table or on the shelf, Tony? – . . . 5 I'd rather go on a bike tour than to school. 6 Bill, I think I heard someone call your name. – That . . . . 7 . . ., but Dad made us stay at home and get ready for the test today. 8 . . . watch TV now. I'd rather take a walk with my dog. 9 . . ., Joe. You'd better tell him about it. 10 . . . very nice. They often let us swim in their pool. 11 I'm sorry, but there is nothing I can do about this situation.
12 . . ., Miss? – I'd rather have a glass of milk, please.

Übung 17 (Seite 45 und 46)
1 Who has heard Mary come home? – All of us.
2 You need not worry; we are fine. 3 Our coach made us run 2 500 m today. 4 I (can) see something move over there. 5 Mike, Bob is here. – Let him wait. 6 I'd rather go to the beach than stay in the room. 7 Where are you now, Jackie? I must (have to) tell you a funny story. 8 Shall I come again on Monday, Mr Williams? – Yes, of course. 9 We'd better ask Andy for advice. Andy is the expert. 10 You'd better take an umbrella with you.

Flagge 6 (Seite 46)
1 We were planning to go to Switzerland in summer, but then Fred got ill and so we decided to stay at home. 2 You must practice harder if you want to be the Number One player. 3 I don't think you can afford to buy two CDs every month. You had better spend the money on other things or save it. 4 I hear you play the violin every day. Are you learning to play it? – Yes, I promised my Mum to practice as often as I could. 5 I promised to write to you and I will write, but don't expect to get a letter very soon. 6 Mrs Benson has offered to take us to the station in her car, but I'd rather walk because it's such a lovely morning. 7 Dad agreed to let me drive when I'm sixteen. 8 Yesterday I watched Mr Dobbs dig a big hole in his garden. He said he wanted to plant a walnut tree. 9 Uncle Peter says he may visit the Statue of Liberty when he is in New York and he promised to send me a postcard. 10 In our summer holidays Dad managed to catch the biggest fish I have ever seen.

Übung 18 (Seite 47)
1 It is difficult/impossible to know what you really want. 2 Little kittens are often fun to watch. 3 Mt. Everest was not easy to climb. 4 We are sorry to bring you bad news: . . . . 5 It was terrible/fun to see those photographs. 6 I think it is impossible to grow rice in Germany or Austria. 7 We should be happy to live in a peaceful country. 8 Caroline, are you ready to go now? – . . .

Übung 19 (Seite 48)
1 You are lucky to be Frank's friend. 2 I was surprised to see Judy walk into the room. 3 Andrew was happy to be in Canada at last. 4 Doris was shocked to discover the broken window. 5 We are very pleased to welcome you here. (We are very pleased to be able to welcome you here.) 6 After the plane had crashed the pilot was happy to be alive. 7 I was sorry to hear about your accident. 8 Betty was glad to get a letter from her boyfriend.

Übung 20 (Seite 49)
1 Who can tell us where to put the books? 2 Christopher was so surprised that he did not know what to say. 3 The old lady was not sure what to do, so . . . . 4 Linda could not remember where to get off the tram. 5 A farmer told us where to find mushrooms. 6 Can anyone tell me who to ask? 7 The children asked themselves when to be back. 8 Daniel had no idea what to do about the problem. 9 I did not know who to send for the doctor. 10 Peter showed me how to install Windows '95.

Übung 21 (Seite 49)
1 Detective: "Mr Jones, you are the last person to see the man alive." 2 Marco Polo was the first European to spend some years in China. 3 Johnny, you were the only one to ask in this situation. 4 The best thing to do was to wait. 5 Franzi von Almsieck is the only swimmer to win four gold medals. 6 The captain is usually the last person to leave a sinking ship.

Übung 22 (Seite 50)
1 The man was too nervous to sit still. 2 My grandpa has (got) enough time to repair my bike. 3 Dad is too careful to have an accident. 4 We have not enough water left to go on. 5 There were enough people to push the car to the nearest garage. 6 There's enough flour to bake three cakes with it. 7 Julius is too young to drive. 8 Our cat is too lazy to chase a mouse.

Flagge 7 (Seite 51)
1 The doctor thinks that Mr Webster is too old to drive a car. 2 The mechanic showed me how to start the engine. 3 We did not know where to hide our cigarettes. 4 Joe was surprised to meet Karin in Madrid. 5 The Coopers cannot decide when to go on holiday. 6 Reinhold Messner was the first person to climb Mt. Everest without the . . . . 7 Veronica and Tim were not sure what to tell their parents. 8 I was glad to go home again. (I was glad to be able to go home again.) 9 I've got enough books to fill a library. 10 . . ., but he was not the only student to do so. 11 We were lucky to find a hotel room. 12 A snowstorm in May was the last thing to expect. (. . . to be expected.) 13 It was too cold to play outside. 14 Are you happy to meet Richard's parents? 15 The best to do against a headache is . . . . 16 I was too tired to think about the problem. 17 There's too little snow to go skiing. (There is not enough snow to go skiing.) 18 The driver was shocked to realize what had happened.

Übung 23 (Seite 53)
1 Joe half uns, unser altes Auto zu reparieren. (Er half uns bei der Reparatur unseres alten Autos.) 2 Darf ich Sie einladen zu bleiben? 3 Wir wissen, daß Mary ein kluges Mädchen ist. 4 Der Captain (Hauptmann) befahl seinen Männern aufzuhören. 5 Erinnere mich bitte daran, Maggie anzurufen. 6 Ich kann euch (dir) zeigen, wie man Pizza macht. 7 Wer hat dir (euch) beigebracht, so gut zu singen? 8 Laura sagte, ich solle hier auf sie warten. 9 Wir wollen (möchten), daß du die Wahrheit sagst. 10 Ich wünsche, daß sie den Raum verlassen.

Übung 24 (Seite 54)
1 I expect you all to work hard. 2 Julia wanted me to come with her. 3 Oliver wants us to visit him at the weekend. 4 My Grandma reminded me to buy a present for Mother. 5 Mr Graham allowed (permitted) us to play in his meadow. 6 We know Sabine to like musicals. 7 Jenny asked me to inform her parents. 8 Can you show me how to open this bottle? 9 I don't want (wish) you to read this article. 10 Mrs Feinstein told (ordered) Martin to return the

money at once. 11 Many men expect women to cook and clean the house. 12 Wendy does not want Alec to dance with her.

Flagge 8 (Seite 54)
1 Mr Tompkins asked me to get (fetch) the newspaper. 2 The audience expects everybody to do their best. 3 The old people on the train told us to be quiet. 4 I would like you to come to my birthday party. (I want you to come . . .)
5 My parents allowed (permitted) me to travel around with my friends for a week. 6 The general ordered the troops to attack. 7 Larry helped us to build the garage. 8 The customs officer told us to open our (the) suitcases.
9 The policeman ordered (told) the man to leave the café. 10 Who can show me how to start this car?

DAS GERUND *(THE GERUND)*

Übung 25 (Seite 57 und 58)
1 Smoking is an expensive habit. 2 Learning English can be hard, but speaking it is getting very important. 3 Programming a computer is more difficult than playing computer games. 4 Skateboarding and snowboarding have become very popular among kids. 5 I really hate listening to boring people. 6 Meeting Gina is always a nice surprise. Do you enjoy talking to her, too?
7 Nancy loves jogging but she doesn't like running fast. 8 I have always disliked watching violent programs on TV.

Übung 26 (Seite 58)
1 The man admitted stealing the jewels. (Der Mann gestand, die Juwelen gestohlen zu haben.)
2 I always avoid getting into a fight if I can. (Wenn ich kann, vermeide ich es immer, in einen Streit/Kampf verwickelt zu werden.) 3 A year ago Jack considered moving back to England. (Vor einem Jahr dachte Jack darüber nach, zurück nach England zu ziehen.) 4 Do you really dislike dancing so much? (Tanzt du wirklich so ungern?)
5 My Dad enjoys drinking a glass of beer in the evening. (Mein Vater trinkt am Abend gern ein Glas Bier.) 6 Fred finished doing his homework in time for "Star Trek". (Fred wurde rechtzeitig vor „Star Trek" mit seiner Hausaufgabe fertig.)
7 Forgive me (for) calling you so late in the evening, but I need your help. (Verzeih mir, daß ich dich so spät am Abend anrufe, aber ich benötige deine Hilfe.) 8 Can you imagine living in Beverly Hills and becoming a filmstar? (Kannst du dir vorstellen, in Beverly Hills zu leben und ein Filmstar zu werden?) 9 Did I mention seeing "Mona Lisa" in Paris? (Habe ich schon erwähnt, daß ich die „Mona Lisa" in Paris sah?) 10 . . ., Paula. I don't mind waiting. (Du mußt dich nicht beeilen, Paula. Es macht mir nichts aus, wenn ich warte.) 11 . . ., Victoria. I really missed talking to you. (Ich bin froh, daß du wieder da bist, Victoria. Ich habe es sehr vermißt, mit dir zu sprechen.) 12 . . . we should practice reading German aloud. (Mrs Reynolds sagte, wir sollten deutsch laut lesen üben.)

Übung 27 (Seite 59)
1 My little brother (has) admitted breaking the vase. 2 If you can, avoid talking to Caspar.
3 I'm considering giving 50 Schillings to the Red Cross. 4 Fritz dislikes getting up early. 5 He enjoys sleeping long at the weekend. 6 The workers finished digging the tunnel yesterday.
7 You risk catching a cold if you go out(side) without a warm jacket. 8 I suggest going to the cinema today. 9 We should practice singing more often. 10 I often imagine travelling to Hawaii. 11 Doris does not mind tidying up (cleaning) the room by herself. 12 My Grandpa misses playing chess with his friends.

Übung 28 (Seite 60)
1 I am afraid of losing my keys, and so . . . .
2 Nobody thought that we were capable of doing it, but we showed them! 3 . . . to bed although he was far from finishing his work.
4 My family and I are fond of inviting friends to a barbeque. 5 Listen to Johnny! He's really good at imitating people. 6 Who is interested in finding out how the story ends? 7 Linda says she is proud of being my friend. 8 What a mess! Who is responsible for tidying up in here?
9 Hello, Andy! I am surprised at seeing you here.
10 Let's go home. I'm tired of listening to this boring speech. 11 . . . – I'm just tired from playing football all afternoon. 12 Mike is not used to running around so much.

Übung 29 (Seite 61)
1 Martin is good at skiing. 2 He is proud of winning so many races. 3 He is used to practicing many hours every week. 4 He is also interested in snowboarding. 5 Sometimes he is very tired from skiing. 6 And sometimes he is afraid of falling. 7 But he is far from quitting.
8 Sometimes he is tired of answering so many stupid questions.

Übung 30 (Seite 62)
1 I apologized for being late, but . . . . (Ich entschuldigte mich für mein Zuspätkommen, aber . . .) 2 My Dad believes in doing important things himself. (Mein Vater glaubt, daß es besser ist, wenn er wichtige Dinge selbst erledigt.)
3 Modern economy depends on getting information from all over the world. (Die moderne Wirtschaft hängt von der Informationsbeschaffung aus aller Welt ab.) 4 . . . today. I don't feel like going out. (Mir ist nicht nach Ausgehen zumute.)
5 Two policemen prevented a young man from jumping into the river. (Zwei Polizisten hinderten einen jungen Mann daran, in den Fluß zu springen.) 6 If you still make mistakes, go on practicing until you can do it. (Wenn du noch immer Fehler machst, übe weiter, bis du es kannst.) 7 Marion insisted on paying for her

drinks herself. (Marion bestand darauf, selbst für ihre Getränke zu zahlen.) 8 Mum had a cold, so we had to put off driving to Munich. (Mutter hatte sich erkältet, und so mußten wir unsere Fahrt nach München verschieben.) 9 Everybody in my class is looking forward to seeing "Frankenstein" at the theatre next week. (Alle in meiner Klasse freuen sich darauf, „Frankenstein" nächste Woche im Theater zu sehen.)
10 Grandma sometimes talks of selling her house and moving to our place. (Oma spricht manchmal davon, ihr Haus zu verkaufen und zu uns zu ziehen.) 11 Thanks for looking after our cats while . . . . (Danke, daß Sie auf unsere Katzen aufgepaßt haben, während wir . . .) 12 Don't worry about losing your way. There are . . . . (Machen Sie sich keine Gedanken darüber, daß Sie sich verirren könnten. Es gibt . . .) 13 Herbert has been talking about crossing the Sahara for years. (Herbert spricht schon seit Jahren davon, die Sahara zu durchqueren.) 14 David Copperfield usually succeeds in fascinating his audiences. (David Copperfield gelingt es für gewöhnlich, seine Zuseher zu faszinieren/begeistern.)

Übung 31 (Seite 62 und 63)
1 We could not keep Uncle Richard from jumping into the pond. 2 I often worry about falling ill. 3 William often talks of climbing Mt. Everest. 4 The tourist thanked me for showing him the way. 5 I had never thought of winning the race. 6 Do you feel like swimming today? – Yes! We are looking forward to seeing who is the fastest. 7 You read very well, Linda. Please go on (keep on) reading! 8 Uncle Richard insisted on driving home from the party himself.

Übung 32 (Seite 63)
1 Carl took the bus home instead of waiting for his mother. 2 Instead of standing around here doing nothing, you could help me. 3 Dad tried to repair the car himself instead of taking it to the garage. 4 Lea was so tired that she went to bed without brushing her teeth. 5 You can't come into this room without knocking. 6 I'm not going to leave without talking to Mr Brown first!

Übung 33 (Seite 64)
1 The little boy ran across the street without looking left or right. 2 Father went fishing with Uncle Richard instead of fixing my bike.
3 Instead of reading the newspaper, Oscar threw it into the wastepaper basket. 4 Oscar threw the newspaper into the wastepaper basket without reading it. 5 René left the room without saying a word. 6 You should be/ought to be happy about Peter's plans instead of worrying.

Übung 34 (Seite 65)
1 It's no use asking Bill for help. He is too busy doing his own things. 2 . . . was over, Susi couldn't help crying. 3 . . . book. It's really worth reading. 4 It's little use trying to grow bananas in Austria. 5 Austria is a country worth visiting. 6 . . . money. Now he is busy spending it again. 7 . . . person! One cannot help liking him. 8 . . . terrible. I can't stand listening to her.

Übung 35 (Seite 65)
1 When Bertie tells jokes, I cannot help laughing. (Wenn Bertie Witze erzählt, muß ich einfach lachen.) Gerund nach *cannot help*. 2 Martha was so tired that she was incapable of driving. (Martha war so müde, daß sie nicht fähig war, zu fahren.) Gerund nach *to be incapable of*. 3 I really like art, but I'm far from understanding this picture. (Ich mag Kunst, aber ich bin weit davon entfernt, dieses Bild zu verstehen.) Gerund nach *to be far from*. 4 Carlo is fond of eating pizza and drinking wine. He is . . . (Carlo ißt gern Pizza und trinkt gern Wein. Er ist . . .) Gerund nach *to be fond of*. 5 Vreni has always been interested in learning more about foreign lands. (Vreni war schon immer daran interessiert, mehr über fremde Länder zu lernen.) Gerund nach *to be interested in*. 6 . . . evening. I'm looking forward to seeing you again soon. (. . . Abend. Ich freue mich darauf, dich/Sie bald wieder zu sehen.) Gerund nach *to look forward to*. 7 Who is responsible for cleaning the floor? (Wer ist für die Reinigung des Fußbodens verantwortlich?) Gerund nach *to be responsible for*. 8 I'm used to drinking tea in the morning. (Ich bin es gewöhnt, am Morgen Tee zu trinken.) Gerund nach *to be used to*. 9 I'm tired of working so much for school. (Ich habe es satt, so viel für die Schule zu arbeiten.) Gerund nach *to be tired of*.
10 Anthony apologized for starting the fight. (Anton entschuldigte sich dafür, daß er mit dem Kampf begonnen hatte.) Gerund nach *to apologize for*. 11 Do you really accuse me of taking the money, Mum? (Beschuldigst du mich wirklich, daß ich das Geld genommen habe, Mutter?) Gerund nach *to accuse of*. 12 . . . by myself, but Harry insisted on helping me. (. . . alleine machen, aber Harry bestand darauf, mir zu helfen.) Gerund nach *to insist on*.

Flagge 9 (Seite 66)
1 My favourite hobby is reading books. 2 Can you imagine wearing yellow shoes? 3 Henry and Charlie! Please stop chatting. 4 Isabella enjoys cooking for her guests. 5 We cannot risk getting lost here. (. . . losing our way here.) 6 I can't stand cleaning up after you all the time.
7 I don't mind sitting beside/next to Rudy.
8 Watching young kittens is always great fun.
9 Finishing an exercise gives you a good feeling.
10 Grandpa stopped driving two years ago.
11 We always avoid making Mr Berger angry.
12 Are you interested in hearing the whole story?

Flagge 10 (Seite 66)
1 We don't mind going to the cinema alone.
2 It's no use waiting for Patrick. 3 We (have) enjoyed being here. 4 How did you get into the

room without knocking? 5 I'm looking forward to travelling (going) to England in summer. 6 Joe is considering (thinking about) buying a sailing boat. 7 We are proud of living in this country. 8 I was surprised at getting such a good mark. 9 Please go on talking. I like listening to you. 10 Feeding the animals is against the law./illegal. 11 I'm tired of staying at home all the time. 12 Charlie cannot imagine living without Susi.

Übung 36 (Seite 68)
1 On seeing Monica with Theo, I became very sad. 2 I usually read for a couple of minutes after going to bed. 3 Before going over to Charlie's place, call . . . . 4 Julia Roberts studies a filmscript carefully before making a film. 5 After finding her car keys, Robin drove off. 6 On finding a fly in her soup, Harriet became sick. 7 Before opening a letter or a parcel, I always check it carefully. 8 On hearing the results of the exam, Maxwell jumped up and down for joy.

Übung 37 (Seite 69)
1 Kurt solved the problem by talking to his sister. 2 Cassie changed her looks by dyeing her hair. 3 Gus surprised everyone by winning the competition. 4 Fred wanted to impress his girlfriend by inviting her to an expensive restaurant. 5 The burglar got into the house by climbing in through a window. 6 The old lady chased off the thief by shouting loudly for help.

Flagge 11 (Seite 69)
1 On reading the headline of the newspaper, Alec got a shock. 2 I was very tired after painting the garden shed. 3 Before writing his answer, Jim thought carefully for a minute. 4 After losing the tennis match, Bruce walked home sadly. 5 On returning from her morning walk, Mrs Jones found a telegram in her letterbox. 6 She made herself a cup of tea before reading the telegram. 7 The Beatles set a world record by selling more records than any other pop group. 8 Mr Pinter ended the meeting by sending us home. 9 Connect these sentences by using a gerund. 10 Little Charlie shocked everybody by eating a grasshopper.

DAS MITTELWORT DER GEGENWART *(THE PRESENT PARTICIPLE)*

Übung 38 (Seite 73)
1 . . . somewhere. I can hear her laughing. 2 From here you can watch the animals drinking. 3 . . . hear it, but I can feel it coming – winter is near! 4 Don't keep me standing here in the cold! 5 I saw you digging a hole in your garden. What . . .? 6 . . . tomorrow. I can feel the air getting colder and colder. 7 . . . over, the children came running out of the building. 8 Some day they will catch you driving without a driving licence. 9 . . . could, but the runner kept coming closer and closer. 10 In winter we usually go skiing two or three times a month. 11 I see you looking at this painting. Do . . .? 12 Don't let me catch you riding my bike again!

Übung 39 (Seite 74)
1 Opening his photo album, Bob showed me a photo of himself./Bob opened his photo album, showing me a photo of himself. 2 Taking Mary by the arm, I led her onto the dancefloor. 3 Standing on the stage, Sue read her own poems./Sue stood on the stage reading her own poems. 4 Leaving the room, I stumbled over the dog. 5 Tom lay in bed reading a book./Lying in bed, Tom read a book. 6 Standing in the kitchen, Olivia cried over the burnt dinner./Olivia stood in the kitchen crying over the burnt dinner. 7 Waving at his neighbour, Bob went into the house. 8 Waking up, Barbara saw a spider above her bed. 9 Eating my ice-cream, I thought about Italy./I ate my ice-cream thinking about Italy. 10 The girl was sitting by the window looking sad. 11 Laughing loudly, Victor and Chris came into the classroom. 12 Sitting down, Jason turned on his computer.

Übung 40 (Seite 75)
1 Walking home from work, Julius saw a little tomcat. 2 Being hungry, the cat miaowed loudly. 3 Not having a pet, Julius took the cat home with him. 4 Not having any cat food at home (oder: Having no cat food at home, . . .), Julius offered him some cheese. 5 Being tired, the cat went to sleep at once. 6 Looking at the sleeping cat, Julius felt he had done the right thing.

Übung 41 (Seite 75)
1 Walking to school, I always meet Lisa and Eric. 2 Having enough money left, we bought some hamburgers and french fries. 3 Being all alone, I decided to ring up Sandy. 4 Riding my sister's scooter down the street, I was stopped by the police. 5 Talking to Helen, I had a wonderful idea. 6 Walking into the house, we heard strange noises. 7 Mum being ill, Dad and I had to do the cooking. 8 The night air being too cold, we decided to sit inside. 9 The bus being late, we missed the beginning of the film. 10 Dad being an expert horseman, people often ask him for advice. 11 Winter being over, Mum put our warm clothes away. 12 Petrol being so expensive now, many people travel by train.

Übung 42 (Seite 76)
1 Leaving the house, I met a man talking to his dog. 2 Turning the corner, Joseph noticed a woman with shopping bags trying to open her car doors. 3 Opening the bag, Peter found a spider hiding in it. 4 Looking out of the window, Clarisse caught sight of a cat chasing a mouse. 5 Opening the door to his flat, Werner found a letter lying on the floor. 6 Being Peter's best

friend, I bought him the vase standing on the table over there. 7 The schoolyear being over, my parents gave me the bike leaning against that tree. 8 My ink cartridge being empty, I took the one lying beside Fred's pencil case.

Flagge 12 (Seite 77)
1 Entering the room, I heard Joe singing "America the Beautiful". 2 Driving through Switzerland, we saw many cows grazing in the mountains. 3 Playing tennis, I can forget all my worries. 4 Opening the book, I saw a picture showing the Tower of London by night.
5 Sitting in her rocking chair, Vera watched TV all day long./Vera sat in her rocking chair, watching TV all day long. 6 Being the only one who knew Mr Hill, I was sent to talk to him. (oder: Being the only one to know Mr Hill, ...).
7 Firing their guns for hours, the hunters killed a dozen pheasants./The hunters fired their guns for hours, killing a dozen pheasants. 8 Running down the stairs, Ida slipped and fell and hurt her elbow. 9 Jake stood outside the house, wondering if he should go in./Standing outside the house, Jake wondered if he should go in.
10 Standing in the middle of the room, Maria looked around./Maria stood in the middle of the room looking around. 11 The car drove into a group of cyclists, knocking three of them over.
12 Can you see Mike flying his kite? It's his newest hobby. 13 I found Dad in the living room reading the paper. 14 Not knowing what to say, I said nothing.

INFINITIV ODER ING-FORM? *(INFINITIVE OR ING-FORM?)*

Übung 43 (Seite 81)
1 Keine andere Form möglich; Gerund zwingend nach *to finish*. 2 Keine andere Form möglich; Infinitiv zwingend nach *I'd like to*. 3 Sammy prefers writing with a ballpoint. (Beide Formen möglich.) 4 . . . I watched my brother playing in the finals. (Beide Formen möglich.) 5 Keine andere Form möglich; Infinitiv zwingend nach *to manage*. 6 He has refused to help me. (Keine andere Form möglich; Infinitiv zwingend nach *to refuse to*.) Auch möglich: I'm very disappointed with Fred for refusing to help me again. (Gerund als Satzverknüpfer nach *for*.) 7 Grandpa loves working in his garden. (Beide Formen möglich.)
8 . . . the tourists continued to climb up the mountain. (Beide Formen möglich.)

Übung 44 (Seite 81)
1 About a month ago Aunt Frieda stopped smoking. 2 She had tried to give it up many times before, but she had never succeeded in doing so. 3 This time she needed to stop because she had asthma. 4 If she had continued to smoke/smoking, she would have risked getting seriously ill. 5 A friend had said to her, "Why don't you try eating sugar-free sweets instead of smoking? It may work."
6 And really, so far she has managed to keep away from cigarettes.

Flagge 13 (Seite 82)
1 The taxi driver stopped at a petrol station to ask for the way. 2 I'd love to fly in a helicopter one day. I love doing (to do) exciting things. 3 . . . are here. I can hear them coming. 4 "Eating sweets is dangerous for your teeth", the dentist said. But it's difficult to give up something one likes so much. 5 I remember reading this book last year. I liked it. 6 Look, somebody forgot to lock the door. I hate coming (to come) home and finding (to find) the door open! Imagine someone walking into the house and stealing something!
7 I'm sure I didn't forget to lock it! I clearly remember checking all the doors and windows before we left. 8 I hate to hear (hearing) my sisters fight all the time! – Why don't you try talking to them about it? Perhaps they will stop fighting when you are near. 9 Have you ever watched Bill doing his card tricks? They are amazing. – No, never. But I'd like to see him do (doing) them one day. 10 Peter has caught a cold. We tried to make him wear a warmer jacket, but he refused to listen to us. 11 My sister loves taking (to take) long walks in the rain. I don't! I hate getting (to get) wet. 12 The walls of my room need painting. I'll try painting them blue and green this time. I like trying out (to try out) new colours.

DIE ZUKUNFT *(THE FUTURE)*

Übung 45 (Seite 86)
1 My cousin Herbert is going to be (will be) at the party, too. I'm sure you will like him. 2 If you are not at home tonight, I'll call you again tomorrow morning. 3 . . . for the afternoon? – Yes, we are going to visit Aunt Edna in hospital. – Good idea! I'll come with you if I may. 4 . . . crazy driver! He's going to crash into one of the other cars! 5 Grandpa will be 65 next week. We are going to have a big party on his birthday.
6 I can't talk to you right now but I promise I will listen to your side of the story as soon as possible.
7 . . . too many mistakes. We are going to lose the game. 8 . . . ? What are you going to do after this year? – I don't know yet, but I think I'll go to a technical school. 9 . . . at the door! Who will go and see who it is? – I'll go!
10 What's Charlie going to do with those roses? – He's going to give them to Susi.

Übung 46 (Seite 88)
1 present 2 present 3 future 4 future 5 future 6 present/future 7 future 8 future 9 present 10 future 11 future 12 present

Übung 47 (Seite 89)
1 When I get next week's pocket money, I'll pay you back the Pound I borrowed from you on Friday. 2 . . . before it gets too dark.

3 Mary has promised that she will write as soon as she arrives in Los Angeles. 4 We will have dinner when all the guests are here. 5 Don't worry! We won't leave before it stops raining. 6 I'll go to bed at once after the visitors leave. 7 As soon as I finish tidying up my room, we can ride our bikes. 8 When Mum and Dad see my school report, they won't believe their eyes!

Übung 48 (Seite 90)
1 From 9:30 to 10:30 he attends a meeting with ministers from France and Spain. 2 From 11 to 11:30 he gives an interview to a BBC journalist. 3 At 12 he calls his wife. 4 From 2 to 5 he meets with his senior staff and they discuss problems. 5 At 5:30 he talks to the Prime Minister on the phone. 6 At 6 p.m. his driver drives (takes) him home. 7 At 8:45 he takes a plane to Paris. 8 On the plane he prepares his speech for the conference next day.

Fahne 14 (Seite 90 und 91)
1 Lynn is leaving for Sweden tomorrow morning. She has . . . . – When does her plane take off? – At 11:40. 2 Frank, you'll catch (a) cold if you don't put on a warmer jacket. – Okay, I'll take the blue one. 3 Do you like Janet? – Oh yes, she's sweet. I'll invite her to my next party. – I'm sure she'll be glad when she hears this. 4 I'm really happy . . . . We're going to have lots of fun. (We'll have . . .) – Yes, I think it'll be great!
5 Our team is leading 4 : 2. We're going to win this match! – I think so, too. I hope they will win the championship this year. 6 We are going to the mountains on Friday. Do you want . . . ? – I'm sorry I can't. We are going to start building a new garage as soon as we get the building materials.
7 . . . was burning. I'll go and see what it is. – I'll stay here and wait. 8 Are you going to the cinema on Saturday, too? – No, I don't think so. I think I'll make a bike tour with Charlie and stay overnight at his place. But perhaps I'll just stay at home and relax. 9 Hurry up, Mother! Father's train arrives in ten minutes! – What? In ten minutes? I'll have to drive faster if we . . . .
10 Some day soon astronauts will land on Mars. I am certain of it. – So am I. They will probably get there within the next 25 years. 11 . . . any more. He says he's looking for a different second half. – I can't believe it. I'm sure they will be friends again soon. 12 That's enough for today. We'll stop now.

DIE RELATIVSÄTZE *(THE RELATIVE CLAUSES)*

Übung 1 (Seite 94)
1 People who speak English have better chances in life. 2 Children whose parents are too strict are usually unhappy. 3 The boys we met at Miriam's party last week gave us their telephone numbers. *(contact clause)* 4 . . . New York is called "the city that never sleeps". 5 Of all the countries I have visited I like New Zealand best. *(contact clause)* 6 How do you like the girls who live in the house across the street? 7 What did you do with the money Grandma gave you at Christmas? *(contact clause)* 8 We all admire the flowers that grow in your garden. 9 Do you know the man whose guests we are tonight? 10 . . . one of the first musicians that (who) used an electric guitar. 11 I'd like to talk to the person who (that) drives the green Volvo that (which) is parked outside.

Übung 2 (Seite 95)
1 I went to the cinema with my parents last night, which was better than staying at home alone.
2 My chemistry teacher sometimes gets mad at us, which makes us all laugh. 3 This morning Dad's car didn't start and so he had to walk to work, which he didn't like at all. 4 We did not believe Walter's story, which made him very angry.
5 Mary got more points on her maths test than anybody else, which was not surprising. 6 My Grandma always kisses me when we meet, which I can't stand. 7 Brian has about 250 CDs, which is more than I have. 8 Our team won the match, which nobody really expected.

Übung 3 (Seite 96)
1 Mr Smith came by bike this morning, which is unusual. 2 Can anybody tell me what this is?
3 . . ., please! I can't hear what the speaker is saying. 4 The trapper found a goldmine, which made him a rich man. 5 Many people drive after drinking alcohol, which is very dangerous.
6 . . . German? I don't know what this word means. 7 Jim fell and broke his leg, which must have hurt terribly. 8 Maxwell, go and ask Sally what she wants for her birthday.

Übung 4 (Seite 99)
1 This is the man who helped us to build the garden shed. – This is Mr Merriwether, who helped us to build the garden shed. 2 Our neighbour has bought a car that (which) can do 230 km.p.h. – Our neighbour has bought a Lamborghini, which can do 230 km.p.h. 3 I have three uncles. My uncle who lives in Boston is a goldsmith. – My Uncle Paul, who lives in Boston, is a goldsmith. 4 The people we met on our America trip were quite nice. – The Hendersons, who (whom) we met on our America trip, were quite nice. 5 The girl we are waiting for is my best friend. – Emma Smith, who (whom) we are waiting for, is my best friend. 6 The Hudson River, which flows past Manhattan Island, empties into the Atlantic Ocean. – The river that (which) flows past Manhattan Island empties into the Atlantic.

Flagge 1 (Seite 99)
1 The ball "Tiger" is playing with is new.
2 Can you show me what we have to do for tomorrow? 3 Those of you who want to see a film today . . . . 4 The Statue of Liberty, which stands in the harbour of New York, has welcomed

millions . . . . 5 A sculptor is a person who makes statues and monuments. 6 The statue you are looking at is called "David". It was made by Michelangelo, who was one of the greatest . . . . 7 Miami, which we are going to visit in December, has more Spanish speakers than English speakers, which is quite surprising, I think. 8 My Dad has painted all the pictures you can see here. My favourite, which hangs in my room, is called "Still Life with Roses". 9 The car I am driving at the moment is the first car that cost me more than $ 10,000. 10 Shakespeare's plays, which were written about 400 years ago, are still performed today. The one I like best is "Romeo and Juliet".

Flagge 2 (Seite 100)
1 Mr and Mrs Gordon, who used to live next door from us, have moved to Florida. 2 They have bought a house in Pinewood, which is a suburb of Miami. 3 Their youngest son, whose name is Marcus, went with them.
4 Benny likes the dress Jessica is wearing.
5 Jessica likes dresses that come from Italy.
6 Benny likes Jessica, who (whom) he has known since kindergarden. 7 Dad said that California has more inhabitants than Canada, which I did not believe. 8 So I looked it up in the "Encyclopaedia Britannica", which Dad had bought the year before.
9 Canada, which is the second largest country in the world, really has fewer people than California.
10 This is Mrs Williams, whose daughter we met at Maxwell's party. 11 A young man who was at the party too introduced us. 12 Maxwell had invited lots of different people, which was an excellent idea.

DIE VORWÖRTER *(THE PREPOSITIONS)*

Übung 1 (Seite 102)
1 I am looking for my pen. 2 I don't want to wait for Tony any longer. 3 Sheila is interested in rock music. 4 Uncle Willie reminds me of my grandfather. 5 Where does she come from?
6 I've never heard of it before. 7 . . . the animals come out of their hiding places. 8 A mother cat takes care of her babies.

Übung 2 (Seite 104)
Hier gibt es keine für alle gültigen und allein seligmachenden Lösungen! Vielleicht kannst du jemand bitten, der gut Englisch kann, deine Sätze durchzulesen.

Übung 3 (Seite 105)
1 . . . directly above the mountain. 2 Meet me at the corner of Union Street and Market Street tonight. 3 Jim kicked his ball through our kitchen window. 4 They have planted some trees behind/in front of/next to our schoolhouse.
5 Mrs Bennet went straight to my mother . . . .
6 I chased our dog across/over/through the fields.
7 From the top of the hill we could see the village below us. 8 Wilma fell from the ladder and landed in the grass. 9 Last year I sat between Tony and Mary in class. 10 The Rykers live in a flat three floors above/below ours. 11 I could hear a helicopter flying over us. 12 The River Thames flows under some very famous bridges.

Übung 4 (Seite 106)
Hier gibt es wieder keine für alle gültigen und allein seligmachenden Lösungen! Vielleicht kannst du jemand bitten, der gut Englisch kann, deine Sätze durchzulesen.

Übung 5 (Seite 106)
1 Helmut lived in Vienna from 1993 to 1995.
2 We have to be back by/at six o'clock and not a minute later. 3 What were you doing at 9 p.m. on Monday, June 22nd? 4 In February we always go skiing for a week. 5 Pat came home at (before/after) Christmas and he stayed until/till January 3rd. 6 You mustn't play the piano or take a shower after 10 p.m. 7 Yesterday I was so tired that I slept for then hours. 8 William Shakespeare died in 1616. He was 52 years old.
9 We've been here since last Friday and we'll stay until/till next Thursday.

Übung 6 (Seite 107)
1 What about asking your mother for help?
2 Mum and Dad are talking about the holidays.
3 The children are running about in the garden.
4 What do you think about our teacher?
5 Claudia is about 17 years old. 6 Peter is somewhere about the house.

Übung 7 (Seite 107)
1 On January 15, the temperature was above plus 10°. 2 Dad likes pizza above everything else.
3 This theory is above my understanding.
4 Our aeroplane is flying high above the city.
5 There are always dark clouds above those hills.
6 The headmaster is above the teachers.

Übung 8 (Seite 108)
1 Look, our cat is running after the mouse!
2 Alec left the room ten minutes after me.
3 After finishing breakfast, Tracy took the bus to school. 4 Help! Somebody is coming after me!
5 After dinner most people go to bed. 6 Two hours after dinner I went to bed. 7 Ludwig bought some new clothes after he had earned/after earning his first money. 8 Bob and Dean met again after twenty years.

Übung 9 (Seite 109)
1 . . . boring. He only wants to talk about computer games. 2 We have to do something about the traffic in our street. 3 High above us the birds were flying south . . . . 4 Only six people got off after the train had stopped. 5 . . . with the ball in your hands is against the rules of basketball. 6 . . . very nice, and above all she is my friend. 7 I'd like to hear more about your holidays in Australia. 8 Some modern art is above me. I just don't . . . . 9 The girl ran

after the pickpocket, but she was too slow. 10 . . . that he threw his glass against the nearest wall. 11 There was a lot of discussion about Monica's birthday present. Everybody . . . . 12 I have nothing against a good joke, but . . .

Übung 10 (Seite 110)
1 There are lovely tiger babies at the zoo. 2 Sorry, but Mum is not at home. 3 My Dad often works at night. 4 The car crashed into the wall at full speed. 5 Mary is better at history than I. 6 At the end of the film Jill had tears in her eyes. 7 Many people sleep best (when they are) at home. 8 We get most of the things we need at the grocer's. 9 I'm staying at the "Hotel Bristol" now. 10 Why are you laughing at me? 11 Everybody left at the end of the film. 12 Your homework is number 3 at the top of the page.

Übung 11 (Seite 111)
1 Wake me up before you leave./I woke up before you left. 2 We came home before the show was over. 3 The bus arrived before the boys had finished the game. 4 Peter has never been here before. 5 We had been waiting long before the train came. 6 Wash your hands before you start to eat.

Übung 12 (Seite 112)
1 The teacher is sitting behind his desk. 2 Francis does not want to sit behind Gregory. 3 The girl hid her face behind her hands. 4 Bill was only one second behind the winner. 5 In 1620 the Pilgrim Fathers left everything behind and sailed to America. 6 Why are you always running behind me?/Why do you always run behind me? 7 The bus was 15 minutes behind schedule. 8 Veronica came in second behind Ricarda.

Übung 13 (Seite 112)
1 On a cold day the temperature is below zero. 2 The diver remained below/beneath the surface for three minutes. 3 A captain is below a major (in the Army). 4 I won't do this because it is below my dignity. 5 The river was deep below the bridge. 6 Charlie kissed Susi below/beneath the full moon.

Übung 14 (Seite 113)
1 Laura had left the party before I could talk to her. 2 . . . nobody was there. At first we thought we were the only guests, but then . . . came. All in all, there were at least twenty people there. 3 . . ., with Martina and Alice close behind her. 4 . . . freezing cold. The temperature dropped to 25 degrees below zero. 5 Many people in our country feel that dirty work is below/beneath them. 6 Before the war 35000 people lived in this town. 7 . . . Los Angeles. I've never been here before. 8 . . . in the paper? It's at the bottom of page 2.

Übung 15 (Seite 114)
1 Look, Mr Thompson is standing beside our English teacher. 2 . . . visit the zoo; besides, it was closed that day. 3 They built the supermarket right beside the old church. 4 Please, sir, I want to sit beside Rebecca. She's . . . . 5 Besides gold, platinum is also very expensive. 6 . . . looked around; then he took the seat beside me. 7 Besides Frank and Jill, two couples have been invited to the party. 8 . . . for the first time, Little Charlie was beside himself with fear.

Übung 16 (Seite 115)
1 Many countries were conquered by the Romans. 2 Dad's book will be finished by next week. 3 All other sprinters were beaten by Linford Christie. 4 They ride to the next village by bike. 5 I'll be back some time next week. 6 We all like(d) to sit by the open fire. 7 I enjoy travelling by plane. 8 I always travel by day.

Übung 17 (Seite 115)
1 You have to (must) bring back the book by Thursday. 2 This poem was written by Milton. 3 I had to learn the poem by heart. 4 You('ll) have to see "Waterworld" by all means. 5 I know this girl only by sight. 6 The people left the room one by one. 7 We went to London by train. 8 They kissed by moonlight.

Übung 18 (Seite 116)
1 While Tobias was working in the garage, . . . 2 Dennis called some time during the afternoon. 3 While I was walking up to the house, the dog . . . . 4 During my stay in Seattle it rained almost every day. 5 We stayed in our hotel room while it was raining. 6 While the fat lady was singing, many people left the room. 7 Many people left the room during the concert. 8 My Mum and Dad met during the summer of 1974.

Übung 19 (Seite 116)
1 The old man asked me for some money. 2 The tourist called for help. 3 Every day I (have to) look for my car keys. 4 The boys are waiting for the bus. 5 Every morning at seven we leave for school. 6 Placido Domingo is famous for singing.

Übung 20 (Seite 117)
1 I'm tired. For this reason I'd like to stay here. 2 Jack was in prison for burglary. 3 The earth is round. We know this for sure. 4 I long for a cool drink. 5 I haven't seen Ulli for months. 6 Fred took the train for Washington. 7 Come on, let's go for a walk. 8 Charlie will do almost anything for money.

Übung 21 (Seite 117)
1 Indiana Jones hid from his pursuers. 2 Ice-cream is made from milk, sugar and fruits. 3 From the top of the mountain (hill) you can see the sea. 4 I go to school from Monday to

Saturday. 5 Inside the house we were safe from the cold. 6 From June 21 on the days are getting shorter. 7 I know Margarita from kindergarden. 8 Mac is suffering from a bad cold.

Übung 22 (Seite 118)
1 Uncle Joe works at night and sleeps by day.
2 While Mum was sleeping, I washed the dishes.
3 At the end of this year, I want to apply for a job in town. 4 How can I keep you from believing this nonsense? 5 Little Ernie had a bad night-mare during the night. 6 Canada is quite different from the USA. 7 I'll make you a sandwich while you are waiting for Wendy.
8 That's Carola over there, by the window.

Übung 23 (Seite 119)
1 Uncle Theo used to live in Bath, but now he makes his home in Paris. 2 Carl jumped into the lake and swam out to his boat. 3 I will be back in a minute. If I'm not, go into the dining room without me. 4 It wasn't as cold in the morning as it was during the night. 5 Sally isn't here. She's in the cinema with Amanda. 6 Mike got in his car and drove away into the night.

Übung 24 (Seite 119 und 120)
1 Our house is made of wood. 2 Katrin's parents lived in the north of London for a while.
3 I saw a picture of you in the newspaper the other day. 4 We met Mr Green on the morning of our second day in London. 5 I wasn't aware of the fact that I had no money. 6 Many people are proud of their work. 7 I am tired of telling you to work harder. 8 Kelly was so sure of winning the first prize. 9 The man died of his injuries after two days. 10 Mum often speaks of her sister, who lives in Australia now.
11 Jacqueline is very jealous of her sister.
12 "Durchstarten in Englisch" consists of four volumes. 13 Boys often dream of their first moped or car. 14 What has become of Charlie's Dad? 15 The summer of 1983 was very hot and dry. 16 Are you afraid of dogs?

Übung 25 (Seite 121)
1 Dad is in London on business. 2 Tim came all the way on foot. 3 Leo broke my pencil on purpose. 4 My birthday is on October 24th.
5 This train is never on time! 6 We'll return on Saturday. 7 Your income depends on your job.
8 We agreed on all points.

Übung 26 (Seite 121)
1 I am your friend. You can rely on me.
2 What shall I wear tomorrow? – Well, it depends on the weather. 3 Paula insisted on inviting us to her party. 4 You can go on board now.
5 Did you do this on purpose? 6 Did you come all the way on foot?

Übung 27 (Seite 122)
1 My son is already over 12. 2 We want to go camping over the weekend. 3 The fight is not over yet. 4 The driver lost control over the car.
5 They walked over the frozen pond. 6 English is spoken all over the world. 7 The Vietnam War was over 25 years ago. 8 I walked over to Mr Singer's car and . . .

Übung 28 (Seite 122)
1 This ring belongs to my sister. 2 You can always turn to your parents if you have problems.
3 This story refers to J. F. Kennedy. 4 Gerry is getting/got married to Andrea. 5 I always paid attention to my teacher when I was in school.
6 The Vietnam War came to an end 25 years ago.
7 Tomorrow I'll/I'm going to talk to my father.
8 Dad works from 9 a.m. to 5 p.m.

Übung 29 (Seite 123)
1 My dog often sleeps under my desk. 2 Mike can stay under water for two minutes. 3 Dad likes working/to work under his new boss.
4 What do Scots wear under their kilts? 5 The old man "lives" under the bridge. 6 They kissed under the mistletoe.

Übung 30 (Seite 124)
1 The girls are playing with their kittens.
2 Have you got any money with you? 3 Can you come to the cinema with me? 4 In our holidays we often stay with friends. 5 Joe is lying in bed with a bad cold. 6 After the film Tim trembled with fear. 7 Why are you so angry with me? 8 You can come to me with all your problems.

Übung 31 (Seite 124)
1 Can I come with you? We could go to your place. 2 . . . so early. I can't get used to it.
3 Do you like spiders? – No, I'm afraid of them.
4 Harry lives in the east of London, on the Thames. 5 Put on a warm jacket over your pullover. It's cold outside. 6 Under these circumstances you can't stay with us any longer.
7 Where's the TV-guide? – Over there, on/under the table. 8 Slow down or you'll lose control over your car.

Flagge 1 (Seite 124)
1 Look, there's a paraglider in the sky, high above the valley. 2 Hurry up, Peter! We are five minutes behind time, and they won't wait for us much longer. 3 Let's go for a walk, Cathy! – Okay, but what shoes shall I put on? 4 As usual, we went to school by bike. 5 Would you like mayonnaise on your hamburger? – No, thanks. I'm not keen on mayonnaise.
6 Normally I'm interested in foreign countries, but under these conditions I wouldn't travel to Nigeria.
7 I'm hungry. – What about a salad? – Okay! I've nothing against salad. 8 In Canada, summer can be quite warm, with temperatures above 30°. But in winter they can drop to below minus 30°.
9 Why are you in such a hurry, Dad? – My train for (to) London leaves in 25 minutes, and it is always on time. 10 Stop running after boys,

Tina! They will only laugh at you. 11 Joe says he is sorry for knocking over the vase, but he did not do it on purpose. 12 I know Bill Smith by sight, but I've never spoken with him.

BINDEWÖRTER UND ANDERE SATZVERKNÜPFER *(CONJUNCTIONS AND OTHER CONNECTERS)*

Übung 1 (Seite 126 und 127)
1 We ran as fast as we could, but we did not catch the bus. So we had to wait for the next one. 2 When we came home in the evening, we closed the windows because it had got cold outside. 3 I have no idea who will be in my class next year. I hope that Betty and Jim will stay. 4 The blue whale is the biggest animal that lives on earth. It must not be hunted because only a few of them are left. 5 Mike Brown, who sits beside me in class, has been a good friend of mine since we went to primary school. Next year he will change to a commercial academy or he will stay on at our school. 6 When we were in Canada last summer, we went to Montreal first. We stayed for a week, and then we went on to Toronto and Niagara Falls. 7 Harry did not feel well yesterday, so he stayed home from school. But today he is here again because he is feeling better already. 8 Charlie is in love with Susi, so he often brings her flowers. Susi enjoys the flowers because she is in love with Charlie, too.

Übung 2 (Seite 128)
1 As the door was open, ... 2 . . . for another night as it was cheap and . . . 3 As it was getting too dark to see, ... 4 We did not try to catch the train as it was too late already. 5 As nobody knew the way, we were soon lost in the woods. 6 Bill called as I was getting ready to leave for school. 7 As the alarm clock started to ring, Sandy . . . 8 As I was talking to Michael, I had a wonderful idea. 9 Conrad found a wallet as he was walking to the post office. 10 As we were driving out of Baltimore, the sun . . . .

Übung 3 (Seite 129 und 130)
1 beside 2 Besides 3 Besides 4 beside 5 beside 6 besides

Übung 4 (Seite 131)
1 Learning foreign languages is important as well as interesting./Learning foreign languages is both important and interesting. 2 July as well as August have 31 days./Both July and August have 31 days. 3 I've talked to Mum as well as Dad about a new mountain bike./I have talked to both Mum and Dad about a new mountain bike.
4 The "Batman" films are funny as well as exciting./The "Batman" films are both funny and exciting. 5 Nigeria as well as India use English as an official language./Both Nigeria and India use English as an official language. 6 Susi is pretty as well as clever./Susi is both pretty and clever. 7 Kimberley sings as well as dances like a professional./Kimberley both sings and dances like a professional. 8 Milk is used for making butter as well as cheese./Milk is used for making both butter and cheese.

Übung 5 (Seite 132)
1 We walked into the room without knocking for the door was open. 2 I decided to stay at the hotel for another night for it was cheap and . . . . 3 We decided to stop for the day for it was getting too dark to see. 4 We did not try to catch the train for it was too late already. 5 We were soon lost in the woods for nobody knew the way. 6 We could not understand the speaker for the people in front of us were making such a noise. 7 The ferryboats were not allowed to leave the harbour for a storm was coming up.
8 I didn't speak to Diana for I did not know what to say.

Übung 6 (Seite 133 und 134)
1 I tried to install a CD drive in my PC; however, I did not know how to begin. 2 Terry invited me to the dance on Saturday. I had to say no, however, because we are spending the weekend at Grandma's place. 3 Columbus wanted to reach India by sailing west. He had no idea, however, that he would discover a new continent for the Europeans. 4 My parents drove to Verona to see "Aida" at the arena. When they got there, they could not get any tickets, however.
5 Reinhold Messner has climbed the highest mountains on earth and he has walked across Greenland. However, an accident forced him to give up his plan to walk from Siberia to Canada.
6 All my friends told me how great the latest Stallone film was. I did not like it, however.

Übung 7 (Seite 134)
1 Learning foreign languages is not only important, but also interesting. 2 Not only July, but also August has thirty-one days. 3 I have talked not only to Mum, but also to Dad. 4 The "Batman" films are not only funny but also exciting. 5 Not only Nigeria, but also India uses English as an official language. 6 Susi is not only pretty, but also clever. 7 Kimberley not only sings, but also dances like a professional.
8 Not only butter, but also cheese is made from milk.

Übung 8 (Seite 135 und 136)
1 . . ., they will either get angry or say I should not worry. 2 New York City can be both fascinating and depressing. 3 Both Kitzbühel and Saalbach had lots of snow last winter./Neither Kitzbühel nor Saalbach had lots of snow last winter. 4 Don't eat at the "Greasy Spoon". Their meals are neither good nor cheap. 5 . . . Wendy's wedding? – Well, I think both the long red dress and the black skirt with the white blouse look good. 6 Mr Strange has spent several

years in China, so he both speaks and writes Chinese perfectly. 7 . . . we want to learn. We can take either French or Latin. 8. The weather was perfect. It was neither too cold nor too hot.

Flagge 1 (Seite 136)
1 You can get to Deerfield both by train and by coach./. . . either by train or by coach./. . . not only by train, but also by coach. 2 Deerfield has got several historical buildings as well as a modern shopping centre. Besides, there are some fantastic seafood restaurants and a very popular summer theatre. 3 . . . the Rolling Stones in concert. Neither the price of the ticket nor the bad weather could keep me from going, and it was worth it. It was so loud, however, that I still have a headache. 4 Charlie is wonderful! He is both handsome and strong./He is not only handsome, but also strong. I like him although he sometimes makes fun of me. 5 As we could not get any tickets for the concert, we decided to go to the cinema instead. However, they were sold out, too. 6 Neither Lisa nor Maggie likes dresses. They always . . . . 7 I completely forgot that your birthday is not on October 14, but on the 24th, although I wrote it down in my notebook. 8 Climbing that mountain was both difficult and dangerous (. . . not only difficult, but also dangerous), as/for there was lots of ice and snow. However, I was neither afraid during the climb nor tired when we got to the top. 9 As we were skiing down the mountain, Peggy fell and hurt both her ankle and her knee. 10 The largest state of the USA is not Texas, but Alaska, although Texas has much more inhabitants than Alaska.

STORIES

Die Sätze in den folgenden Übungen sind nur als Vorschläge gedacht. Selbstverständlich gibt es auch andere richtige Lösungen! Wenn du nicht ganz sicher bist, frage wieder jemand, der Englisch gut beherrscht.

THE WAY TO HEAVEN

Übung 2 (Seite 143)
a) English is a language that is spoken all over the world./There is not one single Indian language.
b) There were many foreigners in the hotel.
c) The rich man was involved in lots of different businesses. d) The young girl didn't look like Charan's sister, she looked rather like a grown-up.
e) Charan was an unusually clever lift-boy.
f) The men in their safety overalls examined the cellar. g) The hotel manager explained to the guests why they could not open the doors.
h) The man from America decided to pay for Charan's education.

Übung 3 (Seite 144)
1 If someone said that India was one country, you would think that they all spoke more or less the same language. 2 Charan is only thirteen, but he works as a lift-boy in a big hotel to feed his family. 3 The man didn't even hear what Charan had said, but another guest had heard Charan and took hold of the tall man's arm. 4 Charan noticed that the man looked better than a couple of days before and that he was even smiling at him. 5 To Charan Wendy looked like a fairy princess from another planet, so unlike the thirteen-year-old girls he knew. 6 Wendy told him that she came from Detroit and that her Daddy sold trucks. 7 While the firemen were trying to fight their way through the smoke, the telephone was ringing in the hotel manager's office. 8 If you gave him, let's say, $ 1000, he could do nothing with it, because criminals would take it away from him.

Übung 4 (Seite 144)
1 India is a big country. It is nearly as big as all of Europe, and about one billion people live there. The country and the people are very poor, and many children have to work to make their living. Charan is one of the millions of Indian boys who work because they have to feed their families. He is only thirteen, but he works as a lift-boy in a big and noble hotel.

2 Everything about him looked expensive; his briefcase, his watch, his shoes, and even the little notebook had golden corners and golden letters on it.

3 A business card fell from the man's notebook. The man did not notice it, he didn't even realize that Charan had bent down and picked it up. Charan said, "Sir, this card has fallen out of your notebook." The man did not even hear what Charan had said, but another guest had heard Charan's words and took hold of the tall man's arm. Charan held out the little card, and then the man said, "Thank you, son!" Then he put it into his jacket. He reached into his pocket and took out a one dollar note. "For you!" the man said.

4 Wendy told Charan that Detroit was a big city in America, that she had a brother who was in college and only came home once a month, and that her parents were divorced and rather rich. Charan told her that he had two sisters, one younger and one Wendy's age, that he saw his mother only twice a month because she worked in a factory far away, and that his father was away on business and he had not seen him for over a year.

5 Most people had gone to their rooms because the afternoons are very hot in India and the monsoon rains had been pouring down for hours and hours.

6 The men in their safety overalls and their oxygen masks examined the cellar, and soon they found out that three of the big aircondition machines had overheated.

7 For the manager the horrible truth was clear. Wendy was in the elevator, and it had got stuck somewhere in the shaft. Nobody knew where, because the control lights were out of order as well. He wanted to explain everything to the guest and be there if help was needed.

8 They were in the lift when suddenly the lights went out and the elevator stopped. Soon they realized that they were stuck. Then the smoke came. Within minutes they started coughing and had problems breathing. Charan told Wendy to stand in a corner, and in the darkness he climbed on her shoulders. Standing on Wendy's shoulders he unscrewed part of the cabin roof and climbed out. Wendy couldn't climb out of the cabin because the walls were too high. So Charan told her to hand him up her dress. Wendy seized it and he pulled her from the cabin. Charan climbed up the shaft behind her, pushing and shoving her up and up and up. Wendy was coughing and vomiting, but they really did reach the top. Charan knew that there was an emergency door that was never locked.

9 Wendy's Dad sent Charan to school and paid for his education, and he left some extra money for Charan's family. It was only the price of a good dinner in the States. He did it because Charan had saved his daughter's life. "It's $ 200 for the way to Heaven," the man from Detroit said.

THE DOG THAT KNEW NO TRICKS

Übung 2 (Seite 148)
a) Mum and Dad had invited people to dinner that Dad knew from work. b) I know this story quite well, and I like it. c) The only thing the dog seemed to understand was to carry things from her to me. d) The lake was completely frozen, so they went skating every day. e) It was unusually warm for that time of the year. f) The ice floes broke loose and drifted a hundred yards or so. g) For the first time we realized the great danger. h) As if he had never done anything else in his life, the dog turned around and disappeared in the fog.

Übung 3 (Seite 148)
1 I was sitting in one of our large sofas with Scraffy on my lap. 2 Mr Nuttle looked like a perfect gentleman in his suit and tie. 3 Two years ago, when our daughter was ten, she brought home a dog on a cold winter evening.
4 We didn't want to keep the dog, but Samantha begged and begged until my wife said, "Alright, keep him, but you have to take care of him."
5 The only thing he really seemed to understand was to take things from her to me and from me to her.
6 Our cabin was right on a lake, and it took us two full hours to walk round it. 7 He ran round and barked and played, and ran right in front of their skates so that they frequently fell down.
8 I had been out with one of the forest rangers, who always showed me some interesting spots.
9 The three of us were sitting in the living room drinking tea, when all of a sudden we heard a terrible noise. 10 When I tried to walk on the ice of the lake it was already too thin to hold me.
11 In panic we asked him go and call for help, but Forrester said, "They wouldn't even start in that fog. Five years ago we lost two helicopters and five men in a fog like this." 12 He tied one end round a big tree that stood near the lake and the other end to the dog's collar.

Übung 4 (Seite 148)
1 I was sitting on one of our large sofas watching TV with Scraffy on my lap. 2 His wife, whom he always called "Dear", was doing the washing-up. 3 Then, in summer, she started teaching him the sort of tricks most dogs know. 4 The only thing he really seemed to understand was to take things from her to me and from me to her.
5 Our cabin was right on a lake, and it took us two full hours to walk round it. 6 He ran round and barked and played, and ran right in front of their skates so that they frequently fell down.
7 The three of us were sitting in the living room having tea, when all of a sudden we heard a terrible noise. 8 He tied one end round a big tree that stood near the lake, and then he tied the other end to the dog's collar. 9 As if he had never done anything else in his life, the dog turned round and disappeared in the dark fog.
10 When the dog appeared from out of the darkness, he was cold, wet, and worn out, and his paws were as bloody as Samantha's hands.

Übung 5 (Seite 149)
1 When Samantha brought the dog home she was ten years old. 2 Samantha tried to teach Scraffy all kinds of tricks most dogs know.
3 The only thing he seemed to understand was to take things from Samantha's Dad to her and from her to him. 4 They spent their winter holidays in one of the wooden cabins up in the mountains.
5 The frightening noise they heard was the breaking of the ice floes. 6 Samantha was out on the ice with the dog while the others were having tea. 7 Forrester tied one end of the rope round a tree and the other end round the dog's collar. 8 When Samantha was safe at last her parents took her into the cabin and comforted her, and then they called the ambulance. 9 The dog's paws were as bloody as Samantha's hands, and the dog was cold, wet, and worn out.

Übung 6 (Seite 149)

1 Mr Nuttle cared so much about hygiene because he worked for a firm that sold paper handkerchiefs and toilet paper. 2 They could skate on the lake because it was completely frozen. 3 The ice was melting because the wind was unusually warm. 4 The helicopters

could not start because it was too foggy. 5 The rope tightened because Samantha had caught it and was pulling herself in. 6 Samantha screamed Scraffy's name from inside the ambulance because she had heard him bark outside. Samantha had first thought Scraffy was dead.

TESTS

1st test (Seite 150–151)

1. a) Is there anything we can do . . . ?
b) There's some cold chicken in the fridge, if you want some (any). c) . . . she couldn't think of anything to say. d) They must be somewhere around here. e) Does anybody know when the concert begins? – I'm not sure, but I think sometime around 8 or 8:30 tomorrow evening. f) . . . for all of us, but somehow we'll make it!
g) Someone I don't know wants to talk to you, Kevin. – What does he want? – I don't know. He didn't say anything.

2. a) Columbus first landed in America on October 12 in the year 1492. That was more than 500 years ago. b) My Mum worked for "Benson & Son" from 1981 to 1988. In other words, she stayed with them for almost eight years. c) The accident at Chernobyl happened in April 1986, five years before the end of the Soviet Union in 1991. d) Danny usually gets up at 7 o'clock in the morning, but on Saturday and Sunday he stays in bed until 9 or 10 o'clock. e) My grandfather's brother emigrated to Canada in the summer of 1947, two years after the end of the Second World War. f) When did you arrive? – On Saturday. – How long will you stay? – Until (Till) the end of next week. – Have you been here before? – Yes, three years ago. – How long did you stay then? – From March to June.

3. a) Look, ... They are coming from their dancing lesson. b) Where do you come from, Mr Clinton? – I'm from Arkansas. I live in Little Rock, which is the state capital. c) Mr Clinton and his wife are staying at the Mayfair Hotel at the moment. d) Cuckoos always lay their eggs in the nests of other birds. e) Look, I understand your problems and I'm really trying to help you, but you . . . . f) Joe, what are you doing with my walkman? – Nothing! I'm just looking at it.
g) My grandmother bakes the world's best cakes.

4. a) What were you doing when I called you Sunday morning? – I was recording a "Universum" film about gorillas. b) From 2 to 4 yesterday afternoon I was waiting for Jenny, but she did not come. c) Helen fell asleep while she was listening to some oldies on the radio. d) We left the house at 7:30 this morning and walked to the bus stop. It took us 3 to 4 minutes to get there.

2nd test (Seite 152–153)

1. a) Most people enjoy summer more than winter. b) I remember the summer of 1983 very well; it was hot all the time. c) The Tower of London is wellknown all over the world. d) Be careful! The tea is still very hot. But you can put cold water in it. e) My brother is going to study at Oxford University next year. He has not yet decided whether he wants to be a doctor or a lawyer. f) The earrings Jamie was wearing yesterday are made of gold. g) An English proverb says: "An apple a day keeps the doctor away." h) Uncle Gerald has been a teacher for 22 years. Now he has been made headmaster of the school in our town.

2. a) My brother is stronger than you. b) I think a good snowboard is more expensive than good skis. c) My sister is almost as tall as my Mum and she walks like her as well. d) The worst thing you can do now is run away. e) I've never seen better films than the "Indiana Jones" series.
f) French is not as easy to learn as English, but many people say that German is (the) most difficult. g) The nearest petrol station is just around the corner, but if it's closed, you'll have to go to the next one, in High Street.

3. a) How long has Charlie been here? – For three days. b) I'm afraid I've left my workbook at home, sir. c) Uncle Leo has been working for my Dad since 1990. d) It has been snowing heavily since the beginning of this week.
e) How long have you known Terry? – Since we went to school together. We have been very good friends all these years.

4. a) Yes! The thermometre shows 25° below zero. b) The two men went into the building half an hour ago, but they have not come out of it yet. c) The castle stands on a hill. You have to walk through a large park before you get to it, however. d) You can't see Charlie because he is hiding behind the tree over there. e) . . . because it is flying above the clouds. f) I'll wait for you at the corner of Church Street and Station Road. I'll be in the park next to the supermarket.
g) Fritz, where are you going? – To the cinema. And you? – I'm walking home from basketball practice. h) I'm sorry, but my Dad is not at home. He is in town with Mum. i) Let's stop for dinner here. There's no restaurant between here and where we want to go. j) Richard ran after the man, but he could not catch him. k) Be careful when you walk across the street! There's always a lot of traffic. l) . . . while he is sitting by the window. m) In the winter holidays we often go skiing to the mountains. n) A woman with a giant hat was sitting directly in front of me.

3rd test (Seite 154–155)

1. a) I've never met the people who moved into

the house next to yours. b) What do you think about the model helicopter I got for Christmas? c) Charlie often calls Mac "chicken", which isn't very funny. d) Do you understand what I have just said? e) This picture was painted by Picasso, who also painted "Guernica". f) Niki Lauda, whose airline consists of more than 10 planes today, often pilots one of these planes himself. g) I'd like to know what you told Marietta about me! h) Aunt Liz, who is famous for her Christmas puddings, uses only things she produces herself. i) The biggest river that runs into the Gulf of Mexico is the Mississippi.

2. a) Columbus discovered America more than 500 years ago. Since then, millions of people from all over the world have moved to the New World. b) Charlie, what are you doing here? – I'm waiting for Susi. – How long have you been waiting? – For almost an hour, but she hasn't come yet. c) Have you ever been to the United States, Doris? – Yes, twice. I first went there three years ago, with my parents, and in the following year I spent three weeks there by myself. d) Listen! Can you hear that funny noise? I think Max is practicing the trumpet again.

3. a) I asked John not to tell his parents about the accident. b) We want you to sing this song at the party. c) You really expect me to believe this nonsense? d) You must tell me how to make this excellent cake. e) Dad decided to repair the moped himself.

4. a) I don't want to go to the cinema tonight. I'd rather stay at home and watch TV. b) Dad agreed to help me with the maths homework if I promised to wash his car. c) You needn't hurry! There's enough time left. d) . . . been here? I didn't hear you come into the room. e) . . . very nice. She offered to take us to the station in her car.

5. (Das ist nur ein Vorschlag von vielen!) a) Charan lived in India and Wendy came from the USA. b) They met in the lift of the hotel while Wendy's father was doing business. c) They soon became good friends. d) One day, right after lunch, smoke was coming from the cellar of the hotel. e) It was streaming up the shaft of the lift. f) Wendy and Charan were caught in the liftcabin. g) When Wendy was safe again, her Dad decided to pay for Charan's education.

4th test (Seite 156–157)

1. a) (Every winter) Thousands of accidents are caused by careless skiers every winter. b) . . . an Indian camp was attacked by the Army. c) The new shopping centre has not yet been opened./ . . . has not been opened yet. d) When we arrived, "God Save the Queen" was being played. e) The new bridge would be built sooner if they had more money. f) . . . on this bench! It has just been painted. g) This report says that "Rocky VIII" is being shot at the moment.

2. a) . . . the latest version of "Phantasmagoria", but then he forgot. b) I was angry and sad because I had really wanted this game for a long time. c) Now he says (that) I will get it on August 1, which is my birthday. d) Give me back my pocket knife or I will tell my parents. e) Mum and Dad were sleeping, so they did not hear us come home. f) I always read a book or a newspaper while (when) I am waiting for the bus.

3. a) Can you imagine dancing with Joe? b) I suggest continuing the practice tomorrow. c) Did you think/Have you thought about asking somebody for help? d) I am tired of coming home so late every day. e) Are you really interested in finding out who is the murderer?/. . . who the murderer is? f) Mike is proud of being the best footballer in his class. g) You should/ought to give up smoking! h) Nobody can keep me from going to the cinema on Saturday. i) Mr Jackson is looking forward to going to Scotland in summer. j) I can't help laughing when you tell a joke. k) It's no use/It's no good talking to Charlie. l) You should/ought to work together instead of quarrelling/fighting.

4. a) After posting the letter, Joe went to a café. b) Before leaving the house in the morning, Kelly checks all the doors. c) On reading the telegram, Stephanie began to cry. d) You can win the "jackpot" by ticking off the correct numbers. e) The storks fly to Africa after leaving Europe. f) Benny surprised us all by scoring four goals in a single match.

5. a) I'm very sorry, but I forgot to inform your parents. b) We'll never forget watching the sun rise over the island. c) Do you remember telling me about Henry's birthday? d) Please remember to ask Albert if he wants to play in our group. e) The tourist stopped to take a picture of the dancers. f) Dad, stop taking pictures! We're hungry. g) Did you try to speak with Mrs Trask yesterday? h) If you can't do it yourself, try finding (to find) somebody to help you.

5th test (Seite 157–158)

1. a) Lisa said that nothing would grow in her garden because it never got any sun. b) Bob remarked that it wasn't as foggy that day as it had been the day before. c) Cal said that he had no idea what time it was, but he would call 1–2–3 to find out. d) Uncle Alec asked why I/we didn't take a taxi. e) The assistant asked me to pay at the desk. f) Dad told me not to shout at him.

2. a) What will you do if you win a million Pounds? – I think I'll buy my parents a bigger house. b) Look at Tim! He's going to fall asleep any time now! c) Emily's train arrives in ten minutes. We'll have to hurry if we want to meet

her at the station. d) Ladies and gentlemen, in a few moments you are going to see something you have never seen before! e) We are going on a class trip tomorrow. Is your class going too?
f) When I see Ronny next time, I'll tell him about your plans.

3. a) Being hungry, we ate everything that was in the fridge. b) The tourists looked at the paintings hanging on the walls. c) Running after the car, the man shouted as loudly as he could./The man ran after the car, shouting as loudly as he could. d) Not having enough money, Bernie could not buy the CD.
e) Entering the room, Conrad noticed several people talking to each other. f) Sitting in the grass, the little boy was crying for his mother./The little boy was sitting in the grass, crying for his mother. g) The water being too cold for swimming, we decided to rent a boat.
h) Standing in the rain, Marcus tried to open his umbrella./Marcus stood in the rain, trying to open his umbrella. i) I can hear Jenny singing next door. k) Coming home from school, Gus found his lunch on the table.

4. a) Samantha's parents were angry when their daughter came home with a dog one day. When Sam said that she would ook after him, they allowed her to keep him, however.

b) They believed that the dog, whose name was "Scraffy", was stupid because he did not learn any tricks. All he could do was take things from Sam to her Dad and from her Dad to Sam.

c) The following winter they all went to the mountains, where they stayed in a cabin by a lake. They took long walks and they went skating every day, when the lake was completely frozen.

d) The fourth day was unusually warm. Sam and her mother went skating in the morning, and Sam's Dad went out with a forest ranger.

e) In the afternoon, while Sam's parents were having tea in the cabin, they heard a terrible noise. It was a deep crack, and it sounded terrible. It was the ice on the lake that was breaking up.

f) Samanta was still skating out on the ice, but her parents did not know.

g) Her father could not get to her because the ice was too thin and there was a very thick fog.

h) In the end they managed to save Samantha because Scraffy had found her and taken the end of a long rope to her. So she could pull herself across the ice. Without Scraffy, Samantha would not be alive today.

Nr. 85047

FRANZ ZACH / RENE GROMES

DURCHSTARTEN IN ENGLISCH

ENGLISCH

FÜR DIE 8. SCHULSTUFE

KERLE

LERNHILFEN

MÜNCHEN
WIEN

DURCHSTARTEN IN ENGLISCH, Englisch für die 8. Schulstufe,
wurde geplant und entwickelt vom Verlag Kerle, München und Wien.

Verfasser: Franz Zach und René Gromes

Verfasser der Durchstartübungen: Do-Ri Rydl und Kim da Silva

1. Auflage 1996

Diesem Lernhilfebuch ist ein Lösungsheft
zu den Übungen beigelegt.

Verlagsredaktion: Klaus Kopinitsch

Layout: Kurt Lackner

Illustrationen: Bruno Haberzettl

Umschlagentwurf: Alexander Strohmeier

Satz: Vogel Medien GmbH, Korneuburg

Druck: Printed in Hungary

Vertrieb: Verlag Herder, Wien

ISBN 3-85303-110-2

Gedruckt auf umweltfreundlichem, chlorfrei gebleichtem Papier.

INHALTSVERZEICHNIS

Hi! Wir stellen uns vor!

Kannst du auch von dir behaupten, *"I ♥ ENGLISH"*? Ganz ehrlich und ohne zu flunkern? Vielleicht geht es dir im Augenblick nicht ganz so gut? Du fühlst dich unsicher, deine Noten sind nicht so, wie du sie gern hättest, und vor den *tests* hast du ein wenig Angst? Vielleicht warst du krank und hast Stunden versäumt, und nun gibt es Probleme mit dem Nachlernen? Vielleicht geht dir aber auch in diesem Schuljahr alles zu schnell, und du brauchst mehr Zeit und Gelegenheit zum Nachdenken und Üben?

Das „Durchstarten-Team" will dir helfen, diese Probleme zu meistern, damit du die Frage mit „Ja, natürlich!" oder noch besser mit *"Yes, of course!"* beantworten kannst. Du wirst dabei nicht allein sein: *Maxwell*, *Mac* und *Charlie* werden dir immer zur Seite stehen. Sie werden dir manchmal sagen, was du tun sollst, und sie wollen dich ganz bestimmt zum Schmunzeln bringen!

Bevor es so richtig losgeht, noch einige Hinweise zur „richtigen" Verwendung von „Durchstarten".

Das Inhaltsverzeichnis sagt dir, worum es in den einzelnen Abschnitten und Unterabschnitten des Buches geht. Es ist übersichtlich gegliedert und durchnumeriert. Der Inhalt deckt die gesamte Grammatik der 4. Klasse ab.

Das Stichwortverzeichnis am Ende des Buches gibt in alphabetischer Reihenfolge – von *about* bis Zukunft – alle wichtigen Stichwörter mit Seitenangabe an, so daß du schnell findest, wonach du suchst.

Alle Kapitel sind gleich aufgebaut. Zuerst kommt eine Erklärung, die du gründlich und genau durcharbeiten sollst. Dann folgen viele abwechslungsreiche Übungen. Die meisten Übungen beginnen mit einem Beispiel (*example*), so daß du sofort weißt, was du in der Folge selbst tun mußt.

Zu „Durchstarten" gibt es ein **Lösungsheft**. Du sollst es aber nur zum Vergleichen und Verbessern deiner Antworten verwenden, nachdem du die Übungen selbständig erarbeitet hast. Denke daran: „Wer mogelt, belügt sich selbst!"

Die Probeschularbeiten *(tests)* sind im Schwierigkeitsgrad und im Inhalt auf den Lehrplan der 4. Klasse abgestimmt. Eine Punktetabelle erlaubt dir, deine Arbeit zu bewerten und selbst zu benoten. *Good luck!*

Die Symbole in der Randspalte sind Signale. Sie wollen dich auf wichtige Dinge aufmerksam machen oder dir sagen, was du tun sollst.

Los geht's. Eine Übung (*exercise*) ist angesagt.

Aha! So geht das!

Achtung! Die Sache ist verdammt wichtig. Lieber noch einmal durchdenken.

Eine Sprachregel, die du auf jeden Fall beherrschen solltest.

Mac hat einen Tip für dich im Sinne von „So kannst du dir das merken" oder „So geht's leichter".

Da hilft nur eins: Auswendiglernen!

Es wird ernst! Am Ende eines Stoffgebietes gibt es einen Wettbewerb mit Punkteauswertung und Beurteilung. Diese Übung zeigt dir, ob du schon am Ziel bist oder noch eine Runde (Wiederholung) benötigst.

Take it easy! Ruh dich aus, mach später/morgen weiter. Es ist schließlich sinnvoller, an mehreren Tagen 30 Minuten zu üben, statt an einem Tag alles machen zu wollen. Übrigens: Hast du ein Kapitel beendet, solltest du ebenfalls eine Pause machen, auch wenn dich kein Symbol daran erinnert.

Die ***stories*** sollen dir nicht nur Freude am Lesen bereiten, sondern auch Hilfe im Umgang mit Texten sein. Hier kannst du lernen und üben, wie man Fragen sinnvoll stellt und beantwortet und wie man kurze und einfache Geschichten zusammenfaßt oder nacherzählt.

Du selbst entscheidest, wie du mit dem Buch arbeitest. Du kannst es vom Anfang bis zum Schluß „durchackern", oder du konzentrierst dich auf das Kapitel, das du gerade nachlernen willst oder mußt. Gleichgültig, wofür du dich entscheidest: Lerne regelmäßig und langsam, damit das Gelernte auch „sitzt"! Hektisches „Pauken" oder „Strebern" knapp vor einem *test* verwirrt und schadet meist mehr, als es nützt.

Aber das ist eigentlich schon ein Tip, wie man richtig lernt. **Lerntips** findest du auf der folgenden Seite. Das kann manchmal mehr helfen, als das Lernen für Englisch selbst.

Wir möchten dir auch noch eine andere Möglichkeit zeigen, deinen Lernerfolg zu steigern. Das Lernen wird dir damit garantiert leichter fallen, vorausgesetzt, du tust mit und übst regelmäßig. Das Ganze beruht auf folgender Erkenntnis: Steigere die Energie deines Körpers, und du steigerst deine Leistungsfähigkeit und damit auch deine Lernleistung. Erlaubtes Doping sozusagen!

Das Tolle daran: Du schaffst das mit einfachen Bewegungsübungen. Wir nennen sie **„Durchstartübungen"**. Sie bringen dich so richtig auf Touren. Sie ermöglichen dir, daß du in kurzer Zeit wesentlich mehr begreifst und dein Wissen bei einer Prüfung auch zur Verfügung hast. Lerngymnastik macht durstig. Genehmige dir vor und nach den Übungen ein Glas Wasser.

Das „Durchstarten-Team" wünscht dir „Gutes Gelingen" und Freude bei der Arbeit mit dem Buch, damit sich der Erfolg bald einstellt. Wir wünschen uns, daß auch du bald sagen kannst:

"YES, I ♥ ENGLISH!"

TOP TEN DER LERNTIPS

Diese zehn Punkte solltest du beim Lernen beachten:

1. Zeitplan.
Trage in einen Kalender alle **Prüfungstermine** ein. Markiere die Tage, die du zum Lernen vor einer Prüfung brauchst. Das schafft Überblick.

2. Stoffübersicht.
Erstelle eine **Liste der** einzelnen **Prüfungsgebiete**, lasse daneben Platz zum Abhaken. Das spornt dich an und gibt dir Übersicht.

3. Entspannen.
Beginne nicht sofort nach der Schule mit den Aufgaben. Eine einstündige **Entspannungspause** fördert deine Konzentration.

4. Arbeitsplatz.
Richte dir einen eigenen Arbeitsplatz ein. Auf diesem **ordne übersichtlich** deine Unterlagen.

5. Aufwärmen.
Verwende dazu unsere Durchstartübungen. **Lerngymnastik** steigert deinen Lernerfolg. Außerdem bist du damit deinen Mitschülern um die berühmte Nasenlänge voraus.

6. Strukturieren.
Was du gliederst, kannst du besser behalten. **Markiere** Wesentliches **bunt**, mache dir am Rand Notizen.

7. Pausen.
Nach 30 bis 45 Minuten Lernen läßt deine Konzentration nach. Lege daher eine etwa **10 Minuten** lange Pause ein. In der Pause mache eine Durchstartübung. Nach der Pause schreibst du eine nicht besonders anstrengende Hausaufgabe. Dann erst lernst du weiter. Auch **dein Gehirn liebt** die **Abwechslung**.

8. Motivieren.
Jeden Tag nach dem Lernen sollte es etwas geben, worauf du dich **freuen** kannst (spielen, ins Kino gehen . . .).

9. Wiederholen.
Beim Wiederholen festigst du den Stoff. Ein heißer Tip: **Abendwiederholung**. Das Gehirn lernt weiter, während du schon schläfst. Das funktioniert aber nur, wenn du nach der Abendwiederholung dein Gehirn mit nichts anderem mehr belästigst.

10. Prüfung.
Wenn du ängstlich bist, **„spiele“** zu Hause **Prüfung**. Das macht selbstbewußter, und du gehst gestärkt zur echten Prüfung.

DER ARTIKEL
THE ARTICLE

Im Englischen gibt es – so wie im Deutschen – zwei Arten von Artikel. Es sind dies:

der **bestimmte Artikel** *the **definite article***	und	der **unbestimmte Artikel** *the **indefinite article***
the [ðə] oder [ði:]		***a / an*** [ə] oder [ən]

Der bestimmte Artikel
the definite article

Der bestimmte Artikel heißt **immer *the***. Unterschiede nach Geschlecht und Fall so wie im Deutschen (der, die, das, des, dem, den) gibt es nicht!

Die Verwendung des bestimmten Artikels ist im Englischen **anders als im Deutschen**. Grundsätzlich gilt:

☆ Der bestimmte Artikel wird dann verwendet, wenn **bestimmte Personen oder Dinge** gemeint sind.

☆ Der bestimmte Artikel wird **im Englischen seltener** verwendet als im Deutschen.

Wann darf man den bestimmten Artikel im Englischen nicht verwenden?

☆ Wenn die **nähere Bestimmung** durch den bestimmten Artikel **nicht nötig** ist:

Mother *is coming.* – **Die Mutter** kommt.

Die Heraushebung durch den bestimmten Artikel ist hier nicht erforderlich, da mit "Mother" ohnehin die eigene Mutter gemeint ist. Es ist also auch ohne Artikel klar, wer gemeint ist.

☆ Wenn die **nähere Bestimmung** durch den bestimmten Artikel **nicht möglich** ist. Gattungsnamen, Materialnamen und Allgemeinbegriffe haben auch im Deutschen keinen bestimmten Artikel:

I like ***beer****.* – Ich trinke gerne **Bier**.

Anders ist die Lage, wenn es sich um eine „nähere Bestimmung" handelt:

How did you like ***the beer*** *<u>(that) we had last night?</u>* –
Wie hat dir **das Bier** geschmeckt, das wir gestern tranken?

☆ **Bei Namen von Personen**

Tony *and* ***Mary*** *usually meet at the station.*
Listen, ***Uncle*** *and* ***Aunt*** *are coming! Are you ready?*
Why are you looking so sad? – ***Uncle Tom*** *has died.*
Queen Elizabeth II *arrived in Berlin yesterday.*
He was called ***Brother Charlie*** *by everybody in town.*

☆ **Bei Namen von Orten**

Zugspitze *is* ***Germany's*** *highest mountain.*
Goran's new home is now in ***America****.*
Mariazell *is a small town in* ***Austria****.*

☆ **Bei Namen von Zeiteinheiten** (Wochen- und Feiertage, Monate, Jahreszeiten)

Do you like summer or winter better?
Eric came home on Sunday.
The first semester usually ends in January.

! **ABER: Bestimmter Artikel bei bestimmten Zeitangaben!**

Leo met Tina in **the summer of 1983**.
The Turners left for California on **the Sunday after Christmas**.
The January of 1994 was unusually warm.

☆ Bei vielen **abstrakten** und **allgemeinen Begriffen**

Time *is* ***money***.
I find ***natural history*** *fascinating.*
My Dad likes ***French wine***.
Horses *run faster than* ***cows***.
Most people *like* ***children***.
(Die meisten Menschen . . .)

! **ABER: Bestimmter Artikel bei bestimmten Begriffen!**

Ulli often remembers ***the time she spent with us***.
I find ***the history of mankind*** *fascinating.*
The French wine he got for Christmas *was excellent.*
The horses that are grazing over there *belong to our neighbour.*

1 Übersetze die folgenden Sätze ins Englische. Beachte: Nirgends kommt der bestimmte Artikel vor!

example: Kinder essen gerne Kaugummi. →
Children like chewing-gum.

1. Mädchen tragen gerne Jeans.
2. Ich mag Butter und Käse.
3. Marmelade wird aus Früchten gemacht.
4. Brasilien exportiert sehr viel Kaffee.
5. Du hast Sand in den Haaren.
6. Wir brauchen die Luft zum Atmen.
7. Schau auf Seite 7 nach.
8. Gold ist schwerer als Eisen.

2 Und ähnlich geht es weiter! Aber es wird schon etwas schwieriger.

1. Ich fahre (= *ride*) oft mit dem Rad in die Schule.
2. Düsenflugzeuge können höher fliegen als Hubschrauber.
3. Die meisten Kinder genießen (= *enjoy*) den Sommer.
4. Für viele Kinder ist das Fernsehen sehr wichtig.
5. Der Fremde hatte schwarze Haare und braune Augen.
6. Mary geht gern in der Stadt einkaufen.
7. Ich möchte jetzt zu Bett gehen.
8. Viele Dschungeltiere sind in großer Gefahr.

Wann muß man den bestimmten Artikel im Englischen verwenden?

☆ Wenn man einzelne Personen oder Dinge **aus einer Gruppe hervorheben** und/oder näher bestimmen will:

Look, ***the boys*** *are playing tennis.*
(Das sind ganz bestimmte Buben, die du kennst.)

ABER: ***Boys*** *like playing tennis.*

(Das gilt für alle Buben, nicht nur für ganz bestimmte.)

☆ Bei **Eigennamen in der Mehrzahl** (Plural)

We went to Canada with ***the Millers*** *last year.*
The Hebrides *are part of Scotland.*
The Habsburgs *dominated Austrian history for hundreds of years.*

☆ Bei **Zeitangaben mit Präposition**

Sometimes I work very long ***in the evening****.*
On the morning *of February 10th Charlie took his first driving lesson.*

3 Übersetze die folgenden Sätze. Beachte: Jeder Satz enthält den bestimmten Artikel!

1. Die Masters haben ein Haus auf den Scilly Isles.
2. Wien liegt (= *is situated*) an der Donau.
3. Charles Lindbergh war der erste, der den Atlantik überquerte.
4. Mr Fredericks arbeitet nur am Morgen und am Abend.
5. Am Nachmittag schläft er meistens (= *usually*).
6. Der Tower von London ist auf der ganzen Welt bekannt.
7. Der Herbst des Jahres 1991 war kühl und feucht.
8. Mein kleiner Bruder wurde am Abend des 5. Mai geboren.

Wenn du alles mit dem Lösungsheft verglichen und eine gehörige **Pause** eingelegt hast, kannst du weiterüben!

4

Bist du soweit? Dann sei gewarnt: Es wird etwas schwieriger! Du mußt jetzt sehr aufpassen, denn hier sind Fallen eingebaut! Es kommen auch Sätze **mit** dem bestimmten Artikel vor.

example: Im Park hinter dem Schloß stehen hohe Bäume. →
In the park behind the castle there are tall trees.

1. Mein Vater erzählte mir am Abend immer Geschichten.
2. Die Luft ist kühl heute.
3. Sally geht in die selbe Schule wie ihre Mutter.
4. Es war Liebe auf den ersten Blick (= *at first sight*).
5. Das Mädchen beim Fenster fühlt sich nicht gut.
6. Die meisten Mädchen mögen keine brutalen Filme.
7. Peter möchte ein Haus am Land haben.
8. Der Kaffe ist sehr heiß; du mußt Milch dazu geben (= *put in*).

5

Weiter geht es bunt gemischt: **mit** oder **ohne** Artike ?

example: The party will be over at two o'clock.

1. In . . . winter . . . days are shorter and . . . nights are longer than in . . . summer.
2. I bought my new bike with . . . money I got from . . . Grandma.
3. All . . . boys of . . . "4a" have to go and see . . . doctor now.
4. I'm sorry I'm late. I'll try to be on time . . . next time.
5. I saw Julia for . . . first time in . . . summer of 1992.
6. The Lake District is in . . . north of England.
7. . . . pepper and . . . salt are not on . . . table.
8. It was . . . love at . . . first sight.

Gehe erst dann zur „Flaggenübung" weiter, wenn du alles richtig gelöst hast und sicher bist, daß du alles verstanden hast!

Letzte Runde: Setze den bestimmten Artikel dort ein, wo er nötig ist, und lasse ihn dort weg, wo er nicht vorkommen darf! Pro „Lücke" darfst du dir einen Punkt gutschreiben – wenn die Lösung stimmt!

✓ richtig

❍❍❍ 1. In _____ evening _____ air is usually cooler than during _____ day.

❍❍ 2. _____ air and _____ water are necessary to survive.

❍❍ 3. _____ love and _____ friendship can help us a lot.

❍❍ 4. "_____ Life of Brian" is one of _____ funniest films I have ever seen.

❍❍ 5. _____ cheese is made from _____ milk.

❍ 6. How did you like _____ cheese we had for supper last night?

❍❍ 7. There were dark clouds in _____ sky when we left _____ village.

❍❍❍❍ 8. _____ fish live in _____ water and _____ birds fly through _____ air.

❍❍ 9. I love _____ music very much, especially _____ music of Kurt Ostbahn.

❍ 10. _____ television is a serious problem for many families.

❍❍❍ 11. It takes _____ time and _____ money to collect _____ diamonds.

❍❍❍ 12. _____ tennis is a very popular sport among _____ young and _____ old.

❍ 13. _____ tennis that Thomas Muster plays is really fantastic sometimes.

❍❍ 14. There is _____ dirt on _____ back of your shirt.

30–29: **HERVORRAGEND!**
28–26: **LOBENSWERT!**
25–23: **PASST!**
22–20: **NA JA, GEHT NOCH!**
19 und darunter: Wiederhole noch einmal die Seiten 9–14.

Der unbestimmte Artikel
the indefinite article

Der unbestimmte Artikel ist viel problemloser als der bestimmte Artikel. Im großen und ganzen wird er so verwendet wie im Deutschen:

> *This was* ***a*** *nice Christmas present. Thank you!*
> *Elias was* ***an*** *unusual child. He played the organ all day long.*

Der unbestimmte Artikel richtet sich genauso wenig nach Geschlecht und Zahl wie der bestimmte Artikel. Dennoch gibt es zwei Formen:

☆ ***a*** → wenn das nachfolgende Wort in der **Aussprache** (nicht in der Schreibung!) **nicht mit einem Vokal** (Selbstlaut) beginnt:

a *uniform* [ə ju:nifo:m]

☆ ***an*** → wenn das nachfolgende Wort in der **Aussprache** (nicht in der Schreibung!) **mit einem Vokal** beginnt:

an *hour* [ən auə]

Setze die richtige Version des unbestimmten Artikels ein. Die Übung ist sehr leicht: Du mußt nur zwischen *"a"* und *"an"* entscheiden! Deshalb solltest du hier auch keine Fehler machen!

1. . . . cat can be . . . good friend.
2. . . . koala bear is not . . . ordinary animal.
3. . . . horse can easily jump over . . . bush.
4. . . . cow gives us milk, . . . bull doesn't.
5. . . . supermarket is . . . boring place for . . . young person.
6. . . . TV-set and . . . telephone can be found in nearly every household.
7. . . . honest person is respected by everybody.
8. . . . banana and . . . orange a day give your body enough vitamins.

Wann darf man den unbestimmten Artikel im Englischen nicht verwenden?

☆ Wenn das **Nomen „unzählbar"** ist:

Milk *comes from a cow.*
(*milk* kann man nicht zählen.)
The ring was made of ***gold****.*
(*gold* kann man nicht zählen.)

☆ Zur **Bezeichnung eines Titels, den es nur einmal gibt**:

Bill Clinton was elected ***President*** *in 1992.*
They made me ***captain*** *of the tennis team.*
Margaret Thatcher was ***Prime Minister*** *for more than ten years.*

☆ **Nach *turn***:

Alan ***turned Muslim*** *after his visit to Arabia.*
(Er **wurde zum Moslem**.)
My uncle ***turned politician*** *at the age of 24.*
(Mein Onkel **wurde** mit 24 **Politiker**.)

Wann muß man den unbestimmten Artikel im Englischen verwenden?

☆ Bei **Berufsangaben**:

My Mum is ***a*** *nurse at the local hospital.*
Uncle Gus is not a composer, but ***an*** *author.*
Dad works as ***an*** *electronics engineer.*

7 Artikel oder nicht? Das ist hier die Frage! Setze den unbestimmten Artikel ein oder lasse ihn weg – je nachdem, wie es sich gehört!

1. Mr Wilson was made _____ headmaster of the new school.
2. He has been _____ teacher for 21 years.
3. Last year Aunt Lisa turned _____ Protestant after being _____ Catholic for 45 years.
4. My Dad was elected _____ chairman (= Vorsitzender) of the conference.
5. Knives are made of _____ metal and _____ plastic or _____ wood.
6. Animals must have _____ food and _____ water to survive.
7. I eat _____ apple every evening before I go to _____ bed.
8. I think Mac will be _____ lawyer when he grows up.

Der unbestimmte Artikel an „nachgeordneter Stelle"

Für uns Deutschsprachige ist dieses „Ereignis" nicht ganz unbekannt. Im Englischen kommt es aber auch in neuer Umgebung vor. Merke dir die folgenden Verbindungen:

You gave me	***half***	***a***	*Pound yesterday?*
	What	***a***	*lovely day!*
Seeing you here was	***quite***	***a***	*shock for me.*
Bob is	***such***	***an***	*intelligent child!*
Bob is	***so intelligent***	***a***	*child that he amazes everybody.*
Running away is	***too easy***	***an***	*answer!*

8

Wandle die folgenden Sätze so um, daß der unbestimmte Artikel an „nachgeordneter Stelle" erscheint. (Es kann mehr als eine „richtige" Lösung pro Satz geben!)

example: Tom had a good idea. →
What a good idea, Tom! (It's such a good idea, Tom!)

1. I've got 500 ml of milk here.
2. That was a sad story.
3. The film was good, but not great. (It was . . .)
4. This development (= *Entwicklung*) is too dangerous. (That's too . . .)
5. Frank's voice is so good that he always sings the leading parts (= *Hauptrollen*).
6. The train was 30 minutes later than usual.
7. The car crash was so bad that the passengers were taken to hospital.
8. The night was too cold for camping.

9

Übersetze die folgenden Sätze ins Englische. Denke dabei an die „nachgeordnete" Stelle!

example: Was für eine gute Idee! Gehen wir! →
What a good idea! Let's go!

1. Was für ein nettes Mädchen Betty doch ist!
2. Das war eine ganz nette Party bei Ulla.
3. Was für ein dummer Fehler!
4. 1994 hatten wir so einen kalten Winter, daß viele Tiere erfroren.
5. Das war eine zu leichte Frage für Jim. Er ist unser Genie (= *genius*)!
6. Heute war so ein heißer Tag!
7. Was für eine nette Überraschung! Peggy und Sue sind da!
8. Mary war ein zu schlauer Gegner (= *clever opponent*) für mich.
9. Du hast eine halbe Woche zum Nachdenken!
10. Conny ist ein recht hübsches Mädchen.

2

Jetzt werden bestimmter Artikel und unbestimmte Artikel gemischt! Setze den richtigen Artikel ein oder lasse ihn weg, wenn er fehl am Platz ist! Pro _____ gibt es einen Punkt zu verdienen.

✓ richtig

❍❍ 1. There is _____ ugly insect in my beer. I hate _____ beer with insects!

❍❍❍❍ 2. _____ video tape on _____ shelf is about _____ woman who walked all the way to _____ North Pole and back.

❍❍ 3. It is nice to play _____ game of chess in _____ café.

❍❍ 4. _____ most people love _____ nature.

❍ 5. I like _____ grapes you brought us yesterday. They're so sweet.

❍❍❍ 6. Look, there are _____ clouds in _____ sky. You'd better take _____ umbrella.

❍❍❍ 7. _____ clouds over _____ lake are lovely. What _____ beautiful day!

❍❍❍ 8. _____ Mother is _____ teacher at _____ school she used to attend when she was young.

❍❍ 9. _____ first day of school was too excit ng _____ day for Steven.

❍❍❍❍ 10. _____ life is hard, but _____ life of my dog isn't! _____ dog has _____ easy life!

❍❍ 11. F. D. Roosevelt was _____ President of the United States from 1932 to 1945. He was _____ President with the longest term of office. (term of office = Amtszeit).

❍❍ 12. Mac and Charlie are fond of _____ grapes with _____ cheese.

28–30 Richtige? ***YOU'RE THE DEFINITE CHAMPION!***
25–27: ***YOU'RE ON YOUR WAY TO BECOMING A CHAMP!***
20–24: ***NOT BAD, BUT NOT TOO GOOD, EITHER!***
19 und darunter: ***YOU KNOW BEST WHAT TO DO . . .!***

HALLO IHR MÜDEN KRIEGER!
WENN IHR WOLLT, ZAUBERE ICH EUCH MIT EIN PAAR LUSTIGEN ÜBUNGEN WIEDER FIT!!
WAS IST MIT MEINER LIMO-DOSE LOS?

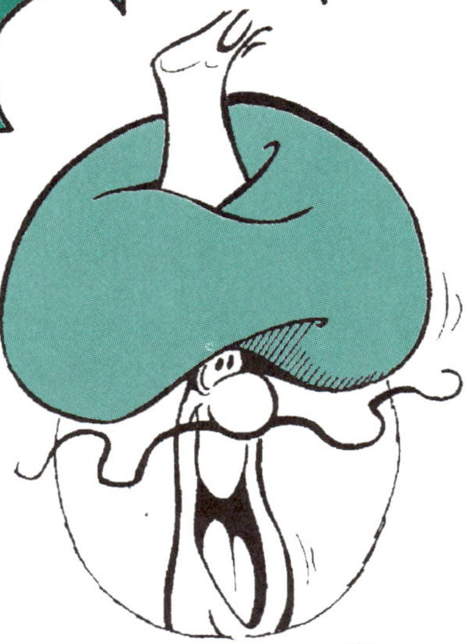

POWERMUDRA

Müde? Erschöpft? Verzweifelt?
Das Powermudra gibt dir Kraft für deine Aufgaben:

Du legst Daumen und Ringfingerkuppen zusammen und den Zeigefinger auf das erste Daumengelenk.
Du kannst es auch nur mit rechter oder linker Hand halten.
Dauer der Übung: mindestens 3 Minuten. Führe das Powermudra mindestens 6mal täglich durch.

Stell dir einmal vor,
du bist Besitzer eines tollen Autos. Es kann schnell fahren, es bringt dich gut und sicher an jedes von dir gewünschte Ziel. Du braust gerade auf der Autobahn dahin, aber plötzlich stottert der Motor. Du drückst stärker aufs Gaspedal, trotzdem wird dein Auto immer langsamer und bleibt sogar stehen. Du kannst nun schimpfen, einen Kopfstand machen, das Auto neu lackieren, die Mitfahrer rausschmeißen – das Auto wird sich keinen Zentimeter bewegen. Wenn dein Auto keinen Treibstoff mehr hat, kannst du tun, was du willst. Du mußt das Richtige tun: **TANKEN!** Dann kannst du deine Fahrt fortsetzen und kommst ans Ziel.

Ebenso ist es mit deiner eigenen Kraft. Wenn deine Energie zu niedrig ist, hast du es sehr schwer, eine gute Lernleistung zu erbringen. Von leicht und locker zu schaffen, was Lehrer und Eltern von dir fordern, ganz zu schweigen.
Unlust, Müdigkeit, Ärger oder Verzweiflung breiten sich in deinem Körper aus. Sie zehren an deiner Energie. Wie willst du aber eine Leistung bringen, wenn dein Tank leer ist?

Daher heißt's auftanken mit dem Powermudra!

DAS ZEITWORT

THE VERB

simple form und progressive form ein Überblick

Werfen wir noch einmal einen Blick auf diese zwei Formen, die für die englische Sprache so typisch sind!

simple form

Simple form bedeutet „einfache Form". Sie heißt deshalb so, weil sie eben ganz „einfach" und ohne irgendwelche Erweiterungen gebildet wird.

Simple forms sind zum Beispiel:

*I **walk** – it **rains** – they **play** – he **did** – we **talked***

Dabei sind ***-s*** und ***-ed*** keine Erweiterungen, sondern die Endung von *3rd person singular (present tense)* beziehungsweise von *past tense*.

Der Ausdruck *simple form* ist allgemein üblich. Auch im Englischunterricht wirst du ihn immer wieder hören.

progressive form

Progressive läßt sich mit „fortschreitend" oder „fortlaufend" übersetzen. Damit bezeichnen wir einen Vorgang, der noch nicht abgeschlossen ist. Die deutsche Bezeichnung für *progressive form* ist daher auch „Verlaufsform" oder „Dauerform".

Progressive form ist nicht **der einzige Ausdruck**, der möglich ist. Vielleicht verwendet ihr an eurer Schule stattdessen auch ***continuous form*** (was das gleiche bedeutet wie *progressive form*) oder ***expanded form***.

Expanded heißt „erweitert", und das beschreibt sehr gut das Aussehen der Form: Du bildest sie mit der Erweiterung ***-ing*** (die du an das Verb anhängst) und der passenden Form von ***to be*** (je nach Person und Zeitstufe). Die „Formel" lautet:

progressive forms sind zum Beispiel:

I	***am***	***doing***	*a difficult exercise.*
He	***is***	***cleaning***	*the table.*
They	***were***	***playing***	*football.*
We	***have been***	***waiting***	*for you for hours.*
	Zeitstufen von *to be*	***base form + ing***	

Wie werden *simple form* und *progressive form* verwendet?

Zunächst ein kleiner Trost, falls du Probleme mit diesen Begriffen und ihrer Anwendung hast! Es ist für uns Deutschsprechende gar nicht so leicht, die völlig korrekte Verwendung von *simple form* und *progressive form* zu erlernen. Dafür gibt es auch einen einfachen Grund: Wir haben in unserer Sprache nichts Vergleichbares!

In den ersten drei Lernjahren hast du aber bereits folgendes gelernt:

R

Simple form wird grundsätzlich dann angewendet, wenn es um eine **Handlung als solche** geht; man erfährt einfach, was geschieht, geschah oder geschehen wird.

*I **write** letters every day.*
*I **went** to town yesterday.*
*I **have done** all my exercises.*

↓

Ich tue (tat, . . .) etwas!

Mit ***progressive form*** wird **der Verlauf eines Geschehens** deutlich ausgedrückt; sie besagt also, daß zu einem bestimmten Zeitpunkt etwas gerade geschieht, geschah oder geschehen wird.

*I **am writing** a letter now.*
*I **was going** to town when . . .*
*I **have been doing** exercises for hours.*

↓

Ich bin (war, . . .) gerade dabei, etwas zu tun!

Guest: "Waiter, call me a taxi!"
Waiter: "Right, Sir. You are a taxi!"

present tense

present simple

Wird verwendet bei

- ☆ **zeitlosen Zuständen;**
- ☆ **allzeit gültigen Tatsachen;**
- ☆ **wiederholten Handlungen.**

The best tea ***grows*** *in India.*
Water ***boils*** *at 212° Fahrenheit.*
Joe ***comes*** *home at 6 every day.*

present progressive

Wird verwendet, wenn

- ☆ **eine Handlung im Augenblick des Sprechens („jetzt eben") passiert.**

My flowers ***are growing*** *very well.*
Be careful! The water ***is boiling****.*
Look, Joe ***is coming*** *home!*

Setze das Verb in die richtige *progressive form* in *present tense*.

Statt eines Beispiels: ***am / is / are*** + ***present participle (base form + "ing")***

1. We (to discuss) the problem at the moment. Please wait a minute.
2. Bob, what (you, do) at the moment? – I (have) a cup of tea, you know.
3. Wait a moment! I (to try) to get my things into my bag.
4. Look, the ambulance (to come) down the street!
5. Now I (to write), but you can talk to me later on.
6. Look, the cat (to sleep). Let's not wake it up.
7. Listen, I (to talk) to you!
8. Dad (to cook) lunch today, but don't go into the kitchen! You know he doesn't like it.

Mit dieser Übung trainierst du "*present simple or present progressive*?". Setze die passende Form ein.

example: Dad usually **drives** to work every morning.

1. Look, your mother (do) a step-dance! – I know. She often (do) that.
2. The sun (shine) by day, the stars (shine) at night.
3. Bad teachers never (do) good work.
4. Herman usually (to play) chess, but at the moment he (play) dominoes.
5. Listen, it (rain)! – That's strange. It never (rain) here in August.
6. Dad is in the cellar. He (repair) my bike. I (need) it to get to school.
7. He always (try) to repair things that (not work).
8. Listen, "Satan" (bark)! – Yes! Something (make) a noise outside.

PAUSE

past tense

past simple

Wird verwendet,

- ☆ um **Ereignisse aus der Vergangenheit** wiederzugeben, die **abgeschlossen und vorbei** sind;
- ☆ zum **Geschichtenerzählen** (*past simple* ist die „ganz normale" **Erzählzeit**).

past progressive

Wird verwendet, wenn

- ☆ **zu einem bestimmten Zeitpunkt in der Vergangenheit gerade eine Handlung im Verlauf war**;
- ☆ **zwei oder mehrere Handlungen zur gleichen Zeit abliefen** (meist *while*-Sätze);
- ☆ **eine Handlung noch andauerte, als eine andere Handlung begann** (kurze Handlung unterbricht lange Handlung; meist *when*-Sätze).

3

Setze das Verb in die richtige *progressive form* in *past tense*.

Statt eines Beispiels: **_was_ / _were_** + **_present participle_**

1. While Sue (play) the piano, Jessie and I (talk) about the holidays.
2. It (just, begin) to snow when we arrived at the airport.
3. Tom and Steve (watch) TV when the phone rang.
4. Sally (paint) her fingernails while Tony (dry) his hair.
5. Yesterday at 4 p.m. we (have) our afternoon tea.
6. The baby (try) to sleep while Mum (hoover) the floor.
7. I (think) of going to bed when Paul arrived with a new video tape.
8. Mac and Charlie (lie) in the sun when a strong wind suddenly carried their sunshade away.

4

Diese Übung trainiert wieder *"past simple or past progressive?"*. Setze die passenden Formen ein.

example: The lights **went** out while I **was preparing** breakfast.

1. While we (watch) TV last night we (hear) a strange noise outside.
2. I (try) to concentrate while Hilary (tell) me about her boyfriend.
3. Teddy (look) for his glasses when the telephone (ring).
4. Sheila (walk) across the street when her hat (blow) off.
5. It (rain) heavily when Frank (get) up in the morning.
6. The sun (shine) when I (come) back home.
7. At 10 in the morning the lights (still, burn).
8. I (cut) my finger while I (peel) apples.
   (to peel = *schälen*)

PAUSE

present perfect tense

present perfect simple

Wird verwendet für

- ☆ **vollendete Handlungen**, deren **Folgen „jetzt und hier"** erkennbar sind; das muß **ohne Angabe des Zeitpunktes** geschehen;
- ☆ **Zustände**, die in der **Vergangenheit anfingen** und **bis in die Gegenwart andauern**.

present perfect progressive

Wird verwendet für

- ☆ **Handlungen**, die in der **Vergangenheit anfingen** und **bis in die Gegenwart** (und vielleicht bis in die Zukunft) **andauern**.

Dazu einige erklärende Beispiele:

→ *Look, somebody* ***has broken*** *the mirror!*
The boys are not here. They ***have gone*** *to the cinema.*

Das sind **abgeschlossene Handlungen**, aber die Folgen sind „jetzt und hier" spürbar: Der Spiegel ist (noch immer) zerbrochen, und die Buben sind (noch immer) nicht zu Hause.
Es ist **unwichtig**, **wann** die Dinge passiert sind; **wichtig** ist nur, **daß** sie passiert sind und daß die Folgen spürbar sind.

→ *We* ***have known*** *the Millers for many years.*
Chuck ***has been*** *here since last week.*

Das sind **Zustände**, **keine Handlungen**. Sie haben (irgendwann) **in der Vergangenheit begonnen** (vor vielen Jahren, letzte Woche) und **dauern** „hier und jetzt" **noch immer an**: Wir kennen die Millers immer noch, und Chuck ist auch noch immer da.

→ *My parents* ***have been saving*** *money for a new car for two years.*
Peter ***has been trying*** *to windsurf since Monday, but he's still not very good at it.*

Das sind **Handlungen**, **keine Zustände**. Sie haben (irgendwann) **in der Vergangenheit begonnen** (vor zwei Jahren, letzten Montag) und **dauern** „hier und jetzt" **noch immer an**: Die Eltern haben noch immer nicht genug Geld für das neue Auto beisammen, und Peter versucht noch immer, Windsurfen zu erlernen).

5

Setze das Verb in die richtige *simple form* in *present perfect tense*.

Statt eines Beispiels:

have ***has***	+	***past participle*** ***(3rd form)***

1. Olivia (like) Sebastian since their schooldays.
2. (you, hear) from Tim? We (not see) each other for some time.
3. I (not have) enough time to finish reading the book since Christmas.
4. Uncle Rick and Aunt Annie (not eat) any meat for years.
5. They (be) vegetarians since their holiday in India.
6. How is Amanda? She (not call) me since my birthday.
7. Dad's old trousers are very dirty. He (wear) them for over a week.
8. It (not rain) in some parts of Africa for more than ten years.

6

Setze das Verb in die richtige *progressive form* in *present perfect tense*.

Statt eines Beispiels: **have been / has been** + **present perfect**

1. I am really tired. I (to do) the same things for hours now.
2. Look at Wendy! She (to sleep) like this since three o'clock.
3. I'm at the station at the moment. I (to wait) for Judy for half an hour.
4. I (to try) to read this story for weeks. I wonder when I will find the time.
5. What (you, do) with yourself since I last saw you? – Well, I finished school and I found a job. I (to train) as an electrician for two years now, and I have two more years to go.
6. I know this town well. I (to live) here since 1989.
7. My grandmother is ill. She (to lie) in bed for two weeks now, and she is slowly getting better.
8. Maxwell (to play) computer games since six o'clock. He really ought to stop now.

7

Diese Übung trainiert "*present perfect simple or present perfect progressive*?". Setze die passenden Formen ein.

example: I **have not seen** you for a week. What **have you been doing** all this time?

1. I (stand) here since 6 o'clock; where (you, be)?
2. Fred (not visit) Spain yet, but he (learn) Spanish for a whole year.
3. How long (you, know) Ellie? – Oh, for three or four years, I think.
4. I (wait) for a taxi for a quarter of an hour, but it (not come) yet.
5. Mr Schmidt (talk) about *present perfect tense* for a week, and now I think I understand.
6. Regina (work) in Paris since last February. She (not be) back since then.
7. Charlie and I had a fight last month, and we (not speak) to each other for weeks.
8. Our cat (sleep) in her basket since this morning. I hope she isn't ill.

Die Zielflagge ist in Sicht! Bei den folgenden drei Übungen sollten dir (fast) keine Fehler mehr unterlaufen! Wenn doch, dann wiederhole die Seiten 23–31.

1 *Present tense: simple form or progressive form?*

❍ richtig

❍❍ 1. The little lady who (pass) by our house right now (live) next door.
❍❍ 2. Valentina is not at home. She (spend) this weekend at her grandmother's. She (visit) her once or twice every month.
❍❍ 3. Why (you, do) your homework now and not at home, Walter?– I usually (do) it at home, sir, but I forgot. I'm sorry!
❍❍ 4. What (you, look) at? – These pictures. They are great. I (like) good pictures.
❍❍ 5. Listen to those girls! They (make) a lot of noise. – Yes! I always (have) to tell them to be quiet.
❍❍ 6. Fritz (fly) to Houston, Texas, today. He often (go) to America on business trips.
❍ 7. On my way to the sports club I often (meet) Jim and Laura. They are in the same club as I.
❍❍ 8. Now I (know) the answer to question 3! – Don't tell me! I (still, think), and I want to answer the question by myself.

PAUSE

2 *Past tense: simple form or progressive form?*

❍ richtig

❍❍ 1. I (look) out of the window when I (see) Martin riding my bike.
❍❍ 2. Ted (have) a cup of coffee when the toaster (fall) from the shelf.
❍❍ 3. Clarissa (sing) while Francis (play) the piano.
❍❍❍ 4. We (drink) tea and (eat) cucumber sandwiches every day when we (be) in London.
❍❍ 5. When I (meet) Veronica in town yesterday, she (wear) a miniskirt.
❍❍ 6. Dad (lay) the table for dinner while the guests (have) a drink at the bar.
❍❍ 7. What (you, do) at 5:30 on Friday morning? – I think I (drive) to work.
❍❍❍ 8. I (think) about Monica when I (have) an idea. I (ring) her up and
❍❍ (ask) her if she (want) to go to the concert with me on Saturday.
❍❍ She (say) yes! I (be) the happiest man on earth!

3 *Present perfect tense: simple form or progressive form?*

✓ richtig

❍ 1. Tell me what (you, do) since I last saw you?
❍❍❍ 2. These photos (lie) on the desk for days. (everybody, look) at them? – No, I (not see) them yet.
❍❍ 3. I (not be) here for ten years, so I wonder what (change) in the village.
❍❍ 4. Dad (not have) a day off this month. He (work) for three weeks now without a break.
❍❍ 5. I (try) to call you since eight o'clock. Where (you, be)?
❍ 6. We (work) hard all week to finish our tree house; I think we'll be able to use it in a week or two.
❍❍ 7. Little Mary (run) around in the rain without shoes for hours. I wonder if she (catch) a cold already!
❍❍ 8. Mr Ross (teach) us music for half a year now, but we (not hear) a single record or CD so far.

past tense or present perfect tense?

Achtung! Das ist keine ganz leichte Frage, und die Antwort ist noch ein wenig schwieriger! Wahrscheinlich bist du selbst auch schon einige Male in diese „Zeitfalle" getappt.

Wo liegt das Problem?

Im Englischen besteht (im Gegensatz zum Deutschen) **ein großer Bedeutungsunterschied** zwischen *past tense* und *present perfect tense*!

Past tense blickt zurück; wir sagen, was in der Vergangenheit passiert ist. Es ist unwichtig, ob sich die vergangene Handlung auf die Gegenwart auswirkt oder nicht! Es steht fest, wann die Handlung passierte (auch wenn es nicht immer ausdrücklich gesagt wird).

Columbus ***discovered*** *America in 1492.*
We ***were listening*** *to "Nirvana" when there* ***was a*** *power blackout.*

Present perfect tense stellt den Bezug zwischen Vergangenheit und Gegenwart her. Wichtig ist, daß „jetzt und hier" Auswirkungen von Handlungen spürbar sind, die in der Vergangenheit begonnen haben. Dabei ist es unwichtig, wann das war; nur die Aussage, seit wann diese Handlung andauert, ist möglich.

Many people ***have emigrated*** *to America since 1492.*
We ***have been listening*** *to your CDs for an hour now. Let's do something else!*

8

Genug der grauen Theorie – wir wollen Taten sehen! Bei dieser Übung haben wir *past tense* und *present perfect tense* gemischt. Also, gut aufgepaßt und mitgedacht!

example: Shakespeare **wrote** his dramas 400 years ago. I **have read** all of them.

1. I (not see) Anita for more than a month. – That's no surprise. She (be) in Australia until last Sunday.
2. Hans (give) me this book a week ago, but I (not read) it yet.
3. When I (come) home last night, you (sleep) like a log. (= *tief schlafen*)
4. I (not see) this film for over a year, but I remember that we (go) to the cinema together then.

5. It (rain) when we (come) home last night, and it (not stop) since then.
6. Ben (try) to call you three times already, but you (be) gone all the time.
7. We (buy) the tickets two months ago.
8. My brother, who is in Australia at the moment, (not write) to us for more than a month. We (get) his latest letter five weeks ago.
9. Look, Mum (make) a cake! – Yes, she (bake) it while you (play) tennis.
10. (you, see) Dennis today? – No, not today, but I (speak) with him yesterday.
11. (you, ever, be) to Monaco for the Grand Prix? – Yes, once. Dad and I (drive) there last year, and we (enjoy) it very much.
12. While we (watch) the race, somebody (break) into our car and (steal) the radio.

Nun bist du reif für die Punkteübung! Aber vorher:

4

Past tense (simple or progressive) oder *present perfect tense (simple or progressive)*? Pro Verb(form) ein Punkt!

✓ richtig

❍❍❍ 1. Where's Kevin? – I've no idea. I (not see) him in the last twenty minutes. The last time I (see) him he (talk) to Lucy.

❍❍ 2. How (be) the "Rolling Stones" concert? – Fantastic! I (never see) such a great show before.

❍❍ 3. You ought to go to bed now, Ernie. You (work) long enough. – I know, but Mr Kane (call) this morning. He said he needed the report tomorrow.

❍❍❍ 4. Arnold Schwarzenegger (leave) Austria when he (be) 21. He (make) more than 15 films since then.

❍❍ 5. Look, the new uniforms (arrive)! We (wait) for them long enough.

❍❍ 6. I (send) a letter to "Greenpeace" last week, and now they (answer).

❍❍ 7. Dad (catch) a big fish yesterday. We (just, eat) it.

❍❍ 8. Alina (write) a long essay last weekend, but she (forget) to bring it today.

17 oder 18 Punkte? ***SIMPLY THE BEST!*** Weniger als 12 Richtige? ***BACK TO PAGE 29!***

future tense

Alles Wissenswerte über ***will-future*** und ***going-to-future*** erfährst du in einem eigenen Kapitel in diesem Buch (ab Seite 84). Wir wollen uns hier daher nur ***future progressive*** zuwenden!

R

future progressive

Kommt selten vor:

☆ bei **Handlungen**, die zu einem **bestimmten Zeitpunkt in der Zukunft** gerade **im Verlauf** sein werden;

Next Monday we ***will be sitting*** *on the train to Paris.*
This time tomorrow Mary ***will be giving*** *her first solo-concert.*

☆ wenn man **einer Sache Nachdruck verleihen** will, damit sie auch sicher passiert;

If I tell Sam to do it, he ***will be doing it****.*
(Du kannst sicher sein, daß er es tut, wenn ich es sage).

9

Wieder geht es nur um *future progressive*. Bilde die Form und überlege dir bei jedem Satz, warum du *future progressive* verwendest.

1. Baby is crying, but in an hour or so he (sleep) soundly.
2. You (still, repair) that clock in the middle of the night if you don't hurry.
3. I tell you, you (do) your homework today and not tomorrow!
4. You can go home with me. I (wait) for you here in an hour.
5. Gloria is your sister, so you (help) her, if you want to or not!
6. This time tomorrow you (play) your first big match. Good luck!
7. If everything goes well, you (cross) the Channel this time next week.
8. It (still, rain) when you come back in the evening.

past perfect tense

Die Anwendung von *past perfect tense* ist leicht zu erklären und zu verstehen: Wenn **zwei vergangene Handlungen** miteinander in Verbindung gebracht werden, dann steht die **frühere Handlung in *past perfect tense***, die **spätere Handlung in *past tense***.

Past tense und *past perfect tense* sind so etwas Ähnliches wie „siamesische Zwillinge"; ***past perfect tense* tritt nie ohne *past tense* auf**.

After Agatha ***had gone*** *home, I* ***went*** *to bed.*

R

past perfect progressive

Wird verwendet:

☆ wenn der **Verlauf der früheren Handlung** betont werden soll.

Before Bill arrived, we ***had been waiting*** *for over an hour.*
It ***had been snowing*** *heavily for days when it suddenly stopped.*

10

Bilde zunächst nur *past perfect simple*.

1. By the time Dad came home, I (not do) any of my tasks.
2. After the guests (leave), we went to bed and fell asleep at once.
3. Mum allowed us to go out after we (finish) our work in the garden.
4. After I (take) a shower, I put on my new jeans and went to the dance.
5. James thanked me for what I (do) for him.
6. We (lose) our way before we got to the hotel.
7. Eve left the hospital after she (be) there for two days.
8. Gertrude went to the doctor after she (fall) and (hurt) her elbow.

11 Bilde nun *past perfect progressive*.

1. Martin told me that he (sleep) all afternoon.
2. Doris said on the phone that she (wait) for me for hours.
3. I heard that Frank (study) for the test for three weeks.
4. Mum was angry because the lights (burn) all night.
5. I found out that Birgit (practice) tennis since she was a little girl.
6. Dad informed his boss that he (try) to find a better job for weeks.
7. I knew that Vanessa (live) in London since 1986.
8. When Oliver returned from his holiday, he realized that somebody (take) his mail out of the mailbox while he was gone.
9. Joe realized that Monica (cry) while he was gone.
10. We (dance) for some time when Julia and Robert arrived.
11. Mr Olson was angry when he saw that we (play) in his driveway (= *Einfahrt*) during his absence (= *Abwesenheit*).
12. The car (stand) in front of our house for two weeks before they removed (= *entfernen*) it.

12 Weiter geht es mit einer Mischung aus *past perfect simple* oder *progressive*.

1. I went home after I (finish) my work.
2. Our guests told us that they (already, see) the Tower of London.
3. Kurt told me that he (wait) for me for several hours.
4. Harry said that he (sleep) at home when I tried to ring him up.
5. In the paper I read that a terrible fire (break) out in my home town.
6. Our geography teacher asked us which European capitals we (visit).
7. We were surprised to hear that Tanja (be) able to read and write at the age of four.
8. I wanted to tell you that the old man (live) in that house for more than forty years.

Salesman: "Can I sell you a vacuum cleaner?"
Woman: "Sorry! I have no vacuum to clean."

13 Und nun noch eine Übung für stille Tage. Hier sind alle Zeitstufen gemischt. Finde die richtige Zeit und setze die passenden Formen ein.

1. The Fords (go) to the theatre last week. They usually (try) to go once or twice every month.
2. I normally (write) with a pen, but today I (use) my Dad's ball-point.
3. After all her friends (arrive), Mary (begin) to play the violin.
4. Quick, hurry! Mum (come) home in a minute and we (not tidy) the kitchen yet.
5. Fritz told me that he (collect) stamps for five years. It is still his number-one hobby.
6. I (never, see) a volcano before we (go) on holiday to Sicily. There we (climb) up Mt. Aetna, which (break out) the year before.
7. Julius (stay) at the same campground for fifteen years. He (never, go) to a different place.
8. Grass (grow) best in a mild and wet climate, such as in England.

5 Den krönenden Abschluß bildet wie immer die Punkteübung. Finde die passende Zeitstufe und setze die richtigen Formen ein. Pro Lücke gibt es einen Punkt. Du solltest mindestens 15 Punkte erreichen! (Mehr ist natürlich noch besser!) *Good luck!*

✓ richtig

○○ 1. I (work) day and night since last week, but I (not finish) the book.

○○○ 2. After I (write) my first short story, I (notice) that I (have) a lot of talent.

○○ 3. When I (see) Harry two days ago, he (just, get off) a bus.

○○ 4. I (throw) away my old "Swatch" yesterday because Grandma (buy) me a new one.

○○○ 5. (you, hear)? Gertie (win) the first prize in a lottery. This time next month she (lie) on a sunny beach somewhere in the Caribbean.

○○ 6. Uncle Edward said that he (be) sorry that he (forget) my Christmas present again.

○○ 7. Michelle told me that she (study) Russian for the last three years. This time next year she (attend) the University of Moscow.

○○ 8. I (not hear) from Linda for some time. I wonder what she (do) at the moment.

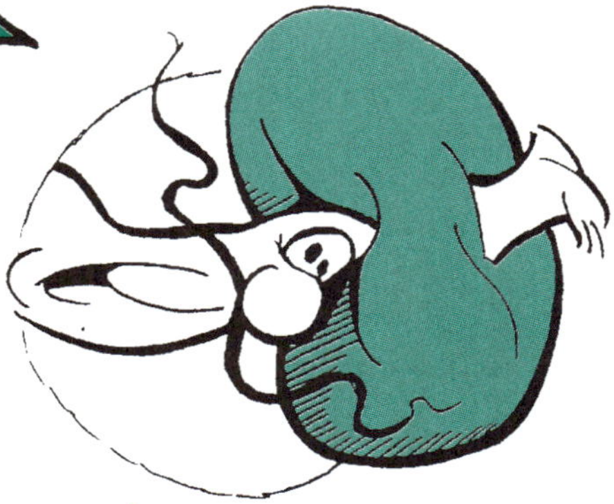

DURCHSTART-ÜBUNG: 2.

ERDKNÖPFE UND RAUMKNÖPFE

Du liest etwas, kannst es dir aber nur schwer merken?

Halte deine Erdknöpfe:

Du berührst mit je zwei Fingern der einen Hand den Rand deines Schambeins und mit zwei Fingern der anderen Hand den Punkt unterhalb der Unterlippe.

Dauer der Übung: 2 Minuten.

Passieren dir Fehler beim Abschreiben von der Tafel?

Halte deine Raumknöpfe:

Du berührst mit zwei Fingern der einen Hand das Steißbein. Es befindet sich am unteren Ende der Wirbelsäule. Mit zwei Fingern der anderen Hand berührst du den Punkt oberhalb der Oberlippe.
Die Erdknöpfe und Raumknöpfe kannst du auch sanft massieren.

Dauer der Übung: 2 Minuten

Die Nennform – the infinitive

Der Infinitiv – wir bleiben in weiterer Folge bei diesem Ausdruck – ist ein alter Bekannter. Du kennst ihn seit langem auch als ***base form***. Da der Infinitiv meist mit ***to*** auftritt, nennt man ihn auch die ***to-form***.

Den Infinitiv verwendest du

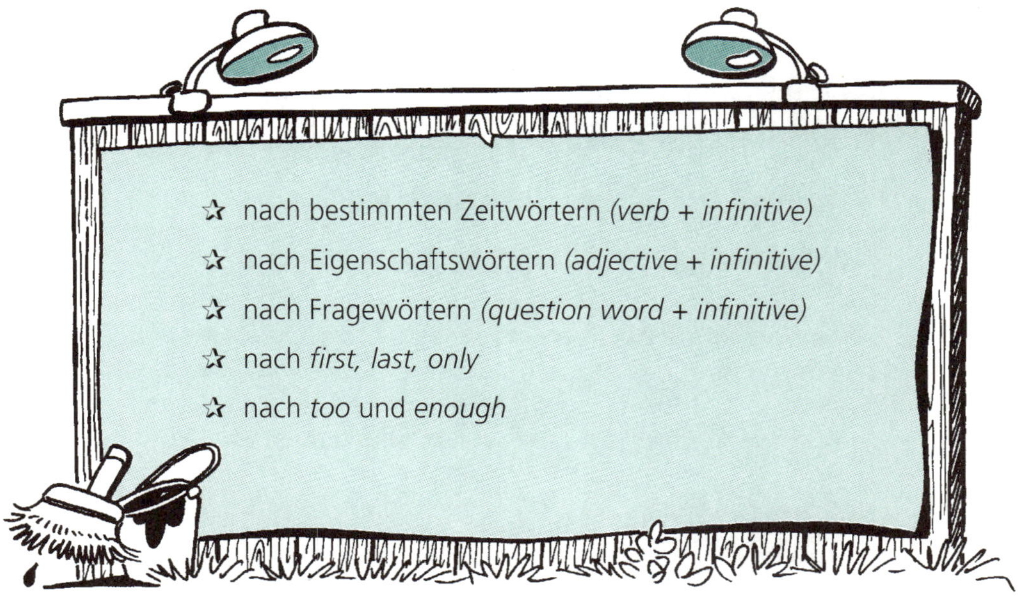

- ☆ nach bestimmten Zeitwörtern *(verb + infinitive)*
- ☆ nach Eigenschaftswörtern *(adjective + infinitive)*
- ☆ nach Fragewörtern *(question word + infinitive)*
- ☆ nach *first, last, only*
- ☆ nach *too* und *enough*

verb + infinitive

Bestimmte Zeitwörter verlangen den **Infinitiv mit *"to"***, andere Zeitwörter verlangen den **Infinitiv ohne *"to"***, und eine dritte Gruppe kommt mit dem **Infinitiv oder einer *"ing"*-Form** vor.

Infinitiv mit *"to"* bei . . .

Die Liste ist natürlich nicht vollständig; weitere Verben aus dieser Gruppe wirst du im Lauf der nächsten Lernjahre noch kennenlernen.

A

afford	(leisten)	*Let's walk! We can't **afford to take** a taxi.*
agree	(zustimmen)	*My parents **agreed to pay** for my piano lessons.*
ask	(bitten)	*Mum has **asked** me **to do** the shopping for her.*
decide	(beschließen, entscheiden)	*Robert and Kate **decided to get** married next month.*
expect	(erwarten)	*We **expect to win** the championship this year.*
happen	(„zufällig")	*I **happened to meet** Jane in town this morning.* (Heute morgen **traf** ich Jane **zufällig** in der Stadt.)
hope	(hoffen)	*Kevin **hopes to find** a better job soon.*
learn	(lernen)	*Where did you **learn to speak** French so well?*
manage	(gelingen, es schaffen)	*Jim **managed to answer** all the questions.* (Jim **gelang es**, alle Fragen **zu beantworten**.)
offer	(anbieten)	*Mr Miller **offered to drive** us home from school.*
promise	(versprechen)	*Will you **promise to call** me as soon as you get home?*
plan	(planen, vorhaben)	*Marianne is **planning to sell** her old car.*
refuse	(ablehnen, verweigern)	*A man called today, but he **refused to tell** me his name.*
seem	(scheinen)	*The people here **seem to be** very friendly.*
want	(wollen)	*I really don't **want to wait** for you every day!*

14 Bilde sinnvolle Sätze, indem du die angegebenen Zeitwörter an passender Stelle einsetzt.

example: I have always liked the sea. I learnt to swim when I was four.

1. We have really enjoyed your visit. We hope ________ you again very soon.
2. The airline has lost my suitcase, but they promised ________ it as soon as possible.
3. Do you want ________ now or later? – Later. I'm not hungry now.
4. You must study harder before the next text, Alan. You can't afford ________ another (= *noch eine*) bad mark.
5. Lord Winterbottom was very friendly. He offered ________ us around the castle himself.
6. Don't shout at me! I refuse ________ to you if you shout at me!
7. If you happen ________ from Sandra, tell her that I am waiting for a letter or a call from her. (*Wenn du zufällig von Sandra hörst, ...*)
8. What's the matter, Dominic? You seem ________ angry at someone.
9. What do you expect ________ in Washington? – Well, we want ________ all the important sights.
10. I told Dad that I wanted a new bike, and he agreed ________ me half of the money.
11. Our English teacher works very fast. He always manages ________ our tests in the next lesson.
12. Charlie decided ________ Susi. He asked her ________ to the cinema with him.

15 Übersetze die folgenden Sätze in gutes Englisch. Beachte: In jedem Satz muß ein Infinitiv vorkommen! Verwende dazu die Tabelle auf Seite 42!

1. Ich gratuliere! Es ist dir gelungen, mich zu überzeugen (= *convince*).
2. Du mußt versprechen, daß du diese Geschichte niemand erzählst.
3. Schau dir Benny an! Er scheint den Spaziergang zu genießen.
4. Können wir es uns leisten, heuer auf Winterurlaub zu fahren?
5. Mehr und mehr Menschen weigern sich, Fleisch zu essen.
6. Zufällig bemerkte ich, daß ich kein Benzin mehr hatte.
7. Mr Brown war damit einverstanden (= *er stimmte zu*), die Eröffnungsrede (= *opening address*) zu halten.
8. Wir beschlossen, Brian um Rat (= *advice*) zu fragen.
9. Wir hoffen, euch nächstes Jahr wiederzusehen.
10. Ich rechne damit (= *ich erwarte*), daß ich dieses Jahr keine Probleme in der Schule haben werde.
11. Wir haben vor, bis Sonntag hierzubleiben.
12. Susi: „Charlie, wo hast du tanzen gelernt?"

Infinitiv ohne *"to"* bei . . .

A

☆ den ***modal verbs*** *can, may, must, shall, will, need not;*

*We **can see** the mountains from our hotelroom window.*
*You **need not answer** this question if you don't want to.*

☆ Zeitwörtern der **Sinneswahrnehmung**: *see, hear, watch, feel* (wenn die Handlung schon abgeschlossen ist);

*You scared me. I did not **hear** you **come** into the room.*
*Where's Bill? – Outside. I'**ve seen** him **leave** the room.*

(Diese Gruppe kommt auch mit einer ***"ing"*-Form** vor! Siehe auch Seite 72!)

☆ den Verben ***let*** und ***make*** in der Bedeutung von „lassen";

***Let** me **show** you my garden. I'm very proud of it!*
*Mum always **makes** me **do** the dishes on Saturday.*

☆ ***had better (not)*** (sollte lieber) und ***had rather (not)*** (würde lieber).

*You'**d better hurry** or the bus will leave without you.*
*I'**d rather not talk** to my Dad tonight; he's in a bad mood.*

16 Setze die angegebenen Verben sinnvoll ein. Beachte: Hier steht der Infinitiv ohne *to*!

example: I cannot **hear** you! Speak louder, please!

1. I think they are still in the house. I didn't see them . . . out.
2. They did not let us . . . our dictionaries, so I don't know if I have translated the sentences correctly.
3. Look at the clock! We'd better . . . at once or we'll be late again.
4. Shall I . . . the books on the table or on the shelf, Tony? – On the table.
5. I'd rather . . . on a bike tour than to school.
6. Bill, I think I heard someone . . . your name. – That was probably Mum.
7. We wanted to go out last night, but Dad made us . . . at home and . . . for the test today.
8. I don't like to watch TV now. I'd rather . . . a walk with my dog.
9. Tim's dog is chasing your cat again, Joe. You'd better . . . him about it.
10. Our neighbours are very nice. They often let us . . . in their pool.
11. I'm sorry, but there's nothing I can . . . about this situation.
12. Tea or coffee, Miss? – I'd rather . . . a glass of milk, please.

17 *And now, translate!* Übersetze die folgenden Sätze in gutes Englisch. Jeder Satz muß einen *infinitive without to* enthalten! Unterstreiche ihn und das auslösende Wort. Schau auf Seite 44 nach, wenn du Hilfe brauchst.

example: Ich würde die Arbeit lieber heute als morgen beenden. →
I'd rather finish the job today than tomorrow.

1. Wer hat Mary heimkommen gehört? – Wir alle.
2. Du brauchst dir keine Sorgen machen; uns geht es gut.
3. Unser Trainer (= *coach*) ließ uns heute 2.500 m laufen.
4. Ich sehe, daß sich da drüben (= *over there*) etwas bewegt.
5. Mike, Bob ist hier. – Laß ihn warten!
6. Ich würde lieber an den Strand gehen als im Zimmer zu bleiben.
7. Wo bist du, Jackie? Ich muß dir eine lustige Geschichte erzählen.

8. Soll ich am Montag wieder kommen, Mr Williams? – Ja, natürlich.
9. Wir sollten lieber Andy um Rat fragen. Andy ist der Experte.
10. Du solltest lieber einen Regenschirm mitnehmen.

6 Infinitiv mit oder ohne *to*? Setze die passenden Formen ein. (Aber dieses Mal ohne Hilfe!)

be – buy – catch – dig – get – go – let – plant – play (2×) – practice (2×) – send – spend – stay – take – walk – write (2×) – visit

✓ richtig

❍❍ 1. We were planning . . . to Switzerland in summer, but then Fred got ill and so we decided . . . at home.
❍❍ 2. You must . . . harder if you want . . . the Number One player.
❍❍ 3. I don't think you can afford . . . two new CDs every month. You had better . . . the money on other things or save it.
❍❍❍ 4. I hear you . . . the violin every day. Are you learning . . . it? – Yes, I promised my Mum . . . as often as I could.
❍❍❍ 5. I promise . . . to you and I will . . ., but don't expect . . . a letter from me very soon.
❍❍ 6. Mrs Benson has offered . . . us to the station in her car, but I'd rather . . . because it's such a lovely morning.
❍ 7. Dad agreed . . . me drive when I'm sixteen.
❍❍ 8. Yesterday I watched Mr Dobbs . . . a big hole in his garden. He said he wanted . . . a walnut tree.
❍❍ 9. Uncle Peter says he may . . . the Statue of Liberty when he is in New York and he promised . . . me a postcard.
❍ 10. In our summer holidays Dad managed . . . the biggest fish I have ever seen.

18 Punkte und darüber? ***CONGRATULATIONS! YOU'VE DONE IT AGAIN.***
16 oder 17 Richtige? ***NOT TOO BAD, BUT . . .***
15 oder darunter? ***WELL, WELL . . . TRY AGAIN!***

adjective + infinitive

English is	***easy***	***to learn****.*	
I am	***happy***	***to see***	*you again.*
This is	***hard***	***to believe****.*	
	adjective +	**infinitive**	

18 Suche dir ein passendes Adjektiv und setze es ein. Dabei gibt es manchmal mehr als nur eine richtige Antwort!

example: It was **great / wonderful / good** to hear from you again.

1. It is . . . to know what you really want.
2. Little kittens (= *Kätzchen*) are often . . . to watch.
3. Mt. Everest was not . . . to climb.
4. We are . . . to bring you bad news: You can't come skiing with us.
5. It was . . . to see those photographs.
6. It think it is . . . to grow rice in Germany or Austria.
7. We should be . . . to live in a peaceful country.
8. Caroline, are you . . . to go now? – Yes, I'm coming.

TIP Die „Formel" *adjective + infinitive* kann auch zur Satzverkürzung verwendet werden. Dadurch werden die Sätze nicht nur kürzer, sondern auch viel „eleganter". Das sieht dann so aus:

Charlie was sorry that he was late. → *Charlie was sorry* ***to be*** *late.*

19

Verkürze die folgenden Sätze mit Hilfe der „Formel" *adjective + infinitive*.

1. You are lucky that you are Frank's friend.
2. I was surprised when I saw Judy walk into the room.
3. Andrew was happy that he was in Canada at last.
4. Doris was shocked when she discovered the broken window.
5. We are very pleased (= *erfreut*) that we can welcome you here.
6. After the plane had crashed the pilot was happy that he was still alive.
7. I was sorry when I heard about your accident.
8. Betty was glad when she got a letter from her boyfriend.

question word + infinitive

I have no idea	**what**	**to do**	*with this thing here.*
Do you know	**where**	**to go**	*from here?*
I'll show you	**how**	**to make**	*pizza.*
	question word	**+ infinitive**	

TIP Diese ebenfalls sehr elegante Methode hilft uns wieder, holprig klingende Satzgebilde zu vermeiden. Du solltest dir also die „Formel" *question word + infinitive* nicht nur gut einprägen, sondern sie auch an passender Stelle selbst anwenden! Das sieht dann so aus:

Anita can teach you how one dances the tango. →
Anita can teach you ***how to dance*** *the tango.*

20 Mache die folgenden Sätze nach diesem Muster „eleganter".

example: The cowboys knew where they could cross the river. →
The cowboys knew where to cross the river.

1. Who can tell us where we must put the books?
2. Christopher was so surprised that he did not know what he should say.
3. The old lady was not sure what she should do, so I offered to help her.
4. Linda could not remember where she should get off the tram.
5. A farmer told us where we could find mushrooms (= *Pilze*).
6. Can anyone tell me who I should ask?
7. The children asked themselves when they should be back.
8. Daniel had no idea what he could do about the problem.
9. I did not know who I could send for the doctor.
10. Peter showed me how I should install Windows '95.

first – last – only – best – worst

The Americans were ***the first to land*** *a man on the moon.*
Lisa is ***the only*** *one among us* ***to speak*** *Greek.*

21 Verkürze und „veredle" die folgenden Sätze mit dem Infinitiv.

1. Detective: "Mr Jones, you are the last person who saw the man alive."
2. Marco Polo was the first European who spent some years in China.
3. Johnny, you were the only one that I could ask in this situation.
4. The best thing that we could do was to wait.
5. Franzi von Almsieck is the only swimmer that won four gold medals.
6. The captain is usually the last person that leaves a sinking ship.

too (+ adjective) – enough (+ noun)

*Lukas was **too** tired **to do** his home-exercises.*
*We haven't got **enough** money **to afford** a bigger apartment.*

TiP Auch mit *too* und *enough* lassen sich Sätze verkürzen oder verbinden und somit stilistisch verbessern. Das sieht dann so aus:

After the long space flight the cosmonauts were so weak that they could not stand up straight. →
*. . . the cosmonauts were **too weak to stand** up straight.*

There's so much food that we could feed an army with it. →
*There's **enough food to feed** an army with it.*

22 Es geht noch einmal: Verkürze, verbinde und „veredle" die folgenden Sätze mit Hilfe des Infinitivs.

1. The man was so nervous that he could not sit still.
2. My grandpa has got lots of time. He can repair my bike.
3. Dad is so careful that he won't have an accident.
4. We have only little water left. We cannot go on.
5. There were so many people that they could push the car to the nearest garage.
6. That's so much flour that we can bake three cakes with it.
7. Julius is so young that he is not allowed to drive.
8. Our cat is so lazy that she won't chase a mouse.

7

Jetzt geht es ans Verkürzen, Verbinden und „Veredeln". Baue in jeden der folgenden Sätze einen Infinitiv ein.

✓ richtig

❍ 1. The doctor thinks that Mr Webster is so old that he should not drive a car.
❍ 2. The mechanic showed me how I should start the engine.
❍ 3. We did not know where we could hide our cigarettes.
❍ 4. Joe was surprised when he met Karin in Madrid.
❍ 5. The Coopers cannot decide when they should go on holiday.
❍ 6. Reinhold Messner was the first person that climbed Mt. Everest without the use of oxygen bottles.
❍ 7. Veronica and Tina were not sure what they should tell their parents.
❍ 8. I was glad when I could go home again.
❍ 9. I've got so many books that I can fill a whole library (= *Bibliothek*).
❍ 10. Raymond answered nine out of ten questions correctly, but he was not the only student that did so.
❍ 11. We were lucky that we could find a hotel room.
❍ 12. A snowstorm in May was the last thing that we expected.
❍ 13. It was so cold that we could not play outside.
❍ 14. Are you happy that you will meet Richard's parents?
❍ 15. The best one can do against a headache is to lie down and rest.
❍ 16. I was so tired that I did not think about the problem.
❍ 17. There is so little snow that we shouldn't go skiing.
❍ 18. The driver was shocked when he realized what had happened.

TO BE THE CHAMP, ist ein Fehler erlaubt, aber mehr nicht!
Ab 15 Richtigen: ***REALLY GOOD!***
Ab 12 Richtigen: ***FAIR ENOUGH TO PASS.***
11 und weniger: ***YOU'D BETTER STUDY THE INFINITIVE AGAIN!***

verb
+ object
+ infinitive

Diese „Konstruktion“ ist keine Unbekannte, denn wir kennen sie auch im Deutschen:

Irene	**bat**	**mich**,	ihre Einkaufstasche	**zu tragen**.
Niemand	**erlaubte**	**uns**,	den Raum	**zu verlassen**.
	Verb	**+ Objekt**	**+**	**Infinitiv**

Im Englischen wird *verb* + *object* + *infinitive* sehr häufig verwendet. Dabei gibt es auch viele Fälle, die im Deutschen nicht möglich sind. Es handelt sich somit um eine „typisch englische“ Konstruktion, die du dir daher auch besonders gut merken solltest.

Irene	***asked***	***me***	***to carry***	*her shopping bags.*
Nobody	***allowed***	***us***	***to leave***	*the room.*
We	***want***	***you***	***to stay***	*at our house a little longer.*
Mr Bell	***expects***	***his son***	***to become***	*a doctor or a lawyer.*
	verb	***+ object***	***+ infinitive***	

Die zwei letzten englischen Beispielsätze verlangen auf Deutsch einen „daß-Satz“:

Wir möchten, daß du noch ein Weilchen bei uns bleibst.
Herr Bell erwartet, daß sein Sohn Arzt oder Anwalt wird.

verb + object + infinitive schreibt man bei folgenden Zeitwörtern:

A

advise	(raten)	*I **advise you to take** a different road.*
allow	(erlauben)	*Mrs Niles **allowed us to stay** overnight.*
ask	(bitten)	*Nick **asked his dad to lend** him £ 10.*
expect	(erwarten)	*Mum **expects me to be** back by 9:30.*
help	(helfen)	*Joe **helped us to repair** our old car.*
invite	(einladen)	*May I **invite you to stay**?*
know	(wissen, kennen)	*We **know Mary to be** a clever girl.*
order	(befehlen)	*The captain **ordered his men to stop**.*
remind	(erinnern)	*Will you **remind me to call** Maggie?*
show how	(zeigen wie)	*I can **show you how to make** pizza.*
teach	(lehren, beibringen)	*Who **taught you to sing** so well?*
tell	(sagen, mitteilen)	*Laura **told me to wait** for her here.*
want	(wollen, mögen)	*We **want you to tell** the truth.*
wish	(wünschen)	*I **wish them to leave** the room.*

Weißt du, was die Mustersätze auf Deutsch bedeuten?
Hier die ersten vier:

Ich rate dir (Ihnen, euch), eine andere Straße zu nehmen.
Frau Niles erlaubte (gestattete) es uns, über Nacht zu bleiben.
(. . . zu übernachten.)
Nick bat seinen Vater, ihm 10 Pfund zu borgen.
Mutter erwartet, daß ich bis 9:30 Uhr zurück bin.

23 Kannst du erraten, was jetzt auf dich zukommt? Genau! Übersetze die verbleibenden Sätze ins Deutsche! Achte besonders darauf, wo das mit Infinitiv möglich ist und wo du dafür einen „daß-Satz" brauchst.

Weiter geht es mit einer „traditionellen" Übung: Übersetze die deutschen Sätze in gutes Englisch. Jeder Satz muß *verb + object + infinitive* enthalten! Aber denke daran: Nicht alle Sätze auf einmal!

1. Ich erwarte, daß ihr alle hart arbeitet.
2. Julia wollte, daß ich mit ihr komme.
3. Oliver möchte, daß wir ihn am Wochenende besuchen.
4. Meine Oma erinnerte mich daran, ein Geschenk für Mama zu kaufen.
5. Mr Graham gestattete uns, auf seiner Wiese (= *meadow*) zu spielen.
6. Wir wissen, daß Sabine Musicals sehr gerne hat.
7. Jenny bat mich, ihre Eltern zu verständigen (= *inform*).
8. Kannst du mir zeigen, wie man diese Flasche öffnet?
9. Ich wünsche nicht, daß ihr diesen Artikel lest.
10. Mrs Feinstein befahl Martin, das Geld sofort zurückzugeben.
11. Viele Männer erwarten, daß die Frauen kochen und das Haus putzen.
12. Wendy möchte nicht, daß Alec mit ihr tanzt.

Diesmal gibt es Punkte für deine Anstrengungen! Übersetze mit Hilfe der *"verb + object + infinitive"*-Konstruktion die folgenden Sätze ins Englische. Du solltest alle Punkte richtig haben! ***Good luck!***

✓ richtig

❍ 1. Mr Tompkins bat mich, die Zeitung zu holen.
❍ 2. Das Publikum (= *audience*) erwartet, daß jeder sein Bestes tut.
❍ 3. Die alten Leute im Zug sagten, wir sollten ruhig sein.
❍ 4. Ich möchte, daß ihr zu meinem Geburtstagsfest kommt.
❍ 5. Meine Eltern erlaubten mir, eine Woche lang mit meinen Freunden herumzureisen.
❍ 6. Der General befahl den Truppen (= *troops*) anzugreifen (= *attack*).
❍ 7. Larry hat uns geholfen, die Garage zu bauen.
❍ 8. Der Zöllner (= *customs officer*) sagte, wir sollen die Koffer öffnen.
❍ 9. Der Polizist befahl dem Mann, das Café zu verlassen.
❍ 10. Wer kann mir zeigen, wie man dieses Auto startet?

GEHIRNKNÖPFE

Schon ein wenig müde vom letzten Kapitel?

Da wollen wir mal deine Gehirntätigkeit wieder auf Vordermann bringen. Man könnte auch aktivieren dazu sagen:
Du berührst mit zwei Fingern der linken Hand den Nabel. Den Daumen der anderen Hand legst du in das rechte Grübchen unterhalb deines Schlüsselbeins. Mit Zeige- und Mittelfinger berührst du das linke Grübchen. Nun massierst du mit leichtem Druck alle drei Stellen gleichzeitig. Nach etwa einer Minute wechselst du die Hände. Nun reiben die Finger der rechten Hand den Nabel, die linke Hand befindet sich beim Schlüsselbein.

Dauer der Übung: 2 Minuten

Das „Gerund“

Das **Gerund** ist ein **hauptwörtlich gebrauchtes Zeitwort**. Es unterscheidet sich von seinem deutschen Gegenstück (das Singen, das Tanzen . . .) in einigen wesentlichen Bereichen. Dies macht das Gerund zu einer „typisch englischen“ Form.

Smoking *cigarettes is bad for your health.* →
Das Rauchen von Zigaretten ist ungesund.
(**Das Zigarettenrauchen** ist ungesund.)

Das **Gerund** ist eine ***ing*-Form**, und die kennst du ja schon von der *progressive form* (als *present participle*):

Nicht jede *ing*-Form ist ein Gerund! Manche *ing*-Formen sind *present participles*, wie etwa bei der *progressive form*. (Mehr über *present participle* und *progressive form* erfährst du ab Seite 71 und 23.)

Swimming *is fun.*	→	*gerund*
Look, Gus is ***swimming***.	→	*present participle (progressive form)*

Das „Einmaleins“ des Gerunds

☆ Das Gerund **kann** am **Beginn des Satzes** stehen, ähnlich wie das Subjekt:

Climbing *is dangerous.*

☆ Das Gerund **kann** an einer **anderen Stelle des Satzes** stehen, ähnlich wie das Prädikat oder das Objekt:

We began ***playing*** *games.*

☆ Das Gerund **muß** nach bestimmten Wörtern und Wendungen stehen:

There is no use ***crying****.*

☆ Das Gerund **darf nicht** nach gewissen Wörtern und Wendungen stehen. (Siehe auch Seite 44, Kapitel „Nennform – *infinitive*“.)

☆ Das Gerund **kann** anstelle bestimmer Gliedsätze stehen:

After ***landing****, the plane rolled to a stop.*
(= After the plane had landed, it rolled to a stop.)

25 Zu Beginn – wie immer – etwas ganz Leichtes! Setze ein Gerund an die Stelle der angegebenen Verben. Überlege, ob es sich dabei um ein Subjekt oder um ein Objekt handelt.

1. (smoke) is an expensive habit (= *Angewohnheit*).
2. (learn) English can be hard, but (speak) it is getting very important.
3. (program) a computer is more difficult than (play) computer games.
4. (skateboard) and (snowboard) have become very popular among kids.

5. I really hate (listen) to boring people.
6. (meet) Gina is always a nice surprise. Do you enjoy (talk) to her, too?
7. Nancy loves (jog) but she doesn't like (run) fast.
8. I have always disliked (watch) violent programs on TV.

Gerund nach bestimmten Verben

☆ Verben, auf die ein Gerund folgen **muß**:

to admit	zugeben, gestehen	***to imagine***	sich (etwas) vorstellen
to avoid	vermeiden	***to mention***	erwähnen
to consider	bedenken, überlegen	***to mind***	(etw.) dagegen haben
to dislike	nicht mögen	***to miss***	(ver)missen
to enjoy	sehr gern tun (haben)	***to practice***	üben, trainieren
to finish	beenden, fertig werden	***to risk***	riskieren
to forgive	vergeben, verzeihen	***to suggest***	vorschlagen

26

Damit du dich an den Klang und das Aussehen von Gerundsätzen gewöhnst: Setze auch hier ein Gerund an die Stelle der angegebenen Verben. Sage dir vor, wie diese Sätze auf Deutsch lauten würden.

1. The man admitted (steal) the jewels.
2. I always avoid (get) into a fight if I can.
3. A year ago Jack considered (move) back to England.
4. Do you really dislike (dance) so much?
5. My Dad enjoys (drink) a glass of beer in the evening.
6. Fred finished (do) his homework in time for "Star Trek".
7. Forgive me (call) you so late in the evening, but I need your help.
8. Can you imagine (live) in Beverly Hills and (become) a film star?
9. Did I mention (see) "Mona Lisa" in Paris?
10. You don't have to hurry, Paula. I don't mind (wait).
11. I'm glad you're back, Victoria. I really missed (talk) to you.
12. Mrs Reynolds said we should practice (read) German aloud.

Eine *-ing*-Form in einen Satz einzusetzen, ist natürlich nicht schwer. Einen (deutsch gedachten) Gedanken mittels einer „Gerundkonstruktion" in gutes Englisch zu übersetzen, ist hingegen schon viel schwieriger! Darin liegt auch das Problem, das wir Deutschsprechende mit dem Gerund haben: zu erkennen, wann ein Gerund verwendet wird und wann nicht. Deshalb findest du in diesem Kapitel immer wieder Übersetzungsübungen. Sie sollen dich mit den „Gerund-Auslösern" nach und nach vertraut machen!

27 Übersetze die folgenden deutschen Sätze mit Hilfe des Gerunds in „elegantes" Englisch.

example: Ich kann mir nicht vorstellen, in dieses Haus einzuziehen. →
I cannot imagine moving into this house.

1. Mein kleiner Bruder hat zugegeben, daß er die Vase zerbrochen hat.
2. Wenn du kannst, vermeide es, mit Caspar zu sprechen.
3. Ich überlege mir, 50 Schilling für das Rote Kreuz zu spenden. (spenden = *to give*)
4. Fritz mag es nicht, wenn er früh aufstehen muß.
5. Er genießt es, am Wochenende lange zu schlafen.
6. Die Arbeiter wurden gestern mit dem Tunnelgraben fertig. (graben = *to dig*)
7. Du riskierst, dich zu verkühlen, wenn du ohne warme Jacke ausgehst.
8. Ich schlage vor, heute ins Kino zu gehen.
9. Wir sollten öfter (= *more often*) Singen üben.
10. Ich stelle mir oft vor, nach Hawaii zu reisen.
11. Doris hat nichts dagegen, das Zimmer allein aufzuräumen.
12. Mein Großvater vermißt das Schachspielen mit seinen Freunden.

☆ Verben, auf die ein Gerund folgen **kann**: siehe ab Seite 78!

Gerund nach bestimmten Fügungen mit *to be*

A

to be afraid of	sich fürchten vor Angst haben vor	***to be proud of***	stolz sein auf
to be (in)capable of	(un)fähig sein zu etwas	***to be responsible for***	verantwortlich sein für
to be far from	weit davon entfernt sein zu	***to be surprised at***	überrascht sein von / über
to be fond of	gerne tun, gernhaben	***to be tired of***	etwas satt haben
to be good at	gut sein bei / in	***to be tired from***	von etwas müde sein
to be interested in	interessiert sein an, sich int. für	***to be used to***	an etwas gewöhnt sein

28

Wieder eine „Gewöhnungsübung": Setze das Gerund ein und überlege dir eine gute deutsche Übersetzung.

1. I am afraid of (lose) my keys, and so I've put them on a long chain.
2. Nobody thought that we were capable of (do) it, but we showed them!
3. Stevie went to bed although he was far from (finish) his work.
4. My familiy and I are fond of (invite) friends to a barbeque.
5. Listen to Johnny! He's really good at (imitate) people.
6. Who is interested in (find) out how the story ends?
7. Linda says she is proud of (be) my friend.
8. What a mess! Who is responsible for (tidy) up in here?
9. Hello, Andy! I'm surprised at (see) you here!
10. Let's go home. I'm tired of (listen) to this boring speech.
11. What's the matter with you, Mike? You don't look well. – Nothing! I'm just tired from (play) football all afternoon.
12. Mike is not used to (run) around so much.

29

Und jetzt die schwierigere Übersetzungsübung vom Deutschen ins Englische.

1. Martin fährt gut Schi. (= Er ist sehr gut im Schifahren.)
2. Er ist stolz darauf, daß er so viele Rennen gewinnt.
3. Er ist daran gewöhnt, viele Stunden in der Woche zu trainieren.
4. Er interessiert sich auch für das Snowboardfahren.
5, Manchmal ist er sehr müde vom Schifahren.
6. Und manchmal hat er Angst vorm Stürzen.
7. Aber er ist weit davon entfernt aufzuhören (= *to quit*).
8. Manchmal hat er es satt, so viele dumme Fragen zu beantworten.

Gerund nach der Kombination *verb + preposition*

Die Liste enthält wieder viel Neues, aber du weißt ja: Nicht versuchen, alles auf einmal zu lernen, denn das verwirrt nur. Nimm dir lieber ausreichend Zeit, denn dann merkst du dir die Vokabeln auch viel besser und länger.

A

to apologize for	sich entschuldigen	***to prevent from***	abhalten von, hindern an
to believe in	überzeugt sein von, glauben an	***to put off***	verschieben
to depend on	abhängen von	***to succeed in***	gelingen
to feel like	zumute sein nach	***to talk about***	sprechen über
to give up	aufgeben, aufhören	***to talk of***	sprechen von
to go / keep on	weitermachen	***to thank for***	danken für
to insist on	bestehen auf	***to think of***	denken an
to keep from	abhalten von, hindern an	***to think about***	(nach)denken über
to look forward to	sich freuen auf	***to worry about***	sich Sorgen machen wegen

30 Das Gerund „zum Angewöhnen": Gerund einsetzen und deutsche Übersetzung überlegen!

1. I apologized for (be) late, but they had started without me.
2. My Dad believes in (do) important things himself.
3. Modern economy depends on (get) information from all over the world.
4. I think I'll stay at home today. I don't feel like (go) out.
5. Two policemen prevented a young man from (jump) into the river.
6. If you still make mistakes, go on (practice) until you can do it.
7. Marion insisted on (pay) for her drinks herself.
8. Mum had a cold, so we had to put off (drive) to Munich.
9. Everybody in my class is looking forward to (see) "Frankenstein" at the theatre next week.
10. Grandma sometimes talks of (sell) her house and (move) to our place.
11. Thanks for (look) after our cats while we were away, Mrs Schneider.
12. Don't worry about (lose) your way. There are street signs everywhere.
13. Herbert has been talking about (cross) the Sahara for years.
14. David Copperfield usually succeeds in (fascinate) his audiences. (audience = *Publikum*)

31 *Translate, please!* Bilde wieder gute englische Sätze.

example: Frank entschuldigte sich dafür, daß er meine Disketten schon wieder vergessen hatte. →
Frank apologized for forgetting my disks again.

1. Wir konnten Onkel Richard nicht daran hindern, in den Teich (= *pond*) zu springen.
2. Ich mache mir oft Sorgen darüber, daß ich krank werde. (krank werden = *to fall ill*)

3. William spricht oft davon, den Mt. Everest zu besteigen.
4. Der Tourist bedankte sich dafür, daß ich ihm den Weg zeigte.
5. Ich hatte nie daran gedacht, daß ich das Rennen gewinnen würde.
6. Ist euch heute nach Schwimmen zumute? – Ja! Wir freuen uns schon darauf zu sehen, wer der Schnellste ist.
7. Du liest sehr gut, Linda. Bitte lies weiter!
8. Onkel Richard bestand darauf, selbst von der Party nach Hause zu fahren.

Gerund nach *instead of* und *without*

Grundsätzlich kann nach jeder Präposition ein Gerund folgen; in den meisten Fällen treten diese Präpositionen aber gemeinsam mit einem Verb auf. (Siehe auch Seite 61!)
Die zwei genannten Präpositionen kommen auch ohne enge Bindung an ein Verb vor.

***Instead of doing** the shopping, Julian went to his friend's place.*
(Anstatt einkaufen zu gehen, ...)

Marc went into the house ***without taking off*** *his shoes.*
(. . . ohne sich die Schuhe auszuziehen.)

32

Setze einfach wieder das Gerund ein *instead of the verb.*

1. Carl took the bus home instead of (wait) for his mother.
2. Instead of (stand) around here (do) nothing, you could help me.
3. Dad tried to repair the car himself instead of (take) it to the garage.
4. Lea was so tired that she went to bed without (brush) her teeth.
5. You can't come into this room without (knock)!
6. I'm not going to leave without (talk) to Mr Brown first!

33

And now English instead of German!

1. Der kleine Bub lief über die Straße, ohne nach links und nach rechts zu schauen.
2. Vater ging mit Onkel Richard fischen, anstatt mein Fahrrad zu richten. (richten = *to fix*)
3. Anstatt die Zeitung zu lesen, warf Oskar sie in den Papierkorb.
4. Oskar warf die Zeitung in den Papierkorb, ohne sie zu lesen.
5. René verließ den Raum, ohne ein Wort zu sagen.
6. Du solltest dich über Peters Pläne freuen (= *to be happy about*), anstatt dir Sorgen zu machen.

A Gerund nach *(to be) busy, cannot help, cannot stand, it's no / little use* und *is / isn't worth*

Look at Vanessa! She ***is busy packing*** *her bags.*
(Sie packt eifrig ihre Koffer.)

I ***cannot help laughing*** *when I see this picture.*
(. . . muß ich einfach lachen.)

I ***cannot stand*** *looking at this picture.*
(Ich kann es nicht ausstehen / ertragen . . . .)

It's no / little use calling *Jim. He's not at home.*
(Es hat keinen / wenig Sinn . . . .)

Have you ever eaten oysters? They ***are worth trying****.*
(Sie sind es wert, daß man sie kostet.)

34 Zum Gewöhnen: Setze das Gerund ein.

1. It's no use (ask) Bill for help. He is too busy (do) his own things.
2. When the film was over, Susi couldn't help (cry).
3. "Dracula" is an exciting book. It's really worth (read).
4. It's little use (try) to grow bananas in Austria. It's too cold.
5. Austria is a country worth (visit).
6. Steven has won some money. Now he is busy (spend) it again.
7. Charlie is such a nice person! One cannot help (like) him.
8. Mrs Hills is terrible. I can't stand (listen) to her.

35 Bevor es um Punkte geht, erhältst du noch einmal die Gelegenheit, alles „gemischt" zu üben! Stelle dir bei jedem Satz zwei Fragen: Wie heißt das auf Deutsch? Warum gehört ein Gerund hierher?

example: *Mum has often kept me from (make) a silly mistake.* →
Mum has often **kept** *me* **from making** *a silly mistake.*
(Mutter hat mich oft daran gehindert, einen dummen Fehler zu machen. → Gerund nach *verb + preposition*)

1. When Bertie tells jokes, I cannot help (laugh).
2. Martha was so tired that she was incapable of (drive).
3. I really like art, but I'm far from (understand) this picture.
4. Carlo is fond of (eat) pizza and drink (wine). He is Italian, of course.
5. Vreni has always been interested in (learn) more about foreign lands.
6. What a lovely evening. I'm looking forward to (see) you again soon.
7. What a mess! Who is responsible for (clean) the floor?
8. No coffee for me, please! I'm used to (drink) tea in the morning.
9. I'm tired of (work) so much for school. I'd like to go to bed.
10. Anthony apologized for (start) the fight. He was really sorry.
11. Do you really accuse me of (take) the money, Mum? I'm not a thief!
12. I wanted to try the exercise by myself, but Harry insisted on (help) me.

9

Jetzt ist es soweit! Jetzt kannst du zeigen, was du kannst! Übersetze die folgenden Sätze in elegantes Englisch. Jeder Satz muß ein Gerund enthalten!

✓ richtig

❍ 1. Mein liebstes (= *favourite*) Hobby ist Bücherlesen.
❍ 2. Kannst du dir vorstellen, gelbe Schuhe zu tragen?
❍ 3. Henry, Charlie! Hört bitt auf zu schwätzen (= *to chat*)!
❍ 4. Isabella kocht gerne für ihre Gäste. (= sie genießt es)
❍ 5. Wir können es nicht riskieren, uns hier zu verirren.
❍ 6. Ich kann es nicht ausstehen, immer hinter dir aufzuräumen.
❍ 7. Es macht mir nichts aus, neben Rudy zu sitzen.
❍ 8. Jungen Katzen (= *kittens*) zuzusehen, ist immer sehr lustig.
❍ 9. Mit einer Übung fertig zu werden, ist ein gutes Gefühl.
❍ 10. Opa hat das Autofahren vor zwei Jahren aufgegeben.
❍ 11. Wir vermeiden es immer, Herrn Berger zu ärgern. (= *to make angry*)
❍ 12. Interessiert es dich, die ganze Geschichte zu hören?

10

Zweiter Durchgang, mit denselben „Spielregeln"!

✓ richtig

❍ 1. Es macht uns nichts aus, allein ins Theater zu gehen.
❍ 2. Es hat keinen Sinn, auf Patrick zu warten.
❍ 3. Es hat uns sehr gefreut (= wir haben es genossen), hier zu sein.
❍ 4. Wie kamen (= *to get*) Sie in das Zimmer, ohne anzuklopfen?
❍ 5. Ich freue mich darauf, im Sommer nach England zu fahren.
❍ 6. Joe überlegt, ob er sich ein Segelboot kaufen soll.
❍ 7. Wir sind stolz darauf, in diesem Land zu leben.
❍ 8. Ich war überrascht, daß ich so eine gute Note bekam.
❍❍ 9. Bitte sprich weiter! Ich höre dir gerne zu. (2x)
❍ 10. Das Füttern der Tiere ist verboten.
❍ 11. Ich habe es satt, immer zu Hause zu bleiben.
❍ 12. Charlie kann sich nicht vorstellen, ohne Susi zu leben.

Wenn du bei jeder Übung mindestens 7 Sätze richtig übersetzt hast – ***GERUND KING/QUEEN!*** Dabei kommt es nicht so sehr auf die *word order* an, sondern nur auf das Gerund an der richtigen Stelle!

Gerund anstelle von Gliedsätzen

Mit Hilfe des Gerunds lassen sich Satzgefüge (also die Kombination aus Hauptsatz und Gliedsatz) verändern, was zu „gehobenerem" Stil führt. Auch zwei Hauptsätze lassen sich unter bestimmten Bedingungen durch ein Gerund verbinden.

Bedingung für diese „Gerundkonstruktion":

Beide Sätze oder Teilsätze haben **das gleiche Subjekt**!

after → ***after***	***before*** → ***before***	***when*** → ***on***

☆ ***After we had left*** *the cinema, we had a hot dog.* →
After leaving *the cinema, we had a hot dog.*

After I had done my homework, . . . → After doing my homework, I . . .
After Bob had arrived in town, . . . → After arriving in town, Bob . . .

☆ *Joe closed the windows* ***before he drove*** *to work.* →
Joe closed the windows ***before driving*** *to work.*

Before Tina went to bed, she called Tom. → Before going to bed, Tina . . .
Read everything before you sign it. → Read everything before signing it.

☆ ***When we returned*** *from Rome, we noticed the broken window.* →
On returning *from Rome, we noticed the broken window.*

When she heard the news, she smiled. → On hearing the news, . . .
When he entered the bank, he pulled a gun. → On entering the bank, . . .

A man was sitting in a pub wearing one blue sock and one red sock.
"That's a strange pair of socks you've got on," said a friend.
"Yes it is," the man replied. "And do you know, I've got another pair at home just like it."

Du bist an der Reihe! Verkürze die folgenden Sätze mit Hilfe von Gerunds.

36

1. When I saw Monica with Theo, I became very sad.
2. I usually read for a couple of minutes after I go to bed.
3. Before you go over to Charlie's place, call and ask if he's at home.
4. Julia Roberts studies a filmscript (= *Drehbuch*) carefully before she makes a film.
5. After Robin had found her car keys, she drove off.
6. When Harriet found a fly in her soup, she became sick.
7. Before I open a letter or a parcel, I always check it carefully.
8. When Maxwell heard the results of the exam, he jumped up and down for joy.

„indem"-Sätze → *by* + gerund

„Indem"-Sätze sagen aus, wie oder auf welche Weise etwas geschieht. Das sieht dann so aus:

Der Mann entkam, **indem er** aus dem fahrenden Zug **sprang**.
Lorie verdient etwas Geld, **indem sie** auf die Nachbarskinder **aufpaßt**.
Du kannst die Nummer Eins werden, **indem du** härter **trainierst** als alle anderen.

Auf Englisch:

The man escaped ***by jumping*** *from a moving train.*
Lorie earns some money ***by looking after*** *the neighbour's children.*
You can become Number One ***by practicing*** *harder than all the others.*

37

Bilde gute englische Sätze, indem du die folgenden deutschen „indem"-Sätze übersetzt.

1. Kurt löste das Problem, indem er mit seiner Schwester sprach.
2. Cassie veränderte ihr Aussehen (= *looks*), indem sie sich die Haare färbte (= *to dye*).
3. Gustav überraschte alle, indem er den Wettbewerb (= *competition*) gewann.
4. Fred wollte seine Freundin beeindrucken (= *to impress*), indem er sie in ein teures Restaurant einlud.
5. Der Einbrecher gelangte (= *to get*) in das Haus, indem er durch ein Fenster kletterte.
6. Die alte Dame verjagte (= *to chase off*) den Dieb, indem sie laut um Hilfe schrie.

11

„Verkürze" die Sätze mit *when*, *before* und *after* mit Hilfe eines Gerunds (Sätze 1 bis 6). „Verknüpfe" die Sätze 7 bis 10, indem du englische „indem"-Sätze bildest. Pro richtigem Satz gibt es einen Punkt, und du solltest mindestens 9 Punkte schaffen!

✓ richtig

❍ 1. When Alec read the headline of the newspaper, he got a shock.
❍ 2. I was very tired after I had painted the garden shed.
❍ 3. Before Jim wrote his answer, he thought carefully for a minute.
❍ 4. After Bruce had lost the tennis match, he walked home sadly.
❍ 5. When Mrs Jones returned from her morning walk, she found a telegram in her letterbox.
❍ 6. She made herself a cup of tea before she read the telegram.
❍ 7. The Beatles set a world record. They sold more records than any other pop group.
❍ 8. Mr Pinter ended the meeting. He sent us home.
❍ 9. Connect these sentences. Use a gerund.
❍ 10. Little Charlie shocked everybody. He ate a grasshopper.

DENKMÜTZE

Hast du Schwierigkeiten, in der Schule gut hinzuhören und alles zu verstehen?

Die Denkmütze ist besonders vor Unterrichtsbeginn nützlich: Entfalte sanft deine Ohren. Beginne oben und massiere am Ohrrand entlang nach unten. Ziehe sanft an den Ohrläppchen. Wiederhole diese Bewegung von oben nach unten 10mal. Wenn du gähnen mußt, öffne dabei bitte den Mund so weit du kannst.

Dauer der Übung: 10mal

Das Mittelwort der Gegenwart

Das ***present participle*** ist das **Mittelwort der Gegenwart** (aus dem Lateinischen: Partizipium Präsens). Es kommt in der deutschen Sprache genauso wie in der englischen vor:

*sleep**ing***	–	schlaf**end**
*go**ing***	–	geh**end**
*runn**ing***	–	lauf**end**

Das ***present participle*** ist **die *ing*-Form**!
Du bildest es nach der altbekannten „Formel":

Dabei mußt du aber besonders auf die Rechtschreibung achten. Du kannst dich sicher an die drei besonderen Regeln erinnern:

1 *writ**e**, com**e**, tak**e**, . . .* →
das „stumme **e**" fällt weg → *writing, coming, taking, . . .*

2 *ru**n**, swi**m**, sto**p**, . . .* →
der Endkonsonant verdoppelt sich → *running, swimming, stopping, . . .*

3 *l**ie**, d**ie*** und ***tie*** →
-ie wird zu *-y* → *lying, dying, tying*

Du kennst das ***present participle*** bereits als einen **Teil der *progressive form*** *(expanded form)*:

*The phone was **ringing** when I left the house.*
*Dad has been **lying** in the sun for two hours.*
*This time next Monday we will be **sitting** on a plane to Miami.*

Das ***present participle*** dient als **Adjektiv** (*adjective*, Eigenschaftswort) zur näheren Bestimmung eines Hauptwortes (Nomen, *noun*). Auch das ist für dich nichts Neues:

*They all looked at the **singing** man.*
*We had a room without **running** water.*
*"**Sitting Bull**" was a famous chief of the Lakota Indians.*

Das **Gerund** – das hauptwörtlich gebrauchte Zeitwort – sieht aus wie das *present participle*, hat aber eine andere Aufgabe zu erfüllen! Siehe dazu auch das Kapitel ab Seite 56!

Das *present participle* – eine „typisch englische" Konstruktion

Neben den bekannten Anwendungen kommt das *present participle* auch noch vor . . .

☆ nach Verben der **Sinneswahrnehmung**: *see, hear, watch, feel . . .* (wenn die Handlung bereits abgeschlossen ist oder wenn sie noch andauert):

*Can you **see** the boys **playing** football over there?*
*I **hear** you **coming** home every evening.*

Diese Gruppe kommt auch mit dem Infinitiv vor! (Siehe dazu Seite 44!)

☆ nach ***go***, ***come***, ***keep*** und ***catch***:

*Let's **go swimming** this afternoon!*
*Gabi **came running** down the stairs to tell me the story.*
*They **kept** us **waiting** for a long time.*
*Max **caught** me **drinking** his Coke.*

38

Setze *present participle* anstelle der angegebenen Verben ein.

1. Irene is here somewhere. I can hear her (laugh).
2. Come here, Larry! From here you can watch the animals (drink).
3. You can't see it and you can't hear it, but I can feel it (come) – winter is near!
4. Don't keep me (stand) here in the cold! Let me in!
5. I saw you (dig) a hole in your garden. What is it for? – I'm going to plant a cherry tree.
6. We'll have snow tomorrow. I can feel the air (get) colder and colder.
7. When the lesson was over, the children came (run) out of the building.
8. Some day they will catch you (drive) without a driving licence.
9. I ran as fast as I could, but the runner kept (come) closer and closer.
10. In winter we usually go (ski) two or three times a month.
11. I see you (look) at this painting. Do you like it?
12. Don't let me catch you (ride) my bike again!

☆ bei **gleichzeitig ablaufenden Handlungen**
anstelle einer der beiden Handlungen:
(Bedingung: gleiches Subjekt in beiden Sätzen)

Mary rode her bike and (she) sang a song.
Mary rode her bike ***singing*** *a song.*
Riding *her bike, Mary sang a song.*

☆ bei **unmittelbar aufeineinanderfolgenden Handlungen**
anstelle der ersten Handlung:
(Bedingung: gleiches Subjekt in beiden Sätzen)

I put on a warm jacket and went out into the night.
Putting on *a warm jacket, I went out into the night.*

39 „Aus Zwei mach' Eins!" Verbinde die folgenden Sätze mit Hilfe des *present participle*.

1. Bob opened his photo album and showed me a photo of himself.
2. I took Mary by the arm and led her onto the dancefloor.
3. Sue stood on the stage and read her own poems.
4. I left the room and stumbled (= *stolpern*) over the dog.
5. Tom lay in bed and read a book.
6. Olivia stood in the kitchen and cried over the burnt dinner.
7. Bob waved at (= *winkte*) his neighbour and went into the house.
8. Barbara woke up and saw a spider above her bed.
9. I ate my ice-cream and thought about Italy.
10. The girl was sitting by the window and looked sad.
11. Victor and Chris came into the classroom. They laughed loudly.
12. Jason sat down and turned on his computer.

☆ anstelle eines **Gliedsatzes**, der **mit *as***, ***because***. ***when*** oder ***while*** eingeleitet wird:
(Mit Ausnahme von *while*-Sätzen müssen Gliedsatz und Hauptsatz nicht das gleiche Subjekt haben.)

<u>As I did not know</u> where Charlie was,
I went to look for him.
***Not knowing** where Charlie was,*
I went to look for him.

(*participle* nur am Beginn des Satzes möglich!)

<u>Because the weather</u> was fine, we decided to make a bike tour.
*The weather **being** fine, we decided to make a bike tour.*

40

Ersetze die Gliedsätze in der folgenden Geschichte durch eine *participle construction*.

1. While Julius was walking home from work, he saw a little tomcat.
2. As the cat was hungry, he miaowed loudly.
3. As Julius had no pet, he took the cat home with him.
4. Julius offered him some cheese because he had no cat food at home.
5. As the cat was tired, he went to sleep at once.
6. When Julius looked at the sleeping cat, he felt he had done the right thing.

41

Bei dieser Übung mußt du darauf achten, ob Gliedsatz und Hauptsatz das gleiche Subjekt oder verschiedene Subjekte haben. Es hilft, wenn du dir die Subjekte unterstreichst!

1. When I walk to school, I always meet Lisa and Eric.
2. As we had enough money left, we bought some hamburgers and french fries.
3. As I was all alone, I decided to ring up Sandy.
4. When I was riding my sister's scooter (= *Mofa*) down the street, I was stopped by the police.
5. While I was talking to Helen, I had a wonderful idea.
6. When we walked into the house, we heard strange noises.
7. As Mum was ill, Dad and I had to do the cooking.
8. As the night air was too cold, we decided to sit inside.
9. As the bus was late, we missed the beginning of the film.
10. As my Dad is an expert horseman, people often ask him for advice.
11. When winter was over, Mum put our warm clothes away.
12. As petrol is so expensive now, many people travel by train.

☆ als **Ersatz für einen Relativsatz *(relative clause)***:

People <u>who work</u> with computers often make a lot of money.
*People **working** with computers often make a lot of money.*

Yesterday I found a wallet <u>that was lying</u> on the ground in the park.
*Yesterday I found a wallet **lying** on the ground in the park.*

In einem Satz können auch **mehrere *present participles*** vorkommen. Das sieht dann so aus:

When I <u>ate</u> the sandwich I <u>saw</u> a fly that <u>was walking</u> all over it.
***Eating** the sandwich, I <u>saw</u> a fly **walking** all over it.*

42 Das kannst du sicher auch alleine! Damit es aber nicht zu schwierig wird, ist das „Haupt"-Zeitwort (das sich nicht verändert) in den ersten drei Sätzen unterstrichen.

1. When I left the house, I <u>met</u> a man who was talking to his dog.
2. When Joseph turned the corner, he <u>noticed</u> a woman with shopping bags who was trying to open her car doors.
3. As Peter opened the bag, he <u>found</u> a spider that was hiding in it.
4. As Clarisse looked out of the window, she caught sight (= *erblickte*) of a cat that was chasing a mouse.
5. As Werner opened the door to his flat, he found a letter that was lying on the floor.
6. As I am Peter's best friend, I bought him the vase that is standing on the table over there.
7. As the schoolyear was over, my parents gave me the bike that is leaning against that tree.
8. As my ink cartridge (= *Tintenpatrone*) was empty, I took the one that was lying beside Fred's pencil case.

12 Wieder ein großes Finale – um viele Punkte! Verwende in jedem der folgenden Sätze *present participles*!

✓ richtig

❍❍ 1. When I entered the room, I heard Joe. He was singing "America the Beautiful".

❍❍ 2. As we were driving through Switzerland, we saw many cows. They were grazing in the mountains.

❍ 3. When I'm playing tennis, I can forget all my worries.

❍❍ 4. When I opened the book, I saw a picture that showed the Tower of London by night.

❍❍ 5. Vera sat in her rocking chair and watched TV all day long. (2 Möglichkeiten)

❍ 6. As I was the only one who knew Mr Hill, I was sent to talk to him.

❍ 7. The hunters fired their guns for hours and they killed a dozen pheasants (= *Fasane*).

❍❍ 8. As Ida was running down the stairs, she slipped and fell and hurt her elbow.

❍❍ 9. Jake stood outside the house and wondered if he should go in. (2 Möglichkeiten)

❍❍ 10. Maria stood in the middle of the room and looked around. (2 Möglichkeiten)

❍ 11. The car drove into a group of cyclists and knocked three of them over.

❍ 12. Can you see Mike? He's flying his kite. It's his newest hobby.

❍ 13. I found Dad in the living room. He was reading the paper.

❍❍ 14. As I did not know what to say, I said nothing.

Wenn du 19 oder mehr geschafft hast, dann bist du **1A**!
Ab 16 bist du ***OKAY***!
Bei 12 oder darunter solltest du das Kapitel noch einmal gründlich durcharbeiten!

Infinitiv oder *ing*-Form?

Die Frage ist berechtigt! Gottseidank ist sie auch recht leicht zu beantworten:

Es gibt Zeitwörter, die

☆ **zwingend den Infinitiv** verlangen
(z. B. *afford, agree, ask . . .*).
Du findest sie in diesem Buch ab Seite →

*Can you really **afford to waste** so much time?*

☆ **zwingend eine *ing*-Form** verlangen. Das kann ein Gerund oder ein *present participle* sein
(z. B. *admit, avoid, consider . . .*
beziehungsweise *go, come, keep . . .*).
Du findest sie in diesem Buch ab Seite →

*I **admit forgetting** my gym shoes, Sir.*
*Did I **keep** you **waiting**? I'm sorry.*

☆ **entweder mit dem Infinitiv oder der *ing*-Form** auftreten können.
Dabei mußt du unterscheiden zwischen

!

gleicher Bedeutung von *verb + infinitive* und *verb + "ing"-form*	**verschiedener Bedeutung** von *verb + infinitive* und *verb + "ing"-form*
*They **began to dance**.* *They **began dancing**.*	*I'll **remember to post** the letter.* *I **remember posting** the letter.*

. . . von *verb + infinitive* und *verb + "ing"-form*

☆ nach ***begin***, ***start*** und ***continue***

*It **began** / **started to rain** when we left the cinema.*
*It **began** / **started raining** when we left the cinema.* → kein Unterschied

☆ nach ***like***, ***love***, ***prefer*** und ***hate***

*My Dad **likes to bake** / **baking** cakes.*
*Helen **prefers to make** / **making** her own clothes.* → kein Unterschied

→ Nach ***would like*** / ***love*** / ***prefer*** / ***hate*** steht **nur** der **Infinitiv**!

***I'd like** to dance.* → Ich möchte (jetzt!) tanzen.
(*I like to dance. / I like dancing.* → Ich tanze gern.)

. . . in der Bedeutung von *verb + infinitive* und *verb + "ing"-form*

☆ nach Zeitwörtern der **Sinneswahrnehmung**: ***see***, ***hear***, ***watch*** . . .

1 ***verb + infinitive*** → *Yesterday I **saw** Tim **return** at 10.*
(siehe Seite 42) *I always **watch** them **play** football.*

Wird meist für die gesamte Handlung verwendet:

Ich sah, wie Tim zurückkam, ins Haus ging usw.
Ich gehe ins Stadion, bleibe 90 Minuten usw.

2 ***verb + "ing"-form*** (siehe Seite 56) → *You can **hear** them **singing**.*
*From here you can **watch** them **playing**.*

Wird meist für eine noch andauernde, nicht abgeschlossene Handlung verwendet:

Du kannst sie jetzt (!) singen hören; sie singen noch.
Du kannst ihnen von hier aus (jetzt!) zusehen.

. . . **. . . in der Bedeutung von *verb + infinitive* und *verb + "ing"-form***

Bei einer Reihe von Zeitwörtern ändert sich die Bedeutung, je nachdem, ob sie mit dem Infinitiv oder mit der *"ing"*-Form auftreten. Dazu gehören unter anderem (keine vollständige Liste!):

A ***forget – need – remember – stop – try***

verb + infinitive	***verb + "ing"-form***
*I'm sorry I **forgot to bring** my pen.* → notwendige Handlung (Hätte ich tun sollen.)	*I'll never **forget meeting** you.* → Erinnerung an Vergangenes (Habe ich schon getan.)
*We **need to start** early today.* → Notwendigkeit, Zwang (aktiv) (Wir müssen etwas tun.)	*Your hair **needs cutting**.* → Notwendigkeit, Zwang (passiv) (Es müßte etwas geschehen.)
***Remember to call** Aunt Liz.* → notwendige Handlung (Vergiß nicht . . .!)	*I don't **remember calling** Aunt Liz.* → Erinnerung an Vergangenes (Ich kann mich nicht erinnern.)
*Dad **stopped to look** at the map.* → eine Tätigkeit unterbrechen (anhalten, um etwas zu tun)	*Dad, **stop looking** at the map!* → eine Tätigkeit einstellen (aufhören, beenden)
*I **tried to bake** a cake yesterday.* → der Versuch, etwas zu tun (Man gibt sein Bestes.)	***Try baking** a cake! It's easy.* → Vorschlag, Problemlösung (Du könntest es ja versuchen.)

43 In dieser Übung findest du Sätze mit *verb + infinitive* und *verb + "ing"- form*. Du sollst entscheiden, welche Sätze auch in der jeweils anderen Kombination möglich sind und welche man nicht verändern kann.

examples: They started playing after we had arrived. →
They started to play after we had arrived.
→ gleiche Bedeutung, daher andere Form möglich

I don't mind waiting for you a little longer. →
→ keine andere Form möglich; "to mind" verlangt zwingend eine "ing"-Form (Gerund)

1. Dad, have you finished working?
2. I'd like to watch "Star Trek" now, okay?
3. Sammy prefers to write with a ball-point (= *Kugelschreiber*).
4. Last Saturday I watched my brother play in the finals. He won.
5. Jack managed to get all his things into the bag.
6. I'm very disappointed with Fred. He has refused to help me again.
7. Grandpa loves to work in his garden.
8. After a short rest the tourists continued climbing up the mountain.

44 In dieser Übung gibt es nur mehr eine richtige Möglichkeit. Die Frage lautet daher: *infinitive or "ing"-form?* Du entscheidest!

examples: Mr Fox is angry because I have forgotten (do) my homework. →
Mr Fox is angry because I have forgotten to do my . . .

I remember (see) this man before,
but I don't know where. →
I remember seeing this man before, . . .

1. About a month ago Aunt Frieda stopped (smoke).
2. She had tried (give it up) many times before, but she had never succeeded in (do) so.
3. This time she needed (stop) because she had asthma.
4. If she had continued (smoke), she would have risked (get) seriously ill.
5. A friend had said to her, "Why don't you try (eat) sugar-free sweets instead of (smoke)? It may work."
6. And really, so far she has managed (keep) away from cigarettes.

13

Same problem, different examples! Setze wieder *infinitive* oder *"ing"-form* ein. Pro Form gibt es einen Punkt!

✓ richtig

❍ 1. The taxi driver stopped at a petrol station (ask) for the way.

❍❍ 2. I'd love (fly) a helicopter one day. I love (do) exciting things.

❍ 3. Gloria and Alfred are here. I can hear them (come).

❍❍ 4. "(eat) sweets is dangerous for your teeth", the dentist said. But it's very difficult (give up) something one likes so much.

❍ 5. I remember (read) this book last year. I liked it!

❍❍ ❍❍ ❍ 6. Look, somebody forgot (lock) the door. I hate (come) home and (find) the door open! Imagine someone (walk) into the house and (steal) something!

❍❍ 7. I'm sure I didn't forget (lock) it! I clearly remember (check) all the doors and windows before we left.

❍❍ ❍❍ 8. I hate (hear) my sisters (fight) all the time! – Why don't you try (talk) to them about it? Perhaps they will stop (fight) when you are near.

❍ ❍❍ 9. Have you ever watched Bill (do) his card tricks? They are amazing. – No, never. But I'd like (see) him (do) them one day.

❍❍ ❍ 10. Peter has caught a cold. We tried (make) him (wear) a warmer jacket, but he refused (listen) to us.

❍❍ 11. My sister loves (take) walks in the rain. I don't! I hate (get) wet.

❍❍ ❍ 12. The walls of my room need (paint). I'll try (paint) them blue and green this time. I like (try out) new colours.

Hast du zwischen 29 und 26 Punkte erreicht? ***HATS OFF TO YOU, MY FRIEND!***
25 bis 22? ***YOU'VE GOT THE FEELING, BABY!***
21 bis 17? ***STILL FAIR!***
16 und darunter? ***I DON'T WANT TO KNOW ABOUT IT!***

ZAUBERPUNKT

Du fühlst dich nicht wohl?
Es streßt dich, lernen zu müssen?
Du hast Heißhunger auf Süßes?

Die Energie deines Körpers ist zu niedrig. Da hilft dir der Zauberpunkt:
Du legst zwei Finger der linken Hand auf die Innenseite des rechten Handgelenks. Diesen Punkt massierst du 2mal täglich 4 bis 12 Minuten und immer dann, wenn es dir nicht gut geht. Du wirst merken, wie das funktioniert. Wenn du an dieser Stelle die Energie aktivierst, verzichtet dein Körper auch freiwillig auf Süßigkeiten. Süßigkeiten sind Energiefresser!

Dauer der Übung: 4 bis 12 Minuten

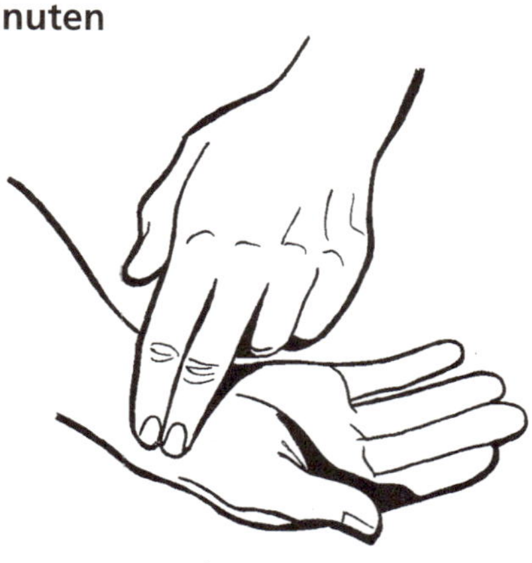

Die Zukunft

Zukunft ist nicht gleich Zukunft! Es kommt darauf an, ob das zukünftige Ereignis geplant ist oder nicht, ob es sich „nur" um eine Vorhersage handelt oder nicht, ob es um eine seit längerem beschlossene Sache geht oder nicht und so weiter.

Kompliziert? Schwierig? Verwirrend? Wir sind der Meinung: Überhaupt nicht! Das meiste kennst du ohnehin schon aus den ersten drei Lernjahren, aber überzeuge dich selbst!

future with "will"

☆ Für Vorhersagen allgemeiner Art: was ohne unser Zutun „einfach geschehen" wird.

*Some time in the future doctors **will find** a cure for AIDS.*
The swallows (= Schwalben) ***will fly** south again in autumn.*

☆ Für ganz plötzliche Entscheidungen (ohne vorher darüber nachzudenken): meist mit *short form.*

*It's hot in here. – I'**ll open** the window.*
*Coke or orange juice? – I'**ll have** a coke, please.*

☆ Für Angebote oder Versprechen:

*Can I go out now, Mum? I'**ll practice** the piano later.*
*If you haven't got the time, we'**ll mow** the lawn for you.*

☆ Für den „Fall der Wirklichkeit" *(conditions)*:

If *Dad misses the train again, he'****ll have*** *to walk.*
Gilbert ***won't keep*** *his mouth shut* ***if*** *we tell him the story.*

☆ Für Vermutungen aller Art: oft mit *think, expect, (be) sure, maybe, perhaps, probably*.

The Millers aren't here yet. I ***expect*** *they'****ll be*** *on the next train.*
They say Seattle is nice. – ***Maybe*** *I'****ll go*** *there on my next trip.*

future with "going to" + base form

☆ Für ein geplantes Ereignis in nicht allzuferner Zukunft *(near future)*: „Was man beschlossen hat."

I ***am going to throw*** *away my sticker albums.*
The children ***are going to make*** *a snowball fight.*

☆ Für eine Vorhersage aufgrund der augenblicklichen Situation: „Alles deutet darauf hin."

Look at those clouds!
*There'****s going to be*** *a storm.*

You've eaten six hotdogs?
*You'****re going to feel*** *sick very soon.*

Und noch einmal, denn „doppelt hält besser"!

	will	***going to***
Vorhaben	plötzliche Entscheidung, ohne vorherige Planung	geplantes Vorhaben (für die „nahe Zukunft")
Vorhersage	allgemeines Ereignis, ohne eigenes Zutun	ausgehend von der augenblicklichen Situation

45

Die Zeit ist reif zum Üben (oder Wiederholen)! Setze die Zeitwörter in die passende Form der Zukunft: *will* oder *going to*?

examples: The next winter (bring) will bring snow and ice again.
Christine (buy) is going to buy a moped. She has told me so herself.

1. My cousin Herbert (be) at the party, too. I'm sure you (like) him.
2. If you are not at home tonight, I (call) you again tomorrow morning.
3. Have you got anything planned for the afternoon? – Yes. We (visit) Aunt Edna in hospital. – Good idea! I (come) with you if I may.
4. Look at that crazy driver! He (crash) into one of the other cars!
5. Grandpa (be) 65 next week. We (have) a big party on his birthday.
6. I can't talk to you right now but I promise I (listen) to your side of the story as soon as possible.
7. We've made too many mistakes. We (lose) the game.
8. What are your plans, Werner? What (you, do) after this year? – I don't know yet, but I think I (go) to a technical school.
9. Somebody is knocking at the door! Who (go) and see who it is? – I (go)!
10. What (Charlie, do) with those roses? – He (give) them to Susi.

Weiter geht's mit echten Neuigkeiten: Auch ***present progressive*** (auch *present continuous* oder *present expanded* genannt) und ***present simple*** können zukünfige Ereignisse bezeichnen!

present progressive

☆ Für geplante Handlungen, für die alle Vorbereitungen getroffen sind; fast immer mit Zeitangabe:

My grandparents ***are returning*** *from their holidays in Malta* ***tomorrow****.*
(Die Flugtickets sind seit langem gekauft, die Hotelrechnung ist beglichen, die Verwandten zu Hause sind informiert, . . .; kurz: alles ist vorbereitet!)

Charlie ***is having*** *a party* ***on Saturday****.*
Are you going?
(Er hat schon alle Einladungen ausgeschickt, seine Eltern sind einverstanden, und er hat sich schon überlegt, was er an Essen und Getränken braucht.)

Present progressive und ***near future*** (mit *going to* + *base form*) sind einander sehr ähnlich! Der (kleine) Unterschied:

R

near future	drückt die Absicht oder den Beschluß aus; steht meist ohne Zeitangabe: ***I'm going to redecorate my room****.* (Ich habe beschlossen, mein Zimmer herzurichten.)
present progressive	drückt ein geplantes Vorhaben aus, für das die Vorbereitungen laufen oder getroffen sind; steht fast immer mit Zeitangabe: ***I'm redecorating my room at the weekend.*** (Ich habe alle Vorkehrungen getroffen: Tapeten und Kleister sind gekauft, Freunde haben ihre Hilfe zugesagt usw.)

Nicht vergessen: *present progressive* ohne Zeitangabe heißt, daß eine Handlung im Augenblick des Sprechens noch nicht abgeschlossen ist!

*What **are** you **doing** here? – We **are waiting** for you!*

46 Diese Übung soll deinen Geist und deine Beobachtungsgabe schärfen! Schau dir jeden Satz genau an und überlege: Beschreibt er einen Vorgang, der sich „hier und jetzt" ereignet? Wenn ja, dann schreibe **PR** (für *present*) dazu. Oder bezieht er sich auf die Zukunft? Dann schreibe **F** (für *future*) dazu.

examples: I am practicing for the next match. → PR
I am playing an important match on Sunday. → F

1. Uncle Frank is in the garden. He is planting an apple tree. → ____
2. Why are you walking so fast? – I want to see the beginning of the new TV show. → ____
3. I'm sorry we can't come tomorrow. Dad is working late again. → ____
4. Joe and Harriet are getting married next week. → ____
5. The Jacksons are leaving for Sweden tomorrow morning. → ____
6. Why are you leaving? It's only 10 o'clock. – I know, but I'm helping my dad in the shop tomorrow. → ____ / → ____
7. Sylvia is planning to organize a tennis tournament in summer. → ____
8. The Pope (= *Papst*) is visiting our country again in June. → ____
9. Look, they are taking away all the park benches! → ____
10. On Wednesday we are taking our American friends with us to our house on the lake. → ____
11. Have you heard? I am playing all the solos in our next concert! → ____
12. Charlie, you are sitting on my chair again, reading my newspaper and wearing my slippers! → ____

present simple

☆ Nach bestimmten *prepositions of time*: ***after***, ***before***, ***when***, ***until***, ***as soon as***.

*I will call you **as soon as** I **hear** from Charlie.*
***When** George **arrives**, we will start the film.*

47 *present simple* oder *future with will*? Setze die richtigen Formen ein.

1. When I (get) next week's pocket money, I (pay) you back the Pound I borrowed from you on Friday.
2. We should finish the game before it (get) too dark.
3. Mary has promised that she (write) to us as soon as she (arrive) in Los Angeles.
4. We (have) dinner when all the guests (be) here.
5. Don't worry! We (not leave) before it (stop) raining.
6. I (go) to bed at once after the visitors (leave).
7. As soon as I (finish) tidying up my room, we can ride our bikes.
8. When Mum and Dad (see) my school report, they (not believe) their eyes!

☆ Bei Angaben über **Fahrpläne** oder andere **genaue Zeitpläne**.

*Our train **leaves** at 8:30 tonight and it **arrives** in Venice at 8 o'clock tomorrow morning.*
*The film **starts** at 6 p.m., and now it's 4:30. We have one and a half hour left.*

48

Aus dem Terminkalender eines Ministers! Bilde Sätze mit *present simple* und verwende dabei die angegebenen Zeitwörter.

example: 12:30–1:30, lunch with Prime Minister (have) →
From 12:30 to 1:30 he has lunch with the Prime Minister.

1. 9:00–10:30, meeting with ministers from France and Spain (attend)
2. 11:00–11:30, BBC journalist, interview (give)
3. 12:00, telephone, wife (call)
4. 2:00–5:00, senior staff (= *Spitzenbeamte*), problems (meet / discuss)
5. 5:30, Prime Minister, telephone (talk)
6. 6:00, his driver, home (drive)
7. 8:45, plane to Paris (take)
8. on the plane, speech, conference next day (prepare)

14

Setze die jeweils beste Form des Zeitwortes ein. Manchmal sind auch zwei richtige Lösungen möglich. Für jede richtige Zeitwortform bekommst du einen Punkt!

✓ richtig

❍❍ 1. Lynn (leave) __________ for Sweden tomorrow morning. She has already packed her suitcases. – When (her plane, take off) __________________________? – At 11:40.

❍❍ 2. Frank, you (catch) __________ a cold if you don't put on a warmer jacket. – Okay, I (take) __________ the blue one.

❍❍❍ 3. Do you like Janet? – Oh yes, she's sweet. I (invite) __________ __________________ her to my next party. – I'm sure she (be) __________ glad when she (hear) __________ this.

❍❍ 4. I'm really happy that you can come skiing with us. We (have) __________ lots of fun. – Yes, I think it (be) __________ great!

❍❍ 5. Our team is leading 4 : 2. We (win) ____________________ this match! – I think so, too. I hope they (win) __________ the championship this year.

❍❍❍ 6. We (go) ____________________ to the mountains on Friday. Do you want to come along? – I'm sorry I can't. We (start) __________ building a new garage as soon as we (get) __________ the building materials.

❍❍ 7. It smells as if something was burning. I (go) __________ and see what it is. – I (stay) __________ here and wait.

❍❍❍ 8. (you, go) ____________________ to the cinema on Saturday, too? – No, I don't think so. I think I (make) __________ a bike tour with Charlie and stay overnight at his place. But perhaps I (just, stay) ____________________ at home and relax.

❍❍ 9. Hurry up, Mother! Father's train (arrive) __________ in ten minutes! – What? In ten minutes? I (must) ____________________ drive faster if we want to meet him at the station.

❍❍ 10. Some day soon astronauts (land) __________ on Mars. I am certain of it. – So am I. They (probably, get) ____________________ there within the next 25 years.

❍❍ 11. Mac doesn't like Charlie any more. He says he (look) ____________________ for a different second half. – I can't believe it! I'm sure they (be) __________ friends again soon.

❍ 12. That's enough for today. We (stop) __________ now!

26 oder 25 Punkte? ***THE FUTURE IS YOURS!***
24 bis 22 Punkte? ***YOUR FUTURE STILL LOOKS GOOD!***
21 bis 18 Punkte? ***MORE CONCENTRATION IN FUTURE!***
17 Punkte oder weniger? ***BACK TO THE FUTURE!*** (Ab Seite 84)

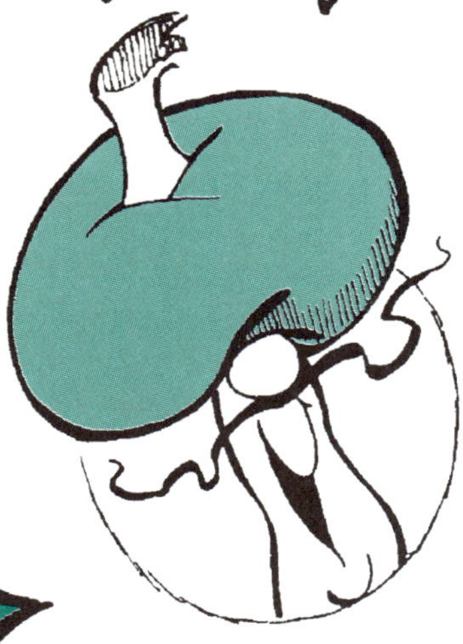

MUDRA FÜR DEN GESUNDEN WILLEN

Du hast keine Lust zu lernen?

Diese Lernunwilligkeit kannst du folgendermaßen abbauen:

Du legst den Zeigefinger in die Daumengrube und bringst Daumen und Mittelfingerkuppe zusammen.

Das Mudra kannst du mit beiden Händen gleichzeitig oder jeweils mit einer Hand halten. Immer dann, wenn du eine Hand gerade nicht brauchst, hältst du die Finger in der beschriebenen Stellung.

Hervorragend geeignet zum Hinhören im Unterricht, beim Schreiben und Nachdenken. Sogar während des Lesens kannst du es halten.

Dauer der Übung: mindestens 7 Minuten

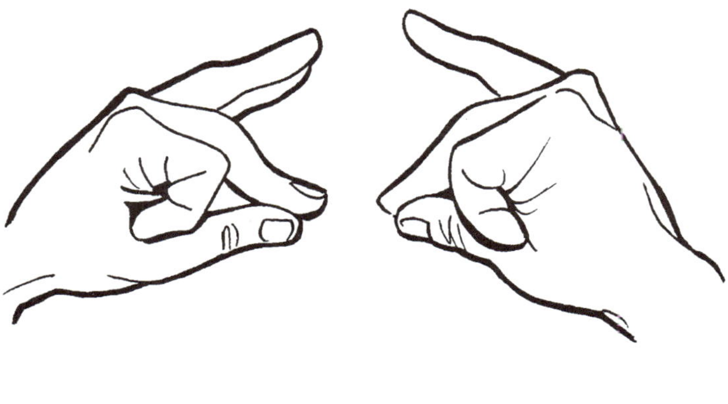

RELATIVSÄTZE: EINSCHRÄNKEND UND ERWEITERND

„Schon wieder *relative clauses*? Das sind doch die mit *who, that, which* und so weiter. Das hatten wir doch schon!" denkst du vielleicht, wenn du das Inhaltsverzeichnis oder die Überschrift liest. Und du hast recht; du hast im zweiten und dritten Lernjahr schon vieles über diese Wörter und Sätze gelernt, und du weißt auch, unter welchen Umständen du das *relative pronoun* weglassen kannst *(contact clause)*.

Im 4. Lernjahr wirst du einige neue Regeln kennenlernen. Sie betreffen die **Zeichensetzung** (Frage: Beistrich oder nicht?) sowie die *relative pronouns* ***which*** und ***what***. Wir lösen damit auch ein Versprechen aus dem Buch „Durchstarten in Englisch für die 7. Schulstufe", Seite 114, ein.

Damit du aber wirklich weißt, worum es geht, folgt ein kurzer Überblick – mit Beispielen – über die wichtigsten bisher gelernten **Regeln**!

R

ÜBERBLICK

- ☆ Bei Personen verwendest du eher *who* statt *that.*
  The familiy who (that) *has moved in next door is from Croatia.*
- ☆ Bei Dingen und Tieren verwendest du eher *that* statt *which.*
  I really like ***the flowers that (which)*** *grow in your garden.*
- ☆ Nach „Extremwörtern" *(superlatives, first, last, all, some, any . . .)* verwendest du immer *that* (außer in *contact clauses*).
  "Waterworld" is ***the most expensive film that*** *has ever been made.*
- ☆ Du kannst und sollst das *relative pronoun (who, which, that)* weglassen, wenn es sich auf das Objekt des Satzes bezieht. Das merkst du daran, daß auf das *relative pronoun* kein *verb* (Zeitwort) folgt, sondern meist ein *personal pronoun* oder ein Name.
  Do you like ***the shoes*** *(that)* ***I****'m wearing today?*
  Who was ***that woman*** *(who)* ***you*** *were talking to?*
- ☆ *whose* darfst du niemals weglassen.
  Are you ***the person whose picture*** *was in all the newspapers?*

!

Zum Wiederholen und Einüben: Setze *who, which, that* oder *whose* ein oder lasse das *relative pronoun* weg, wo das möglich ist *(contact clause)*.

examples: Oscar arrived on the plane **that (which)** has just landed.

Would you like to see the pictures . . . I took last summer? →
Would you like to see **the pictures I took** last summer?

1. People . . . speak English have better chances in life.
2. Children . . . parents are too strict are usually unhappy.
3. The boys . . . we met at Miriam's party last week gave us their telephone numbers.
4. In a famous song New York is called "the city . . . never sleeps".
5. Of all the countries . . . I have visited I like New Zealand best.
6. How do you like the girls . . . live in the house across the street?
7. What did you do with the money . . . Grandma gave you at Christmas?
8. We all admire (= *bewundern*) the flowers . . . grow in your garden.
9. Do you know the man . . . guests we are tonight?
10. Elvis Presley was one of the first musicians . . . used an electric guitar.
11. Policeman: "I'd like to talk to the person . . . drives the green Volvo . . . is parked outside."

Bist du mit deinem Ergebnis zufrieden? Hat das Erinnerungsvermögen ausgereicht? Wenn nicht, solltest du dir die „Regeln" auf Seite 93 noch besser einprägen!

Nun aber zu den neuen „Regeln"!

☆ Ein Relativsatz, der sich auf den **gesamten vorherigen Satz** bezieht (und nicht nur auf einen Satzteil), wird immer mit ***which*** eingeleitet.
Vor *which* wird ein **Komma** gesetzt.

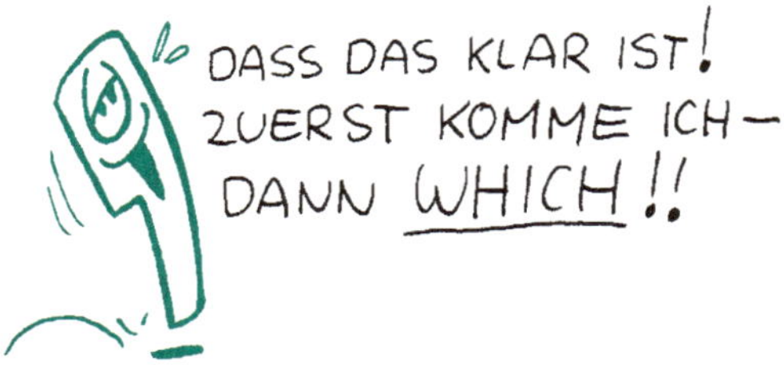

Gabriella finished the race first.
***This** made her very happy.*

*Gabriella finished the race first**,***
***which** made her very happy.*
(. . ., **was** sie sehr glücklich machte.)

2 „Aus zwei mach' eins!" Verbinde die folgenden Sätze. Vergiß dabei nicht auf die Beistriche (Kommas)!

example: Charlie says he can eat seven burgers. I don't believe this. →
Charlie says he can eat seven burgers, which I don't believe.

1. I went to the cinema with my parents last night. This was better than staying at home alone.
2. My chemistry teacher sometimes gets mad at us. This makes us all laugh.
3. This morning Dad's car didn't start, and so he had to walk to work. He didn't like it at all.
4. We did not believe Walter's story. This made him very angry.
5. Mary got more points on her maths test than anybody else. This was not surprising.
6. My Grandma always kisses me when we meet. I can't stand it.
7. Brian has about 250 CDs. That's more than I have.
8. Our team won the match. Nobody really expected this.

R

☆ ***what*** steht für *that which* (= was).
Vor *what* steht **kein Komma**!

*I don't know **what** I should do.*
(. . . **was** ich tun soll.)

3

which oder *what*? Setze das passende Wort ein.
Achte auf die Zeichensetzung (Komma).

1. Mr Smith came by bike this morning . . . is unusual.
2. Can anybody tell me . . . this is?
3. Be quiet, please! I can't hear . . . the speaker is saying.
4. The trapper found a goldmine . . . made him a rich man.
5. Many people drive after drinking alcohol . . . is very dangerous.
6. Which of you speaks German? I don't know . . . this word means.
7. Jim fell and broke his leg . . . must have hurt terribly.
8. Maxwell, go and ask Sally . . . she wants for her birthday.

PAUSE

Dir ist sicher aufgefallen, daß bei den Relativsätzen in den ersten drei Lernjahren nirgendwo ein Beistrich (ein Komma) vorkam. Das war weder Schlamperei noch ein Versehen, sondern richtige englische Zeichensetzung. (Im Unterschied zur deutschen Zeichensetzung, die bei jedem Relativsatz einen Beistrich verlangt!).

Es gibt aber auch im Englischen Relativsätze, die Beistriche (Kommas) verlangen!

Vergleiche die beiden folgenden Sätze miteinander. Wodurch unterscheiden sie sich?

!

1 *The reporters interviewed **the driver who** had won the race.*

2 *The reporters interviewed **Damon Hill, who** had won the race.*

Hast du eine Erklärung, eine Vermutung, einen Verdacht? *Check it out!*

Satz **1** ist ein **einschränkender Relativsatz** *(defining relative clause)*. Er schränkt die große Zahl der möglichen Fälle auf einen konkreten Fall ein.

Erst durch ihn wissen wir, welcher Fahrer gemeint ist. Ohne ihn wäre der Satz unklar, unvollständig oder nicht eindeutig. Er ist für das Verstehen des Satzes **notwendig**.

Es gibt keine Beistriche!

Betrachten wir unseren Mustersatz:

The reporters interviewed ***the driver****.* =

Da es viele *drivers* gibt, bleibt völlig unklar, welcher *driver* gemeint ist. Die große Zahl möglicher Fälle muß also eingeschränkt werden, damit die Aussage eindeutig ist.

. . . (the driver) who won the race. =

Der Relativsatz schränkt die Zahl der möglichen Fälle auf einen bestimmten Fall ein: Gemeint ist der Fahrer, welcher das Rennen gewonnen hat. Damit wird die Aussage klar und eindeutig.

Satz **2** ist ein **erweiternder Relativsatz** *(non-defining relative clause)*.

Er bietet zusätzliche (= erweiterte) Informationen an. Er ist für das klare und eindeutige Verstehen des Satzes **nicht erforderlich**.

Er wird vom Hauptsatz durch Beistriche abgetrennt.

Betrachten wir wieder unseren Mustersatz:

The reporters interviewed ***Damon Hill****.* =

Hier ist alles klar und eindeutig: Es gibt nur einen Damon Hill.

(. . . Damon Hill), who won the race. =

Der Relativsatz bietet zusätzliche Information: Damon Hill hat das Rennen gewonnen. Diese Information brauchen wir aber nicht, um den Satz zu verstehen.

Noch zwei Beispiele zur Verdeutlichung:

The ship we talked about yesterday has arrived.

- *"The ship has arrived."* ist nicht klar und eindeutig. Man fragt sofort: „Welches Schiff?" Daher wird auf ein bestimmtes Schiff eingeschränkt – auf dasjenige, worüber wir gestern sprachen.
- Man setzt keine Beistriche, weil es sich um einen (notwendigen) einschränkenden Relativsatz handelt.
- Man läßt das *relative pronoun (that/which)* weg, weil es um einen *contact clause* geht.

The ***"Queen Elizabeth", which*** *we talked about yesterday, has arrived.*

- *"The 'Queen Elizabeth' has arrived."* ist eine klare und eindeutige Aussage. Die Zusatzinformation – wir unterhielten uns gestern über sie – ist für das Verstehen des Satzes nicht notwendig.
- Man setzt Beistriche, weil es sich um einen (nicht notwendigen) erweiternden Relativsatz handelt.
- Man wählt *which*, weil *that* nicht nach einem Komma stehen darf und somit in einem erweiternden Relativsatz nicht vorkommen kann.

Die **„neuen Regeln"** lauten daher:

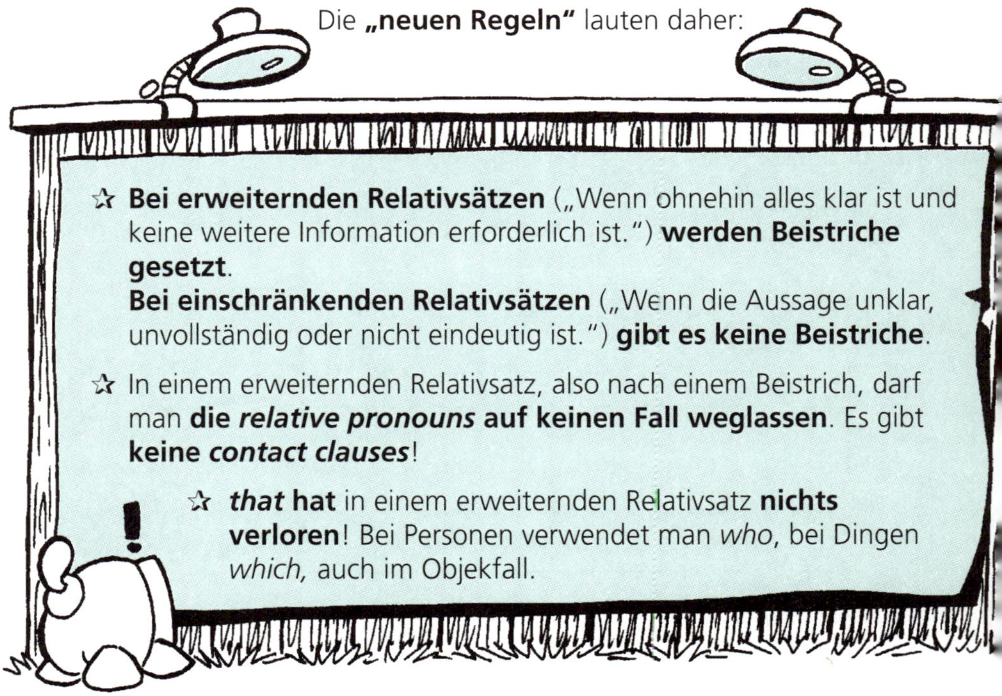

☆ **Bei erweiternden Relativsätzen** („Wenn ohnehin alles klar ist und keine weitere Information erforderlich ist.") **werden Beistriche gesetzt**.
Bei einschränkenden Relativsätzen („Wenn die Aussage unklar, unvollständig oder nicht eindeutig ist.") **gibt es keine Beistriche**.

☆ In einem erweiternden Relativsatz, also nach einem Beistrich, darf man **die *relative pronouns* auf keinen Fall weglassen**. Es gibt **keine *contact clauses***!

☆ ***that* hat** in einem erweiternden Relativsatz **nichts verloren**! Bei Personen verwendet man *who*, bei Dingen *which*, auch im Objekfall.

4 Bei dieser Übung triffst du auf „Satzpaare". Ein Satz erfordert einen einschränkenden Relativsatz *(defining relative clause)* ohne Beistriche, der andere verlangt einen erweiternden Relativsatz *(non-defining relative clause)* mit Beistrichen. Verwende die passenden *relative pronouns* oder lasse sie weg (bei *contact clauses*) und setze Beistriche, wo sie hingehören.

1. This is the man . . . helped us to build the garden shed.
   This is Mr Merriwether . . . helped us to build the garden shed.
2. Our neighbour has bought a car . . . can do 230 km.p.h.
   Our neighbour has bought a Lamborghini . . . can do 230 km.p.h.
3. I have three uncles. My uncle . . . lives in Boston is a goldsmith.
   My Uncle Paul . . . lives in Boston is a goldsmith.
4. The people . . . we met on our America trip were quite nice.
   The Hendersons . . . we met on our America trip were quite nice.
5. The girl . . . we are waiting for is my best friend.
   Emma Smith . . . we are waiting for is my best friend.
6. The Hudson River . . . flows past Manhattan Island empties into the Atlantic Ocean.
   The river . . . flows past Manhattan Island empties into the Atlantic.

PAUSE

1 *Relative pronouns* und Kommas: Setze sie dort ein, wo es sein muß!

✓ richtig

❍ 1. The ball . . . "Tiger" is playing with is new.
❍ 2. Can you show me . . . we have to do for tomorrow?
❍ 3. Those of you . . . want to see a film today, please raise your hands!
❍ 4. The Statue of Liberty . . . stands on an island in the harbour of New York has welcomed millions of immigrants to the New World.
❍ 5. A sculptor is a person . . . makes statues and monuments.
❍❍ 6. The statue . . . you are looking at is called "David". It was made by Michelangelo . . . was one of the greatest sculptors of all times.
❍❍ 7. Miami . . . we are going to visit in December has more Spanish speakers than English speakers . . . is quite surprising, I think.
❍❍ 8. My Dad has painted all the pictures . . . you can see here. My favourite . . . hangs in my room is called "Still Life with Roses".
❍❍ 9. The car . . . I am driving at the moment is the first car . . . cost me more than $ 10,000.
❍❍ 10. Shakespeare's plays . . . were written about 400 years ago are still performed today. The one . . . I like best is "Romeo and Juliet".

Du solltest mindestens **12 Richtige** haben! Wenn nicht, bitte das Kapitel noch einmal gründlich durcharbeiten!

Eine etwas schwierigere Übung: „Aus zwei mach eins!" Verbinde die beiden Angabesätze miteinander, indem du Relativsätze bildest.
Übungsziele: Verwendung der richtigen *relative pronouns* oder Erkennen von *contact clauses*; richtige Beistrichsetzung.
Dafür gibt es je einen Punkt!
Beachte: Je drei Sätze gehören inhaltlich zusammen.

✓ richtig

❍❍ 1. Mr and Mrs Gordon have moved to Florida. They used to live next door from us.
❍❍ 2. They have bought a house in Pinewood. This is a suburb of Miami. (suburb = *Vorort*)
❍❍ 3. Their youngest son went with them. His name is Marcus.

❍❍ 4. Benny likes the dress. Jessica is wearing the dress.
❍❍ 5. Jessica likes dresses. They come from Italy.
❍❍ 6. Benny likes Jessica. He has known her since kindergarden.

❍❍ 7. Dad said California has more inhabitants than Canada. I did not believe that.
❍❍ 8. So I looked it up in the "Encyclopaedia Britannica". Dad had bought it the year before.
❍❍ 9. Canada really has fewer people than California. Canada is the second largest country in the world.

❍❍ 10. This is Mrs Williams. We met her daughter at Maxwell's party.
❍❍ 11. A young man introduced us. He was at the party, too.
❍❍ 12. Maxwell had invited lots of different people. This was an excellent idea.

Na, wie sieht das Ergebnis aus?
Wenn du mindestens 17 Punkte erreicht hast, kannst du schon **RELATIV** zufrieden sein.
Ab 20 Richtigen: **HUT AB!**
Und mit 22 oder mehr richtigen Antworten bist du ***ABSOLUTELY TOP***!

Teacher (on the phone): "So you say John is too ill to come to school today?"
Voice at the other end: "That's right."
Teacher: "Who am I talking to?"
Voice at the other end: "This is my father."

NILPFERD

Du kannst dich nicht mehr konzentrieren?
Du sitzt schon viel zu lange bei deinen Hausaufgaben?

Tanke wieder Energie:
Du stehst, die Beine sind hüftbreit auseinander, die Füße zeigen gerade nach vorne. Die Knie sind gebeugt und leicht federnd. Du schwingst nun die gestreckten Arme abwechselnd nach vorne und hinten.
Achte darauf, daß der Arm vorne und der Arm rückwärts mit den Schultern eine Linie bilden.

Dauer der Übung:
50mal mit jedem
Arm nach vorne

DIE VORWÖRTER

Vorwörter (Präpositionen) und ihre richtige Anwendung zählen zu den kniffligeren Kapiteln der englischen Grammatik. Der Grund dafür: Es gibt keine Regeln, die man sich merken könnte! Das macht das Erlernen natürlich nicht einfacher.

Nimm die folgenden Sätze als Beispiel für die Unterschiede zwischen Englisch und Deutsch:

Das Bild hängt **an** der Wand. → *The picture hangs* ***on*** *the wall.*
Ich denke oft **an** dich. → *I often think* ***of*** *you.*

„an" wird also einmal mit ***on*** übersetzt, das andere Mal mit ***of***. Da ist keine Regel erkennbar! Allerdings gibt es einen guten Tip:

TIP

Merke dir Präpositionen immer im Zusammenhang mit einem Verb oder einem Nomen: zum Beispiel ***on the wall*** und ***to think of someone***.

1

Du kannst gleich selbst überprüfen, an welche (und wie viele) solcher „Merkkombinationen" *verb + preposition* du dich erinnern kannst. Du bist ihnen in den vergangenen Lernjahren schon oft begegnet! Setze also die fehlenden Präpositionen ein.

1. Help me, please. I am looking . . . my pen.
2. Let's go! I don't want to wait . . . Tony any longer.
3. Sheila is interested . . . rock music. She likes Elvis Presley best.
4. Uncle Willie reminds me . . . my grandfather.
5. I've never seen this woman. Where does she come . . .?
6. What's "cryolyte"? I've never heard . . . it before.
7. In the evening the animals come out . . . their hiding places.
8. A mother cat takes care . . . her babies.

Die wichtigste **Aufgabe der Präposition** besteht darin, eine **Beziehung zwischen einem Verb und einem anderen Satzteil** herzustellen:

Peter is going	→	***into***	→	*the house.*
(Peter geht	→	**in**	→	das Haus.)
The car was standing	→	***at***	→	*the corner.*
Das Auto stand	→	**an**	→	der Ecke.

Was ändert sich, wenn du im zweiten Beispiel statt *at* die Präpositionen *near* oder *behind* verwendest? . . . Das Auto steht nun nicht mehr **an** der Ecke, sondern **in der Nähe** der Ecke oder gar **hinter** der Ecke, so daß man es gar nicht mehr sieht.

Welche Beziehungen können also durch Präpositionen hergestellt werden?

Es gibt

- ☆ ***prepositions of place*** (Vorwörter des **Ortes**): *under, over, in . . .*
- ☆ ***prepositions of time*** (Vorwörter der **Zeit**): *from . . . to, since, till . . .*
- ☆ ***"other" prepositions*** (andere Präpositionen): *with, in spite of . . .* (Das sind Präpositionen, die weder Raum noch Zeit ausdrücken, sondern in „übertragener" Bedeutung auftreten.)

Viele Präpositionen werden sowohl zeitlich als auch räumlich und auch in anderen Bedeutungen verwendet.

prepositions of place – Vorwörter des Ortes

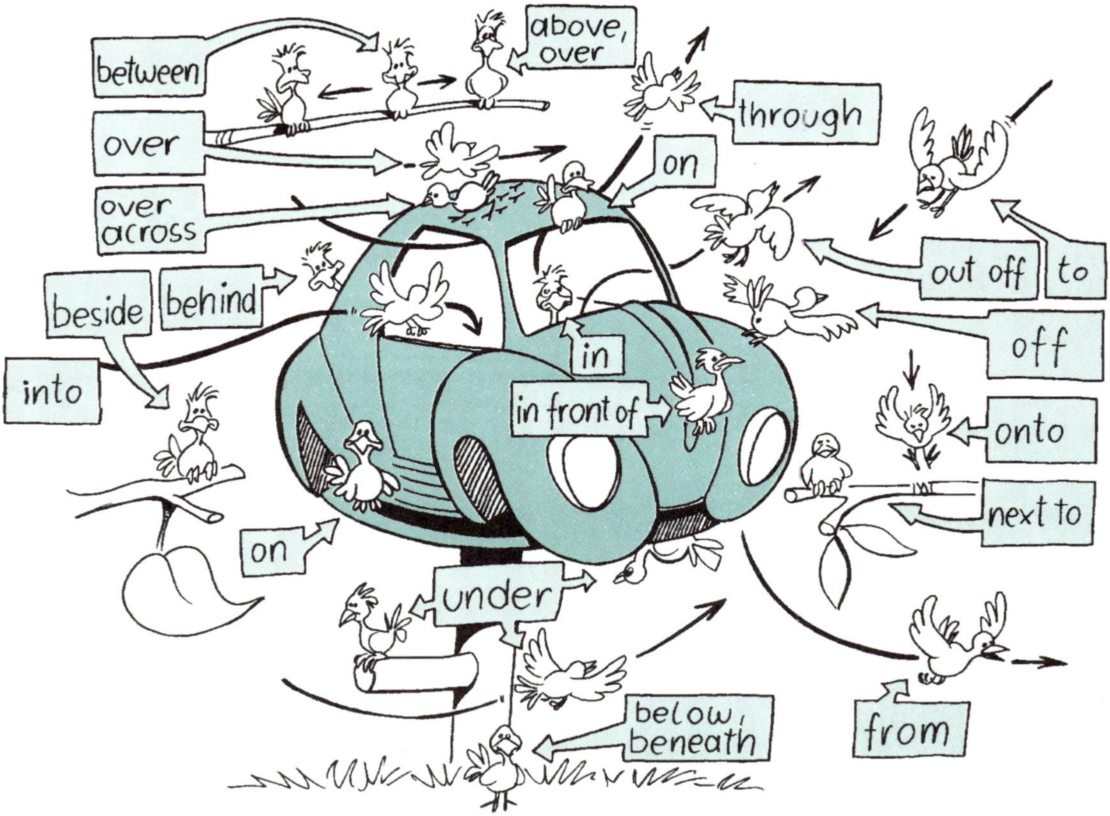

Bilde nun mit jeder *preposition of place* zwei Sätze, die mit der Zeichnung in Zusammenhang stehen. Es sind insgesamt 20 Präpositionen enthalten, von denen einige mehr als nur eine Bedeutung haben. Bilde zwei Zehnergruppen und lege zwischen ihnen eine erholsame **Pause** ein!

A boy was caught climbing **up** a farmer's apple tree. The farmer shouted **up at** him, "Come **down** this minute or I'll tell your father!"
"You can tell him now," said the boy, "he's **up** here **with** me."

Für diese Übung begeben wir uns hinaus in die große, weite Welt. Setze passende *prepositions of place* ein!

1. The full moon was standing directly . . . the mountain. It was beautiful.
2. Meet me . . . the corner of Union Street and Market Street tonight.
3. Jim kicked his ball . . . our kitchen window. Luckily it was open!
4. They have planted some trees . . . our schoolhouse. (3x!)
5. Mrs Bennet went straight . . . my mother to tell her the news.
6. I chased our dog . . . the fields. (mehrere Möglichkeiten!)
7. From the top of the hill we could see the village . . . us.
8. Wilma fell . . . the ladder and landed . . . the grass.
9. Last year I sat . . . Tony and Mary in class.
10. The Rykers live in a flat three floors . . . ours.
11. I could hear a helicopter flying . . . us.
12. The River Thames flows . . . some very famous bridges.

prepositions of time – Vorwörter der Zeit

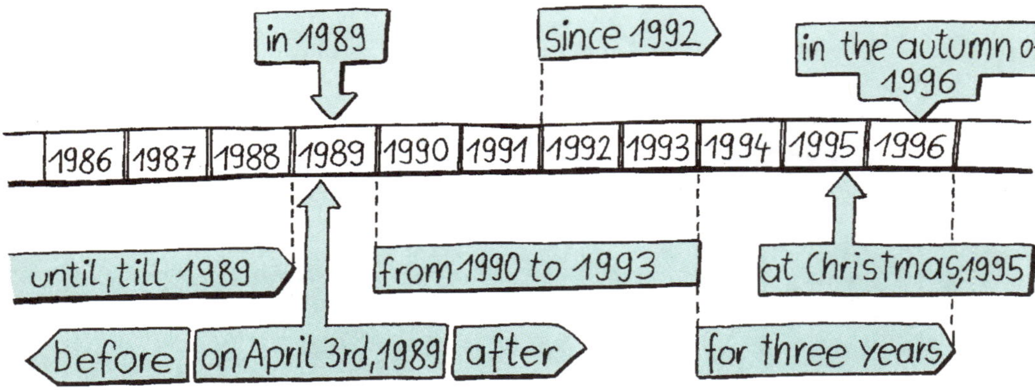

4

Bilde je zwei sinnvolle Sätze mit jeder *preposition of time*.

example: We lived in Schladming from 1986 to 1992.
I waited for you from 8 to 10. Where were you?

5

Setze sinnvolle *prepositions of time* ein.

1. Helmut lived in Vienna . . . 1993 . . . 1995.
2. We have to be back . . . 6 o'clock and not a minute later! (2x)
3. What were you doing . . . 9 p.m. . . . Monday, June 22nd?
4. . . . February we always go skiing . . . a week.
5. Pat came home . . . Christmas and he stayed . . . January 3rd. (3x)
6. You mustn't play the piano or take a shower . . . 10 p.m.
7. Yesterday I was so tired that I slept . . . ten hours.
8. William Shakespeare died . . . 1616. He was 52 years old.
9. We've been here . . . last Friday and we'll stay . . . next Thursday.

Auf den folgenden Seiten schauen wir uns einige Präpositionen genauer an. Wir tun das in alphabetischer Reihenfolge. So kannst du schnell und leicht nachschauen, wenn es Fragen gibt.

place	***time***	***"other"***
irgendwo, herum, in / um . . . herum	ungefähr, etwa (eigentlich ein Adverb)	über, darüber, wegen; mit *do*: dagegen
*I'd like **to walk about** a little*	*What's the time? – **About 2 o'clock!***	***What about going** to my place now?*

!

Wichtige „Kombinationen": *talk / tell (me) / think / walk about;*
***What about** . . .?* (Wie wär's mit . . .?)
*I can **do nothing about** it.*

6 Bilde Sätze mit *about* nach dem Muster des Beispielsatzes.

example: let – talk – new plan →
Let's talk about Perry's new plan.

1. what – ask your mother – help
2. Mum and Dad – talk – holidays
3. the children – running – garden
4. what – think – our teacher – ?
5. Claudia – seventeen years old
6. Peter – somewhere – house

place	*time*	*"other"*
oberhalb, (dar)über (→ ohne Berührung)	——	über, darüber, höher als
The polar star stands directly ***above the Pole****.*	——	*Your idea is* ***above me****.* (. . . ist mir zu hoch)

! **Wichtige „Kombinationen":** *The temperature is* ***above 30°*** *(degrees).*
Above all*, I like dogs.* (vor allen Dingen)

7 Bilde Sätze mit *above*. Richte dich nach dem Beispielsatz und nach *exercise* 6.

1. on January 15 – temperature – plus 10°
2. Dad – like – pizza – everything else
3. this theory – my understanding
4. our aeroplane – high – the city
5. always – dark clouds – hills
6. the headmaster – the teachers

place	*time*	*"other"*
hinter . . . her, nach	nach	nachdem + *past perfect* (eine Konjunktion)
Max ***ran after*** *his dog.*	***After lunch*** *you can go out and play.*	***After I had finished*** *my lunch, I went out and . . .*

Wichtige „Kombinationen": *The policeman* ***ran after*** *the thief.*
(= nachlaufen mit dem Ziel: „erwischen")
My Mum is always ***after me****.*
(Sie kontrolliert mich immer.)

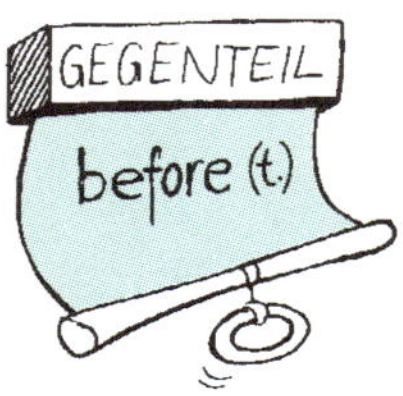

Bilde Sätze mit *after*. Du weißt ja jetzt, wie's geht!

1. look – our cat – run – the mouse
2. Alec – left room – ten minutes – me
3. finish breakfast – Tracy – take bus to school (→ *Konjunktion*)
4. Help! – somebody – come – me
5. dinner – most people – go to bed
6. two hours – dinner – I – to bed
7. Ludwig – buy new clothes – earn his first money (→ *Konjunktion*)
8. Bob and Dean – meet again – twenty years

place	*time*	*"other"*
in allen Verwendungen: gegen, dagegen		
Tom put the ladder ***against the wall****.*	——	*I have nothing* ***against your new haircut****.*

Wichtige „Kombinationen": *Don't* ***fight against*** *windmills!*
Dad ***is against*** *it!* (Er ist dagegen.)

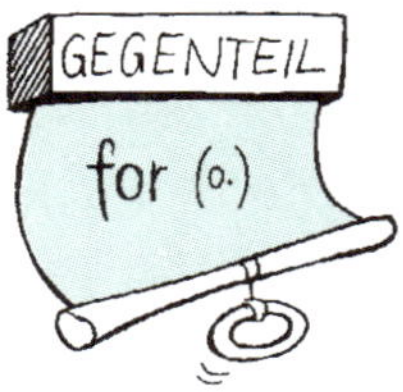

„etwas dagegen unternehmen" →
to do something ***about*** *it*
(≠ to do something against it)

9 Setze *about, above, after* oder *against* sinnvoll ein.

1. Martin is really boring. He only wants to talk . . . computer games!
2. We have to do something . . . the traffic in our street.
3. High . . . us the birds were flying south because winter was coming.
4. Only six people got off . . . the train had stopped.
5. Running more than three steps with the ball in your hands is . . . the rules of basketball.
6. Helen is clever, helpful and very nice, and . . . all she is my friend.
7. I'd like to hear more . . . your holidays in Australia.
8. Some modern art is . . . me. I just don't understand it.
9. The girl ran . . . the pickpocket, but she was too slow.
10. Harry was so upset that he threw his glass . . . the nearest wall.
11. There was a lot of discussion . . . Monica's birthday present. Everybody wanted to buy something different.
12. I have nothing . . . a good joke, but putting sugar in the petrol tank just isn't funny!

at

place	*time*	*"other"*
an, bei, in, zu (genauer Punkt im Raum)	an, bei, in, um, zu (genauer Punkt in der Zeit)	in, bei, auf, für
Tom was waiting for me ***at the corner****.*	*Jim arrived* ***at 3:20****.*	*Julian* ***is*** *very* ***good at*** *imitating people.*

!

Wichtige „Kombinationen": ***at*** *home – at the top / bottom of page 3* (auf Seite 3 oben / unten) – *at the grocer's / butcher's / doctor's / . . . – at night – at half the price – at the beginning / end of – at Christmas / Easter / . . . – at full / half speed* (mit voller / halber Geschwindigkeit) – *at first* (zuerst, zunächst) – *at last* (zuletzt, endlich) – *at least* (mindestens, zumindest);
look at (anschauen), *laugh at* (auslachen), *arrive at* (ankommen in)

10

Bilde Sätze mit *at* nach bekanntem Muster. Überlege bei jedem Satz, wie du *at* auf Deutsch übersetzen würdest!

1. lovely – tiger babies – zoo
2. sorry – Mum – not home
3. Dad – often – work – night
4. car – crash – into wall – full speed
5. Mary – better – history – I
6. end of film -Jill – tears in her eyes
7. many people – sleep best – home
8. we – get most things – grocer's
9. am staying – Hotel Bristol – now
10. why – you – laugh – me – ?
11. everybody – leave – end of film
12. homework – number 3 – top of page

PAUSE

place	*time*	*"other"*
——	vor, bevor, zuvor (ab einem vergangenen oder zukünftigen Zeitpunkt)	schon einmal (bejaht), noch nie (verneint)
——	*I'm sure we will return **before 10 o'clock**.*	*We've never done this **before**.*

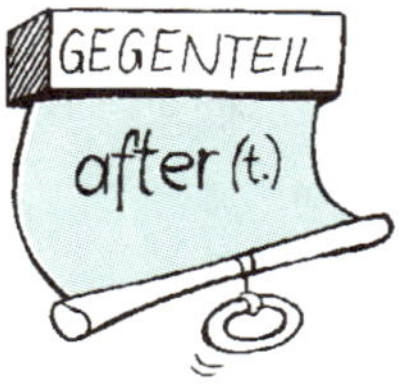

11

Bilde Sätze mit *before*. Du weißt, wie's geht!

1. wake up – me – you – leave
2. we – come home – the show – over
3. the bus – arrive – the boys – finish the game
4. Peter – never – be here
5. we – wait long – the train – come
6. wash hands – start to eat

place	*time*	*"other"*
in allen Verwendungen: hinter, hinten nach, hinterher; zurück		
*Meet me **behind the church** at 5:30.*	*We are already ten minutes **behind plan**.*	*Let's go back! I've **left** my umbrella **behind**.*

! **Wichtige „Kombinationen":** *to **leave** something **behind*** (etwas vergessen, zurücklassen)

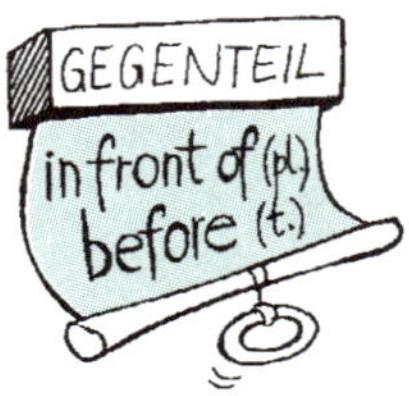

12

Bilde Sätze mit *behind*.

1. the teacher – sit – desk
2. Francis – not want to sit – Gregory
3. the girl – hide – face – hands
4. Bill – only one second – the winner
5. in 1620 – the Pilgrim Fathers – leave everything – and – sail – America
6. why – you – always – run – me – ?
7. bus – 15 minutes – schedule (= *Plan*)
8. Veronica – come in second – Ricarda

place	***time***	***"other"***
in allen Verwendungen: unter, unterhalb (ohne Berührung)		
*From the top of the hill we saw **the town below / beneath** us.*	——	*This is **beneath** my **dignity*** (= Würde).

! **Wichtige „Kombinationen": *below zero*** (unter Null → Temperatur)

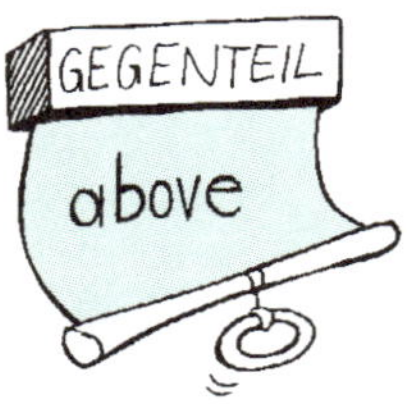

13

Bilde Sätze mit *below* und / oder *beneath*.

1. cold day – temperature – zero
2. diver – remain – surface (= *Wasseroberfläche*) – three minutes
3. a captain – be – a major
4. I – not do – this – my dignity
5. river – deep – bridge
6. Charlie – kiss – Susi – full moon

14 Setze *at, before, behind* und *below / beneath* sinnvoll ein.

1. Laura had left the party . . . I could talk to her.
2. When we arrived, nobody was there. . . . first I thought we were the only guests, but then more and more people came. All in all, there were . . . least twenty people there.
3. Sue was running in first position, with Martina and Alice close . . . her.
4. It was freezing cold. The temperature dropped to 25 degrees . . . zero.
5. Many people in our country feel that dirty work is . . . them.
6. . . . the war (= *Krieg*) 35000 people lived in this town.
7. This is my first visit to Los Angeles. I've never been here . . . .
8. Have you seen my picture in the paper? It's . . . the bottom of page 2.

Diese zwei Wörter sehen einander zum Verwechseln ähnlich, und sie werden auch oft miteinander verwechselt (siehe auch Seite 129)!

☆ ***beside = next to***

place	***time***	***"other"***
neben, daneben	——	außer
*In the physics lesson I **sit beside** Mary.* (= neben)	——	*Dad was **beside himself** when he came home.* (= er war außer sich)

! **Wichtige „Kombinationen":** ***to be beside oneself*** (außer sich sein)

☆ ***besides = in addition to*** (→ zusätzlich, außerdem; außer)

***Besides us**, there were three people at the party.* (= außer uns)
*I have many other things to do **besides**.* (= zusätzlich)
***Besides**, I want to go home now.* (= außerdem)

15

Setze beside und besides richtig in die folgenden Sätze ein.

1. Look, Mr Thompson is standing . . . our English teacher.
2. It was raining, so we couldn't visit the zoo; . . ., it was closed that day.
3. They built the supermarket right . . . the old church.
4. Please, sir, I want to sit . . . Rebecca. She's my best friend.
5. . . . gold, platinum is also very expensive.
6. The handsome stranger looked around; then he took the seat . . . me.
7. . . . Frank and Jill, two couples have been invited to the party.
8. After watching a horror film for the first time, Little Charlie was . . . himself with fear.

place	***time***	***"other"***
bei, an, über, durch	ungefähr um (3 Uhr), bis spätestens; bei, nach	mit passive voice: von, durch; mit
*Tim caught me **by the arm**.*	***By the time** we saw the police, it was too late.*	*"Fidelio" was composed **by Beethoven**.*

Wichtige „Kombinationen": *by* *day* – *by car / bus / coach / . . .* (mit dem Auto, . . .) – *by force* (mit Gewalt) – *by Friday* (bis spätestens) – *by then* (bis dahin) – *by chance* (zufällig) – *by mistake* (unabsichtlich) – *one by one* (einzeln) – *two by two* (paarweise) – *by the way* (übrigens) – *by heart* (auswendig) – *by means of* (mittels) – *step by step* (Schritt für Schritt) – *by all / no means* (auf jeden / keinen Fall) – *by sight* (vom Sehen) – *by nature* (von Natur aus)

16

Bilde sinnvolle Sätze mit *by*.

1. many countries – conquered – the Romans
2. Dad's book – finished – next week (*future!*)
3. all other sprinters – beaten – Linford Christie
4. they – ride – to the next village – bike
5. I – be back – some time – next week (*future!*)
6. we all – like to sit – the open fire
7. I – enjoy – travel – plane
8. I – always – travel – day

17

Übersetze ins Englische. *Make good sentences!*

1. Du mußt das Buch bis spätestens Donnerstag zurückbringen.
2. Dieses Gedicht wurde von Milton verfaßt (= geschrieben).
3. Ich mußte das Gedicht (= *poem*) auswendig lernen.
4. Ihr müßt euch auf alle Fälle „Waterworld" ansehen.
5. Ich kenne dieses Mädchen nur vom Sehen.
6. Die Leute verließen einzeln den Raum.
7. Wir fuhren mit dem Zug nach London.
8. Sie küßten sich bei Mondschein.

Akute Verwechslungsgefahr! Beide Wörter bedeuten **„während"**, aber:

☆ ***during*** → ist eine **Präposition** und steht **vor einem Nomen**;

during the day, during the first week, during last winter

☆ ***while*** → ist eine **Konjunktion** und **leitet einen Gliedsatz ein**.

While you were sleeping, . . .; . . . while Joe was ill.

18

Setze *during* und *while* richtig ein. Achte auf das, was folgt!

1. . . . Tobias was working in the garage, I was taking a rest.
2. Dennis called some time . . . the afternoon.
3. . . . I was walking up to the house, the dog was watching me carefully.
4. . . . my stay in Seattle it rained almost every day.
5. We stayed in our hotel room . . . it was raining.
6. . . . the fat lady was singing, many people left the room.
7. Many people left the room . . . the concert.
8. My Mum met my Dad . . . the summer of 1974.

place	***time***	***"other"***
zu, zur, nach (als Ziel)	seit, . . . lang	für, wegen, um, vor, aus, nach
*Dad **left for work** at 6.*	*I haven't see you **for two years**.*	*Mila wept **for joy**.*

!

Wichtige „Kombinationen": ***for*** *money* (für / um Geld) – *for joy* (aus / vor Freude) – *for robbery* (wegen Raubes) – *to leave for work* (in die Arbeit gehen / fahren) – *for nothing* (gratis, für nichts) – *the train for Dover* (. . . nach Dover) – *for instance / example* (z. B.) – *for this reason* (aus diesem Grund) – *for sure* (ganz sicher) – *once and for all* (ein für allemal);
to wait for (warten auf) – *to go for a walk* (spazieren gehen) – *to apply for a job* (sich bewerben) – *to ask for something* (um etwas bitten) – *to care for* (mögen) – *to long for* (sich sehnen nach) – *to look for* (suchen)

19

Bilde sinnvolle Sätze mit *for*.

1. old man – ask – me – money
2. tourist – call – help
3. every day – I – look – car keys
4. the boys – wait – the bus
5. at 7 – we – leave – school
6. Placido Domingo – famous – singing

20 Übersetze ins Englische. *Make good sentences!*

1. Ich bin müde. Aus diesem Grund möchte ich hier bleiben.
2. Jack war wegen Einbruchs (= *burglary*) im Gefängnis.
3. Die Erde ist rund. Wir wissen das ganz sicher.
4. Ich sehne mich nach einem kühlen Getränk.
5. Ich habe Ulli seit Monaten nicht gesehen.
6. Fred nahm den Zug nach Washington.
7. Komm, gehen wir spazieren!
8. Charlie macht fast alles für Geld.

place	*time*	*"other"*
von, aus (von einem Ort weg)	von . . . an (von einem Zeitpunkt weg)	vor, aus (etwas bestehen / gemacht sein)
*Pat was walking **home from school**.*	*We waited for Caroline **from** six **to** eight.*	*Steel is **made from** iron coal.*

Wichtige „Kombinationen": *to hide **from*** (sich verstecken vor) – *to be made from* (bestehen aus) – *to be different from* (sich unterscheiden von) – *to be safe from* (sicher sein vor) – *to prevent / keep from* (hindern an) – *to protect from* (beschützen vor) – *to suffer from* (leiden an / unter);
from . . . to (von . . . bis) – *from . . . on* (von . . . an)

21 Übersetze ins Englische. *Make good sentences!*

1. Indiana Jones versteckte sich vor seinen Verfolgern (= *pursuers*).
2. Eiscreme wird aus Milch, Zucker und Früchten gemacht.
3. Von der Spitze des Berges kannst du das Meer sehen.
4. Ich gehe von Montag bis Samstag in die Schule.
5. Im Haus waren wir sicher vor der Kälte.
6. Vom 21. Juni an werden die Tage kürzer.
7. Ich kenne Margarita vom Kindergarten.
8. Mac leidet an einer bösen Erkältung.

22

Setze *by, during, while, for* oder *from* sinnvoll ein.

1. Uncle Joe works at night and sleeps . . . day.
2. . . . Mum was sleeping, I washed the dishes.
3. At the end of this year, I want to apply . . . a job in town.
4. How can I keep you . . . believing this nonsense?
5. Little Ernie had a bad nightmare . . . the night.
6. Canada is quite different . . . the USA.
7. I'll make you a sandwich . . . you are waiting . . . Wendy.
8. That's Carola over there, . . . the window.

place	*time*	*"other"*
in, auf	am, in, im (Jahr)	in, mit, auf
Grandma lives ***in the country****.*	*I'll be back* ***in twenty minutes****.*	*What's "pneumonia"* ***in German****?*

Wichtige „Kombinationen": ***in*** *the morning* (am Morgen / Vormittag) – *in the street* (auf der Straße) – *in the picture* (auf dem Bild) – *in the country* (auf dem Land) – *in a hurry* (eilig) – *in danger* (in Gefahr) – *in good / bad health* (bei guter / schlechter Gesundheit) – *in a loud voice* (mit lauter Stimme) – *in time* (rechtzeitig); *to believe in* (glauben an) – *to succeed in* (Erfolg haben, gelingen) – *to take part in* (teilnehmen an) – *to be interested in* (interessiert sein an, sich interessieren für)

place	*time*	*"other"*
in . . . hinein (Bewegung)	bis in . . . hinein (Zeit)	in
Jim ran ***into the house***	*Dad worked* ***deep into the night****.*	*Please translate this* ***into English****.*

! **Wichtige „Kombinationen":** *to run **into** somebody* (jemand zufällig treffen) – *to run into trouble* (in Schwierigkeiten geraten) – *to burst into tears* (in Tränen ausbrechen) – *to divide into* (teilen in)

23 Setze *in* oder *into* sinnvoll ein.

1. Uncle Theo used to live . . . Bath, but now he makes his home . . . Paris.
2. Carl jumped . . . the lake and swam out to his boat.
3. I'll be back . . . a minute. If I'm not, go . . . the dining room without me.
4. It wasn't as cold . . . the morning as it was during the night.
5. Sally isn't here. She's . . . the cinema with Amanda.
6. Mike got . . . his car and drove away . . . the night.

Dieses sehr oft vorkommende Wörtchen ist trickreich. Man kann nämlich seine Bedeutung nicht genau angeben! Es ist daher am besten, du übst die folgenden Sätze solange, bis du sie fehlerfrei beherrscht. Merke dir dabei auch immer gleichzeitig die deutsche Bedeutung!

24 Setze *of* ein.

1. Our house is made . . . wood. (*made of* → Material verändert sich nicht)
2. Katrin's parents lived in the north . . . London for a while. (*genitive*)
3. I saw a picture . . . you in the newspaper the other day.
4. We met Mr. Green on the morning . . . our second day in London.
5. I wasn't aware . . . the fact (*der Tatsache bewußt*) that I had no money.
6. Many people are proud . . . their work. (*stolz auf*)

7. I am tired . . . telling you to work harder. (*ich habe es satt*)
8. Kelly was so sure . . . winning the first prize, but she didn't.
9. The man died . . . his injuries (*Verletzungen*) after two days.
10. Mum often speaks . . . her sister, who lives in Australia now.
11. Jacqueline is very jealous (*eifersüchtig*) . . . her sister.
12. "Durchstarten in Englisch" consists . . . (*besteht aus*) four volumes (*Bänden*).
13. Boys often dream . . . their first moped or car.
14. What has become . . . Charlie's dad? – (*Was ist aus ihm geworden?*)
15. The summer . . . 1983 was very hot and dry.
16. Are you afraid . . . dogs? – No, I love dogs!

place	***time***	***"other"***
auf (oben), an	am, an	von, auf
Don't sit ***on the desk****!*	*We always go to church* ***on Sunday****.*	*Lots of people* ***live on*** *a handful of rice a day.*

Wichtige „Kombinationen": *to live* ***on*** (leben von) – *to put on* (anziehen) – *on the 20th of July* – *on business* (geschäftlich) – *to go on board* (an Bord gehen) – *on time* (pünktlich) – *to be keen on* (scharf sein auf) – *to agree on* (übereinstimmen in) – *to congratulate on* (gratulieren zu) – *to insist on* (bestehen auf) – *to depend on* (abhängen von) – *to rely on* (sich verlassen auf) – *on foot* (zufuß) – *on purpose* (absichtlich)

25

Bilde Sätze mit *on*.

1. Dad – London – business
2. Tim – came all the way – foot
3. Leo – break my pencil – purpose
4. my birthday – October 24th
5. train – never – time
6. we – return – Saturday
7. income – depend – job
8. we – agree – all points

26

Übersetze ins Englische. *Make good sentences!*

1. Ich bin dein Freund. Du kannst dich auf mich verlassen.
2. Was soll ich morgen anziehen? – Nun, das hängt vom Wetter ab.
3. Paula bestand darauf, uns zu ihrem Fest einzuladen. (Gerund!)
4. Ihr könnt jetzt an Bord gehen!
5. Hast du das absichtlich gemacht?
6. Seid ihr den ganzen Weg (= *all the way*) zu Fuß gekommen?

place	***time***	***"other"***
über, über . . . hin (mit / ohne Berührung)	über (einen Zeitpunkt hinaus)	über, mehr als, vorbei, aus
The dog jumped ***over the wall****.*	*Can Jim stay* ***over the weekend****?*	*The last lesson is* ***over*** *at 1:10 p.m.*

Wichtige „Kombinationen": *to stay* ***over****night* (über Nacht bleiben) – *over and over* – *to rule over somebody* (über jemand regieren) – *to have / keep / lose control over* – *dirty all over* (überall schmutzig) – *all over the world* (auf der ganzen Welt) – *over here / there* (hier herüben / dort drüben)

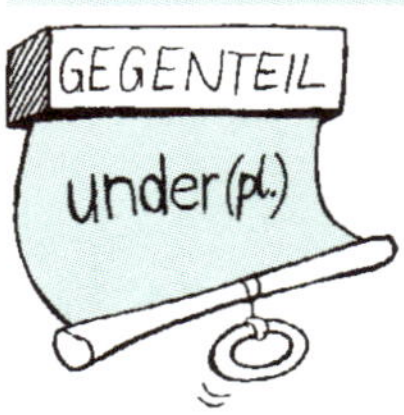

27 Bilde Sätze mit *over*.

1. my son – already – 12
2. we – want – go camping – weekend
3. the fight – not . . . yet
4. the driver – lose control – car
5. they – walk – frozen pond
6. English – speak – all . . . world
7. Vietnam War – 25 years ago
8. I – walk – Mr Singer's car

place	***time***	***"other"***
nach, zu (in Richtung Ziel)	vor, bis (zu einem Zeitpunkt)	mit, zu, bei, in
Ron goes ***to school*** *in this town.*	*It's* ***a quarter to*** *five.*	*Jack is* ***married to*** *Jill.*

! **Wichtige „Kombinationen":** *to talk* ***to*** (sprechen mit) – *to be married to* (verheiratet sein mit) – *to go to pieces* (in Stücke / Scherben brechen) – *to come to an end* – *to agree to* (zustimmen) – *to belong to* (gehören) – *to refer to* (sich beziehen auf) – *to turn to* (sich wenden an) – *from . . . to* – *to pay attention to* (aufpassen)

28 Bilde Sätze mit *to*.

1. this ring – belong – my sister
2. you – turn – parents – problems
3. this story – refer – J.F. Kennedy
4. Gerry – married – Andrea
5. I – pay attention – teacher – always
6. Vietnam War – end – 25 years ago
7. tomorrow – talk – my father
8. Dad – work – 9 a.m. . . . 5 p.m.

<table>
<tr><th>place</th><th>time</th><th>"other"</th></tr>
<tr><td colspan="3">in allen Verwendungen: unter</td></tr>
</table>

Let's sit down ***under that tree****.*	*I finished the race in* ***under 20 minutes****.*	*Are you still* ***under 16****?*

wichtige „Kombinationen": ***under*** *these / such conditions / circumstances* (unter diesen / solchen Bedingungen / Umständen)

Bilde Sätze mit *under*.

1. my dog – often sleep – my desk
2. Mike – stay – water – two minutes
3. Dad – like – work – new boss
4. what – Scots – wear – kilts – ?
5. the old man – "live" – bridge
6. they – kiss – mistletoe

place	*time*	*"other"*
bei	——	aus, mit, vor
Sam is staying ***with his Uncle and Aunt****.*	——	*Mr Webster came* ***with his daughter****.*

Wichtige „Kombinationen": *to tremble* ***with*** *fear* (vor Angst zittern) – *to be pleased / bored with* (erfreut sein über / gelangweilt sein mit) – *to be angry with* (böse / zornig sein auf / mit)

30

Bilde Sätze mit *with*.

1. the girls – play – kittens
2. you – got – any money – you – ?
3. come – me – cinema
4. in holidays – we – stay – friends
5. Joe – lie in bed – bad cold
6. after film – Tim – tremble – fear
7. why – you – angry – me –?
8. come – me – all your problems

31

Setze ein: *of, on, over, to, under* oder *with.*

1. Can I come . . . you? We could go . . . your place.
2. I hate getting up so early. I can't get used . . . it.
3. Do you like spiders? – No, I'm afraid . . . them.
4. Harry lives . . . the east . . . London, . . . the Thames.
5. Put . . . a warm jacket . . . your pullover. It's cold outside.
6. . . . these circumstances you can't stay . . . us any longer
7. Where's the TV-guide? – . . . there, . . . the table.
8. Slow down or you'll lose control . . . your car.

PAUSE

1

Jetzt, da es um Punkte geht, stehen alle besprochenen Präpositionen zur Auswahl, *from "about" to "with"*! Setze also passende Vorwörter ein.

❍❍ 1. Look, there's a paraglider . . . the sky, high . . . the valley.

❍❍ 2. Hurry up, Peter. We are five minutes . . . time, and they won't wait . . . us much longer.

❍❍ 3. Let's go . . . a walk, Cathy! – Okay, but what shoes shall I put . . .?

❍❍ 4. As usual, we went . . . school . . . bike.

❍❍ 5. Would you like mayonnaise . . . your hamburger? – No, thanks. I'm not keen . . . mayonnaise.

❍❍ 6. Normally I'm interested . . . foreign countries, but . . . these conditions I wouldn't travel to Nigeria.

❍❍ 7. I'm hungry. – What . . . a salad? – Okay! I've nothing . . . salad.

❍❍ 8. In Canada, summer can be quite warm, with temperatures . . . 30°. But in winter they can drop to . . . minus 30°.

❍❍❍ 9. Why are you . . . such a hurry, Dad? – My train . . . London leaves in 25 minutes, and it is always . . . time.

❍❍ 10. Stop running . . . boys, Tina! They will only laugh . . . you.

❍❍ 11. Joe says he's sorry . . . knocking over the vase, but he didn't do it . . . purpose.

❍❍ 12. I know Bill Smith . . . sight, but I've never spoken . . . him.

Wieviele der 25 Punkte hast du erreicht? Wenn es mehr als 20 waren, darfst du mit dir zufrieden sein. Bei weniger als 14 solltest du aber diejenigen Vorwörter, die fehlerhaft waren, wiederholen!

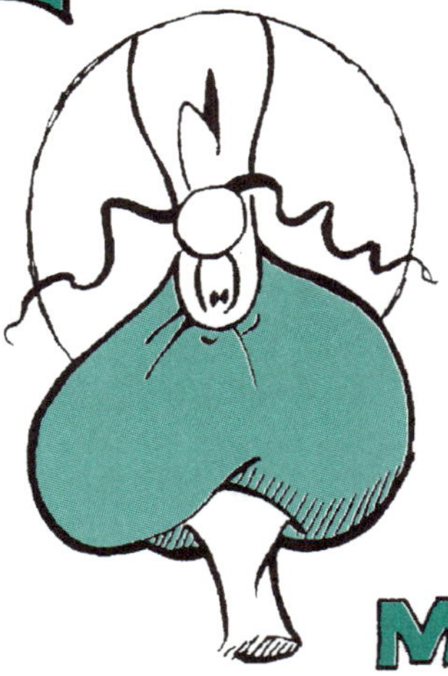

MUDRA ZUM GEHIRNEINSCHALTEN

Dir fehlt die zündende Idee?
Du hast Angst, daß dir bei der Prüfung nichts mehr einfällt?
Dir fehlt die Motivation zum Lernen?

Schalte dein Gehirn wieder ein:
Du legst die Daumenkuppen auf Ring- und Kleinfingernagel.
Halte diese Stellung mit beiden Händen gleichzeitig.
Das Mudra solltest du 6mal täglich machen. Natürlich auch dann, wenn du dein Gehirn dringendst brauchst; vor einer Prüfung zum Beispiel.

Dauer der Übung:
mindestens 4 Minuten

BINDEWÖRTER UND ANDERE SATZVERKNÜPFER

Bindewörter *(conjunctions)* sind Satzverknüpfer *(connecters).* Wie alle *connecters* dienen sie der **gedanklichen und sprachlichen Verbindung von Sätzen**. Erst die *connecters* erlauben es uns, kompliziertere Zusammenhänge einfach und eindeutig auszudrücken. Ohne *connecters* wäre die Sprache ein kümmerliches Aneinanderreihen von Wörtern und Wortgruppen.

Die wichtigsten *connecters* begleiten dich schon seit deinen ersten Englischstunden: *and* und *but.* Nicht viel später hast du *because, so, that* und die *relative pronouns (who, that, which . . .)* kennen- und anwenden gelernt, und auch *when* und *then* gesellten sich bald dazu.

Zu Beginn eine Übung zum „Auffrischen"! Setze die oben genannten *connecters* an die passende Stelle.

examples: It was hot in the room, **so** we opened all the doors.

1. We ran as fast as we could, . . . we did not catch the bus. . . . we had to wait for the next one.
2. . . . we came home in the evening, we closed the windows . . . it had got cold outside.
3. I have no idea . . . will be in my class next year. hope . . . Betty and Jim will stay.
4. The blue whale is the biggest animal . . . lives on earth. It must not be hunted . . . only a few of them are left.

5. Mike Brown, . . . sits beside me in class, has been a good friend of mine since we went to primary school. Next year he will change to a commercial academy (= *Handelsakademie*) . . . he will stay on at our school.
6. . . . we were in Canada last summer, we went to Montreal first. We stayed for a week, and . . . we went on to Toronto and Niagara Falls.
7. Harry did not feel well yesterday, . . . he stayed home from school. . . . today he is here again . . . he is feeling better already.
8. Charlie is in love with Susi, . . . he often brings her flowers. Susi enjoys the flowers . . . she is in love with Charlie, too.

In der Folge findest du alphabetisch geordnet weitere *connecters.* Natürlich sind das nur die „wichtigsten", die du am Ende des vierten Lernjahres auf jeden Fall kennen solltest. Präge dir diese Wörter im Laufe der Zeit wirklich gut ein, damit du sie in Zukunft bei Bedarf richtig und ohne lange nachzudenken anwenden kannst!

although, though
obwohl, obgleich

Drückt einen Widerspruch aus;
kein Unterschied zwischen Langform und Kurzform bei Bedeutung und Anwendung.

We decided to go for a walk ***although*** *it was raining.*
I ate three sandwiches ***though*** *I wasn't really hungry.*
Although *flying is safer than driving, many people are afraid of flying.*

as
da / als, während

☆ Ähnlich *because*: gibt einen Grund an;
kann auch am Beginn des Satzes stehen.

***As** we were tired, we did not want to play another game.*
*Mum did not allow us to go out **as** it was already 9 o'clock.*
*I'm never going to smoke **as** it is expensive and dangerous and causes bad breath and stained fingers.*

☆ Kann statt *while* oder *when* verwendet werden:

***As** we were driving through Oklahoma, we expected to see a tornado.*
*We noticed a strange smell in the house **as** we walked into the hall.*
(hall = Vorzimmer, Diele*)*
***As** the sun went down, all the animals came out of their hiding places.*

2 Verwende in den folgenden Sätzen *as* statt *because* und *when / while*.

examples: Fred did not finish reading the book because it was boring. →
Fred did not finish reading the book as it was boring.

When we were leaving the house, we heard a loud crash in the street. →
As we were leaving the house, we heard a loud crash in the street.

1. Because the door was open, we walked into the room without knocking.
2. I decided to stay at the hotel for another night because it was cheap and the people were friendly.
3. Because it was getting too dark to see, we decided to stop for the day.
4. We did not try to catch the train because it was too late already.
5. Because nobody knew the way, we were soon lost in the woods.
6. Bill called while I was getting ready to leave for school.
7. When the alarm clock started to ring, Sandy slowly opened her eyes.
8. While I was talking to Michael, I had a wonderful idea.
9. Conrad found a wallet while he was walking to the post office.
10. When we were driving out of Baltimore, the sun was rising over the horizon.

as well as
sowie, wie auch, und

Wird meist als Verstärker anstelle von *and* verwendet.
Ähnliche Bedeutung wie *both . . . and* (siehe Seite 130).

The Dillingers are our neighbours ***as well as*** *our friends.*
(. . . our neighbours and our friends.)

The film about sharks was informative ***as well as*** *exciting.*
(The film . . . was both informative and exciting.)

besides
außerdem

Nicht verwechseln mit *beside* (*next to* = neben, daneben; siehe Seite 113); steht für gewöhnlich am Beginn des Satzes und wird von einem Beistrich (Komma) gefolgt.

We're too tired to go for a walk;
besides, *we'd like to watch TV now.*

I don't like the colour of this dress;
besides, *it's too expensive for me.*

Charlie is a fantastic basketball player;
besides, *he also plays volleyball very well.*

3

Du entscheidest: *beside* oder *besides*? Streiche das falsche Wort durch.

example: Cornelia is sitting beside / ~~besides~~ me in English.

1. Mr and Mrs Grant's new house has a three-car garage. They have built it behind the house, not beside / besides it.

2. Would you like to have dinner with us? – That would be nice. Beside / Besides, I am really hungry.
3. "Cats" is a wonderful musical, with fantastic songs and lyrics. Beside / Besides, you will like the dance scenes.
4. Where did you put the newspapers I gave you this morning? – Over there, on the desk, right beside / besides the lamp.
5. The pirates buried their treasure at the end of the canyon, beside / besides a big black rock.
6. Are you coming to the cinema with us? – No, thanks. I don't like westerns; beside / besides, we are having guests tonight.

PAUSE

both . . . and
sowohl . . . als auch

Sagt aus, daß von zwei Möglichkeiten beide in Frage kommen. „Gegenspieler" sind *neither . . . nor* (weder . . . noch); verwandt mit *either . . . or* (entweder . . . oder). Siehe Seite 131.
Mit sehr ähnlicher Bedeutung: *as well as* (vergleiche Seite 129).

Verwende dieselbe Wortart nach *both* und *and*; damit erreichst du einen „ausgewogenen" Stil!

Sammy collects ***both*** *minerals* ***and*** *CDs. (both + noun, and + noun)*
(Sammy collects minerals as well as CDs.)
Too many kids ***both*** *smoke* ***and*** *drink. (both + verb, and + verb)*
Both *Jane* ***and*** *Sue like dark-haired boys. (both + name, and + name)*

4 Verwende *as well as* und *both . . . and* anstelle von *and*.

example: Barbara's shoes look elegant and expensive. →
Barbara's shoes look elegant as well as expensive.
Barbara's shoes look both elegant and expensive.

1. Learning foreign languages is important and interesting.
2. July and August have thirty-one days.
3. I have talked to Mum and Dad about a new mountain bike.
4. The "Batman" films are funny and exciting.
5. Nigeria and India use English as an official language.
6. Susi is pretty and clever.
7. Kimberley sings and dances like a professional.
8. Milk is used for making butter and cheese.

but
sondern (aber)

In diese „Falle" bist du vielleicht schon einmal getappt: *but* heißt eben nicht nur „aber", sondern auch „sondern"!

(Siehe auch *not only . . . but also* = nicht nur . . . sondern auch, Seite 134.)

Willy's birthday is not on September 1st, ***but*** *on October 1st.*
Not money ***but*** *friendship is the most important thing in the world.*
That's not Mary, ***but*** *her sister Maggie.*

either . . . or
entweder . . . oder

Sagt aus, daß eine von zwei Möglichkeiten in Frage kommt.
Nach beiden Wörtern dieselbe Wortart (oder Satz) verwenden (zwecks Ausgewogenheit des Stils)!

We can ***either*** *walk* ***or*** *take a taxi.* (+ verb)
People are ***either*** *rich* ***or*** *happy, but rarely both.* (+ adjective)
Either *you pay for the broken window* ***or*** *I'll tell your parents.* (+ Satz)

for
denn

Dient zur Erklärung oder Begründung;
kann manchmal anstelle von *because* oder *as* verwendet werden (gilt aber als „gehobener" Stil);
for kann niemals an der ersten Stelle im Satz stehen.

Everyone expected us to win the finals ***for*** *we had the best players.*
Jacob was the last to arrive ***for*** *he had to walk all the way.*
Let's ask Charlie, ***for*** *he is the expert!*

5

Hier sind noch einmal die ersten fünf Sätze von *exercise 2* und drei neue Sätze. Setze dieses Mal *for* anstelle von *because* oder *as* ein. Beachte dabei, daß du die *word order* von drei Sätzen verändern mußt!

example: Fred did not finish reading the book because it was boring. →
Fred did not finish reading the book for it was boring.

1. We walked into the room without knocking because the door was open.
2. I decided to stay at the hotel for another night because it was cheap and the people were friendly.
3. As it was getting too dark to see, we decided to stop for the day.
4. We did not try to catch the train because it was too late already.
5. As nobody knew the way, we were soon lost in the woods.
6. We could not understand the speaker as the people in front of us were making such a noise.
7. As a storm was coming up, the ferryboats were not allowed to leave the harbour.
8. I did not speak to Diana because I did not know what to say.

PAUSE

however
jedoch

Einer der ganz wichtigen *connecters*! Damit kannst du die ständige Wiederholung von *but* vermeiden und deinen Ausdruck entscheidend verbessern!

However kann am Anfang, in der Mitte oder am Ende des Satzes stehen und tritt immer in Verbindung mit Beistrichen (Kommas) auf:

However, ..., *however*, ..., *however.*

We all thought that Charlie would be late again, as usual. ***However,*** *he was the first to arrive.*

I was sure Dad would lend me the money for a new CD-ROM drive. When I asked him, ***however,*** *he said no!*

Everbody told me that snowboarding was easy. I had lots of problems staying on my feet, ***however***.

6 Formuliere die folgenden *but*-Sätze mit Hilfe von *however* um. *However* sollte dabei nicht immer an der gleichen Stelle im Satz stehen!

example: We wanted to take the train to New Orleans, but when we arrived at the station, the train had already left. →
. . . to New Orleans; when we arrived at the station, however, the train had already left.
(. . . to New Orleans. However, when we arrived . . .)

1. I tried to install a CD drive in my PC, but I did not know how to begin.
2. Terry invited me to the dance on Saturday, but I had to say no because we are spending the weekend at Grandma's place.
3. Columbus wanted to reach India by sailing west, but he had no idea that he would discover a new continent for the Europeans.

4. My parents drove to Verona to see "Aida" at the arena, but when they got there, they could not get any tickets.
5. Reinhold Messner has climbed the highest mountains on earth and he has walked across Greenland, but an accident forced him to give up his plan to walk from Siberia to Canada.
6. All my friends told me how great the latest Stallone film was, but I did not like it.

not only . . . but also
nicht nur . . . sondern auch

Liefert eine Erweiterung oder Ergänzung der Aussage.
In der Bedeutung ähnlich *both . . . and*.

Next year I will ***not only*** *have new teachers,* ***but also*** *new subjects.*
The questions were ***not only*** *difficult,* ***but also*** *unfair.*
Not only *Catherine,* ***but also*** *her two sisters will be at the dance.*

7 Verwende *not only . . . but also* anstelle von *both . . . and*.

example: Barbara's shoes look both elegant and expensive. →
Barbara's shoes do not only look elegant but also expensive.
(Barbara's shoes look not only elegant but also expensive.)

1. Learning foreign languages is both important and interesting.
2. Both July and August have thirty-one days.
3. I have talked to both Mum and Dad about a new mountain bike.
4. The "Batman" films are both funny and exciting.
5. Both Nigeria and India use English as an official language.
6. Susi is both pretty and clever.
7. Kimberley both sings and dances like a professional.
8. Both butter and cheese are made from milk.

neither . . . nor
weder . . . noch

Sagt aus, daß keine von zwei oder mehr Möglichkeiten in Frage kommt. „Gegenteil" von *both . . . and* (sowohl . . . als auch), „verwandt" mit *either . . . or* (entweder . . . oder); siehe Seite 130 und 131.

Auf beide Wörter muß die gleiche Wortart folgen! Das Zeitwort *(verb)* steht dabei entweder im *singular* (gehobener Stil) oder im *plural* (Umgangssprache).

> ***Neither*** *Jack* ***nor*** *Bill like****s*** *going to school.*
> *(****Neither*** *Jack* ***nor*** *Bill like going to school.)*

> *Most of my older friends* ***neither*** *drink* ***nor*** *smoke.*
> *When we were in London last year,* ***neither*** *the Tower* ***nor*** *Buckingham Palace was (were) open to tourists.*

8 Bilde Sätze mit *both . . . and, either . . . or* und *neither . . . nor*. Manche Sätze sind eindeutig, bei anderen ergeben sich mehrere Möglichkeiten. Damit die Sache für die Sätze 1–3 einfacher wird:
\+ bedeutet *both . . . and*, – bedeutet *neither . . . nor*; 0 bedeutet *either . . . or*.

examples: . . . Uncle Joe . . . Uncle Tom live in Canada. + →
Both Uncle Joe and Uncle Tom live in Canada.

My cat is ill. He . . . drinks . . . eats. – →
My cat is ill. He neither drinks nor eats.

You must . . . tidy up you room . . . wash the dishes. 0 →
You must either tidy up your room or wash the dishes.

1. If I tell my parents that I've lost my new pullover, they will . . . get angry . . . say I shouldn't worry. 0
2. New York City can be . . . fascinating . . . depressing. +
3. . . . Kitzbühel . . . Saalbach had lots of snow last winter. +, –

4. Don't eat at the "Greasy Spoon". Their meals are . . . good . . . cheap.
5. What should I wear at Wendy's wedding (= *Hochzeit*)? – Well, I think . . . the long red dress . . . the black skirt with the white blouse look good.
6. Mr Strange has spent several years in China, so he . . . speaks . . . writes Chinese perfectly.
7. Next year we will be able to choose which language we want to learn. We can take . . . French . . . Latin.
8. The weather was perfect. It was . . . too cold . . . too hot.

Setze die angegebenen *connecters* sinnvoll ein. Manchmal gibt es mehr als eine richtige Lösung!

> although – as – as well as – besides – but – both . . . and – either . . . or – for – however – neither . . . nor – not only . . . but also

✓ richtig

❍❍ 1. You can get to Deerfield . . . by train . . . by coach. The coach is faster, of course. (2×)

❍❍ 2. Deerfield has several historical buildings . . . a modern shopping centre. . . ., there are some fantastic seafood restaurants and a very popular summer theatre.

❍❍ 3. I really wanted to see the Rolling Stones in concert. . . . the price of the ticket . . . the bad weather could keep me from going, and it was worth it. It was so loud, . . ., that I still have a headache.

❍❍ 4. Susi: "Charlie is wonderful! He is . . . handsome . . . strong. I like him . . . he sometimes makes fun of me."

❍❍ 5. . . . we could not get any tickets for the concert, we decided to go to the cinema instead. . . ., they were sold out, too.

❍ 6. . . . Lisa . . . Maggie likes dresses. They always wear jeans.

❍❍ 7. I completely forgot that your birthday is not on October 14, . . . on the 24th, . . . I wrote it down in my notebook.

❍❍❍ ❍ 8. Climbing that mountain was . . . difficult . . . dangerous, . . . there was lots of ice and snow. . . ., I was . . . afraid during the climb . . . tired when we got to the top.

❍❍ 9. . . . we were skiing down the mountain Peggy fell and hurt . . . her ankle (= *Knöchel*) . . . her knee.

❍❍ 10. The largest state of the USA is not Texas, . . . Alaska, . . . Texas has much more inhabitants than Alaska.

Hast du 18 oder mehr Richtige? ***YOU ARE WELL-CONNECTED!*** Bei weniger als 14: ***USE YOUR CONNECTIONS TO "DURCHSTARTEN"*** und wiederhole die letzten 11 Seiten!

BECKENACHTEN UND ARMKREISEN

Du fühlst dich schlaff?

„Male“ mit deinem Becken eine Acht, damit dein Körper Energie zum schöpferischen Träumen bekommt:
Du stehst mit leicht gebeugten Knien, die Füße sind hüftbreit auseinander. Du streckst die Arme nach hinten und verschränkst die Daumen ineinander.
Nun machst du mit den Hüften eine Vor- und Rückwärtsbewegung, so daß daraus eine Acht entsteht. Der Oberkörper bleibt dabei aufrecht, die Atmung ist fließend. Achte darauf, daß die Ellbogen möglichst gestreckt bleiben.

**Dauer der Übung:
30mal**

Eine letzte Übung zur Aktivierung deiner Energie:

Du stehst hüftbreit, die Knie locker. Du kreist nun mit beiden Armen gleichzeitig von vorne nach oben, über den Kopf nach hinten.
Achte darauf, daß die Ellbogen gestreckt bleiben.

**Dauer der Übung:
50mal**

STORIES

Das Kapitel *stories* will dir helfen, eine ganz wichtige Fertigkeit in Englisch zu entwickeln: nämlich einen Gedanken, einen Text zu erfassen und auf verschiedene Weise wiederzugeben.

Auch dein Leseverständnis soll gefördert werden, damit du eine englische Geschichte und später einmal auch eine englische Zeitung oder ein Buch lesen kannst, ohne gleich die Flinte ins Korn zu werfen.

Von alleine geht das aber nicht, und deshalb findest du im Anschluß an jede Geschichte Übungen und Arbeitsaufgaben. Sie sind natürlich schon schwieriger als in den früheren Bänden von „Durchstarten in Englisch", aber du hast ja auch schon drei volle Lernjahre hinter dir!

Folgende Arbeitsaufgaben kommen vor, und es geht immer nach der gleichen Reihenfolge:

 1. *read the story* (Lesen)

 2. *make sentences* (Sätze bilden)

 3. *fill in* (Wörter einfügen)

 4. *finish sentences* (Sätze weiterführen)

 5. *answer questions* (Fragen beantworten)

 6. *why-questions* (Warum-Fragen)

Noch ein Tip fürs Lesen: Die Verwendung des Wörterbuches *(dictionary)* ist jetzt sinnvoller denn je. Schlage aber nicht sofort jedes Wort nach, das du nicht verstehst, sondern versuche zunächst, seinen Sinn aus dem Zusammenhang heraus zu erraten.

The Way to Heaven

1 Read the story

Lies dir die Geschichte einmal durch, ohne eine Pause einzulegen. Wenn du ein Wort nicht verstehst, lies zunächst weiter. Wenn du wirklich nicht dahinterkommst, was es bedeutet, kannst du in deinem Wörterbuch *(dictionary)* nachsehen.

India is a big country. It is nearly as big as all of Europe, and about one billion people live there. But it isn't a country at all. If someone said that it was one country, you would think that they all speak more or less one language and have more or less the same colour of skin, like in Austria, or Spain, or Finland, or in any other country in Europe. But we don't speak of one "European people", and there is no "European language", and there isn't an "Indian people" or an "Indian language", either. They speak about 150 different languages there, and some Indians from the North look like Europeans, and some from the South are very dark-skinned. Anyway, whatever language they speak, and whatever colour they are, there is one thing that is quite different from our way of living: the country and the people are very poor, and many children have to work to make their living.

Charan is one of the millions of Indian boys who work because they have to feed their families. He is only thirteen, but he works as a liftboy in a big and noble hotel, which is great for him and his family, because he gets food, money, a room and clothes and, best of all, he even gets some extra money from the guests: he gets tips (= Trinkgeld).

Once, it was during the monsoon season, the hotel was full of guests, mostly foreigners, because there was a U.N. conference in the city. So Charan was very busy taking people from America, Japan, the Netherlands, from Germany and other countries, up and down the hotel in "his" lift. He knew he wouldn't get any tips if people were in a hurry, but he did his job as carefully as usual.

One day a tall man in an expensive suit got on the lift. Everything about him looked expensive; his briefcase (= Aktentasche), *his watch, his shoes, and even the little notebook that he opened on his way to the 16th floor had golden corners and golden letters on it. Suddenly a business card fell from his notebook. The man did not notice it, he*

didn't even realize that Charan bent down and picked it up. He seemed to be lost in his thoughts. When Charan looked into the man's face he saw that it was very tense (= angespannt).
The lift had stopped on the 16th floor and the man was ready to get off when Charan said, "Sir, this card has fallen out of your notebook." The man did not even hear what Charan had said, but another guest had heard Charan's words and took hold of the tall man's arm. "Sir, I think the liftboy wants to tell you something." Then the rich man turned and looked at Charan. Charan held out the little card. The man took it slowly. Charan saw that the man's hands were trembling a bit, and then the man said, "Thank you, son, thank you. If I had lost this card . . ." Then he put it into his jacket. He reached into his pocket and took out a one dollar note. "For you," the man said. "You have deserved (= verdient) *it." Then he went away.*
The lift was called downstairs again so Charan hurried into the cabin. On his way down he looked at the money. He knew that it was very much for him and his family. Then other guests entered and Charan had no time to think about it anymore.
A few days later the U.N. conference was over, and other people came to the hotel. Only the man with the expensive suit was still there. Charan noticed that he looked better a couple of days later, and the man sometimes smiled at the boy when he saw him. Charan always smiled back: it was his job but he would have done it anyway. One day late in the evening, Charan took the man once again to the 16th floor. This time the man's daughter was with him, and they laughed and were happy. The man told the girl of his "little adventure" with the business card and the girl smiled at Charan. When they had reached the 16th floor the girl said, "Oh, Daddy, I've forgotten my hair ring in the restaurant downstairs. I'll be back in a minute." "Alright," the man said and he went into his room. Charan had to take the girl down to the ground floor where the restaurant was. As soon as the door closed the girl said, "What's your name?" As he had been told to answer all questions that were put to him, he said his name. "I'm Wendy," she said, "and we come from Detroit. My Daddy sells trucks." Charan did not know where Detroit was, but he thought it was a rich town. "You and I, we're both the same age," the girl said. Charan looked at her. To him she looked like a fairy princess from another planet. She was so unlike all the thirteen-year-old girls he knew. She looked like a grown-up. She looked like a young lady.
There were not many people around now, so Charan waited for Wendy until she returned from the restaurant, and he took her upstairs again. And from this day on the two children, who were so

unlike in every way, and who came from completely different worlds, and who had nothing in common but their age, talked with each other whenever they met. The hotel management did not like contacts between guests and people who worked in the hotel. Charan spoke his Indian English, and Wendy spoke American English, and when they talked it sounded like the discussions at the U.N. conference, because the people there also used English, and they also came from different countries. Wendy told Charan that Detroit was a big city in America, and that she had a brother who was in college and only came home once a month, and that her parents were divorced and rather rich. And Charan told her that he had two sisters, one younger, and one Wendy's age, and that he saw his mother only twice a month because she worked in a factory far away, and that his father was away working and he had not seen him for over a year. So, in a way, they had very much in common. But two days later something happened that showed how much all young people have in common.

It all started right after lunch. Most people had gone to their rooms because the afternoons are very hot in India and the monsoon rains had been pouring down for hours and hours. The hotel was unusually quiet when a trail of smoke found its way out of the kitchen. Hotel kitchens are very big so it didn't seem surprising at first, but then one of the waiters told the receptionist (= Mann am Empfangsschalter, Reception) *that the smoke didn't smell of kitchen. Then everything happened very quickly. After a short phone call to the hotel management the two men ran through the kitchen and into the cellar. Thick smoke met them on their way down. They could not see what was the matter, but they knew that the smoke was not coming from the kitchen. Then the waiter shouted, "The lifts!" The receptionist ran upstairs. He was an experienced man. He called the fire brigade, and soon some men arrived through the back entrance. The men in their safety overalls and their oxygen masks* (= Atemschutzgeräte) *examined the cellar, and soon they found out that three of the big air-condition machines had overheated.*

They were not burning, but they had become so hot that all the synthetic material on the machines and on the ceiling of the room had melted and produced an extremely biting smoke, which was now streaming up through the lift shaft. While the firemen were trying to fight their way through the smoke the telephone was ringing in the hotel manager's office. "Yes, sir, can I help you?" the manager said. "My daughter left our room half an hour ago. She said she was going to the restaurant. Now I see that the elevator is out of order. Could you . . .". But the manager stopped listening.

"Your room number, please!" And in a couple of minutes the manager was in the guest's room. Very soon the horrible truth was clear. Wendy was in the elevator, and it had got stuck somewhere in the shaft. Nobody knew where, because the control lights were out of order as well. "We can't open the doors, because then the shaft might catch fire," the manager explained. The two men stood silently in the hotel room. Then the manager said, "I, too, have a daughter." Thirty minutes passed; thirty minutes that seemed like a lifetime. The two men hardly spoke. Both were afraid that something had happened that would ruin each one's life in a different way. And then the door opened. Both men looked in the same direction, and in stumbled Wendy, dirty, weeping and exhausted, but safe. And outside the door stood Charan, trembling and shivering, his face black with smoke. Soon a doctor arrived and examined the two children. They were still under shock but not hurt or in any danger. For some time Wendy could not talk, but then she told her story.

"We were in the lift when suddenly the lights went out and the elevator stopped. First I thought we only had to press the emergency button and everything would be alright, but then we realized that we were stuck.

I heard Charan telling me through the darkness that the security systems would soon tell the management that we were in the elevator, and we sat down on the floor. But then the smoke came. Within minutes we started coughing (= husten) *and had problems breathing* (= atmen). *Then Charan told me we had to leave the cabin. He told me to stand in a corner, and in the darkness he climbed on my shoulders. He said he always had a screwdriver with him to repair little things.*

So he unscrewed part of the cabin roof and climbed out. The shaft was full of smoke but he said, 'It's only five floors to heaven.' This is what the people call the top of the hotel. You can see the sky from up there, Charan told me. When he had gone the smoke came in faster, but we could see a little light from the top. It was so terrible. I couldn't climb out of the cabin because the walls were too high. So Charan told me to hand him my dress so he could pull me up. I did and he let it down again. I seized it and he pulled me from the cabin. There is a long ladder in the shaft. He climbed up behind me, he pushed me and shoved me up and up and up. I was coughing, and vomiting (= erbrechen), *but I was so afraid that I did reach the top. Charan knew that there was an emergency door. It is never locked. After we had left the shaft, we sat down on the roof and breathed deeply. Then Charan showed me the way down, and here I am again, Daddy."*

An hour later the safety engineers informed the manager that the problem was under control. Nobody had been harmed. In the evening the man from Detroit came into the manager's office. "How can I thank the lift boy?" he asked. "I mean, how much would you think is alright? I'm not a poor man." The manager was serious und looked into his face. "Do you really want to do something for him?" "Anything I can afford. And I mean it." "Then send him to school." The man from Detroit did not understand at first, but the manager told him. "If you gave him, let's say, a thousand dollars, he could do nothing with it. If people found out about it, some criminals would find him and take it from him. His father was shot a year ago; he had become involved with drug dealers. I haven't told the boy the truth yet. But if you could pay for his education and give some extra money to his family, it would make sense. There are not many boys who can open elevator doors in the dark. I believe he is gifted." When the American didn't say anything the manager added, "It would cost about $ 200 a year." "What?" said the man. "That's the price of a good dinner in the States." "But here we are in India," the manager said. "$ 200 for the way to Heaven," the man from Detroit said. "There is a missionary station two blocks away that will organize things for the boy," the manager said. "And here's the number of my credit card; that will organize things for the missionaries." Then they both shook hands.

2 Make sentences

Make sentences using the following words:

a) language
b) foreigner
c) to be involved
d) grown-up
e) unusually
f) to examine
g) to explain
h) education

3 Finish sentences

1. If someone said that India was one country, ...
2. Charan is only thirteen, but ... .
3. The man didn't even hear ..., but another guest . . .
4. Charan noticed that the man looked ... .
5. To Charan Wendy looked ... .
6. Wendy told him that ... .
7. While the firemen were trying ... .
8. "If you gave him, let's say, $ 1000 ... .

4 Answer questions

1. What do you know about India and Charan?
2. What can you say about the man from Detroit?
3. What was the incident (= *Vorfall*) in the lift about?
4. What did Charan and Wendy tell each other?
5. Why was the hotel so quiet "right after lunch"?
6. What had happened to the air-condition machines?
7. Why did the manager go into the guest's room?
8. How did Charan and Wendy get out of the cabin and the shaft?
9. How did Wendy's father help Charan? Why did he do it?

The Dog That Knew No Tricks

1  **Read the story**

Lies dir die Geschichte einmal durch, ohne eine Pause einzulegen. Wenn du ein Wort nicht verstehst, lies zunächst weiter. Wenn du wirklich nicht dahinterkommst, was es bedeutet, kannst du in deinem Wörterbuch *(dictionary)* nachsehen.

"Aren't you afraid your daughter will catch fleas (= Flöhe) *or lice or something else?" Mr. Nuttle said to my Dad. I was sitting on one of our large sofas watching TV with Scraffy on my lap* (= Schoß). *Scraffy was our dog. Mum and Dad had invited people to dinner that Dad knew from work. Mr. Nuttle looked like a typical businessman in his dark suit, white shirt, and tie. His wife, who he always called 'Dear', was doing the washing-up with Mum. We had had one of those big dinners Dad used to give for business friends. He had a position in a firm that sold paper handkerchiefs and toilet paper, so hygenie was very important to him.*
Dad looked at Scraffy and me, but he didn't smile. He took the bottle of red wine and filled the glasses for his guest and himself. And then he told him the story. I know this story quite well, and I like it. It is a wonderful story, and I am part of it.

— ☆ —

Three years ago, when our daughter Samantha was ten, she brought home a dog on a cold winter evening. He was dirty, thin, hungry and looked terrible. We didn't want to keep him, but she begged and cried so that in the end my wife said, "Alright, keep him, but you will have to take care of him. I do not want to have him in the house." We weren't very happy, but Samantha certainly was.
In summer she started to teach him the sort of tricks most dogs know: how to sit still, how to stand on his hind legs (= Hinterbeine), *how to jump over low fences* (= Zäune) *and the like. But nothing worked. The dog wouldn't learn anything. We said that he was as stupid as a stone. And I think even Samantha was a bit sad about that. But the saddest thing for her was that we didn't like the dog. She loved him. He could do nothing wrong. The only thing he really seemed to understand was to take things from her to me and from me to her. He could bring you stones, sticks, and all kinds of things. When Samantha gave him a little red ball and said, "Go!", he would*

come to me, and then I could send the ball back to Samantha. But that's not much of a clever dog.

Well, anyway, the following winter we spent our holidays in one of those wooden cabins (= Holzhütte) up in the mountains. We didn't go skiing there, but we enjoyed the open country. We took long walks in the snow, and what I liked best, it was so quiet there.

Our cabin was right on a lake, and it took us two full hours to walk around it. The lake was completely frozen, so Samantha and my wife went skating every day.

Scraffy, the dog, was always with them, because Samantha wouldn't go anywhere without him. He ran round and barked and played, and ran right in front of their skates so that they frequently fell down.

On the fourth day, I remember it quite well, the sun was bright as ever, but the wind was unusually warm. It was one of the days when you shouldn't turn on the heating (= Heizung). It was clearly too warm for that time of year. Samantha and my wife went skating without their jackets, and when my wife returned to prepare dinner, Samantha and the dog stayed out on the ice. In the afternoon it suddenly became foggy (= nebelig). I had been out with one of the forest rangers, who always showed me some interesting places. We hurried home from our walk in order not to worry anybody. The three of us were sitting in the living room having tea, when all of a sudden we heard a terrible noise. It was a deep crack which seemed to run round our house. It was frightening, to say the least . Jack Forrester, the ranger, told us that it was the ice melting. "Nothing dangerous", he said, "the ice floes (= Schollen) break loose, drift a hundred yards (= fast 100 Meter) or so, and then freeze again over night."

Then my wife said, "Where is Samantha?" We hurried out. The fog was so dense that we couldn't see more than ten yards. And it was getting dark.

"Samantha!" we all shouted in panic. When I tried to walk on the ice of the lake it was already too thin to hold me. For the first time in my life I felt the terror of death. Then, in a moment of complete silence, we heard the thin and distant voice of our girl. She seemed to be screaming as loud as she could. Then there was the deep crack again, louder than before.

I said to Forrester, "Please, go and call for help. Call a helicopter, call . . ." but he said, "They wouldn't even start in that fog. Five years ago we lost a helicopter and three men in a fog like this."

Helplessly we shouted her name again and again. Suddenly we understood the words "broken" and "hurt". "I'll go for it (= Ich geh hinaus)," I said, but Forrester held me back. "You won't get ten yards. And the cold water will kill you within two minutes."

And then we heard the barking of the dog. It was quite close. And when we called his name he was there in seconds. In panic we asked him questions about our daughter, we were screaming and shouting and weeping, but then Forrester asked, "Is this your dog?" "No," I said, "it's her dog." For the first time I realized (= erkennen) *the importance of this difference. "Do you think he will go back to her, if you tell him to?" Forrester went on. "I hope to God he will!" I said. Forrester went to his car and got a long thin rope. It was the sort people climb mountains with. He tied one end round a big tree that stood near the lake, and then he tied the other end to the dog's collar* (= Halsband). *I knelt down to the dog, patted* (= tätscheln) *his fur* (= Fell) *and said, "Please, please, go to Samantha! Go to Samantha!"*

As if he had never done anything else in his life, the dog turned round and disappeared in the dark fog. My wife covered her face with her hands and wept bitterly. "Please, dear God, let him find Samantha!" Again there were loud cracks from melting ice blocks, and they echoed through the whole valley. "What if the rope isn't long enough?" I asked doubtfully. "We wouldn't have heard her then, would we?" Forrester said tensely (= gespannt). *"If she is a clever girl, she will take the rope and pull herself along. It's not difficult on ice. And the ice blocks don't melt suddenly. Even the thin places are strong enough for her to slide over."*

Suddenly the rope tightened (= spannte sich). *We screamed with joy. Again and again we shouted her name. Then her voice sounded louder and closer and a minute later we saw Samantha lying on the ice, pulling herself along with the rope. Her face and her hands were bloody, she was wet all over, but alive. When we lifted her up the first thing she said was, "Where's Scraffy?"*

But the dog was gone. We quickly took her inside and comforted her. We called for the ambulance, and they said the car would get there in about an hour.

When the ambulance arrived we carried Samantha out. But suddenly we heard a dog barking near the lake. From inside the ambulance Samantha screamed the dog's name at the top of her voice. We explained it to the driver. When the dog appeared from out of the darkness he was cold, wet, and worn out, and his paws were as bloody as Samantha's hands. My wife knelt down and held him close to her face. Then she whispered with tears in her eyes, "We won't ever let you go, Scraffy."

2 Make sentences

a) to invite
b) quite well
c) to seem to understand
d) completely
e) unusually
f) to break loose
g) to realize
h) anything else

3 Fill in

1. I was sitting in one . . . my lap.
2. Mr. Nuttle looked like . . . and tie.
3. Two yers ago . . . was ten, she brought . . .
4. We didn't want . . . wife said, "Alright, . . .
5. The only thing he . . . from her to me and . . .
6. Our cabin was . . . round it.
7. He ran round . . . fell down.
8. I had been out with . . . interesting spots.
9. The three of us . . . terrible noise.
10. When I tried to walk . . . to hold me.
11. In panic we asked him . . . but Forrester said . . .
12. He tied one end . . . dog's collar.

4 Finish these sentences

1. I was sitting ...
2. His wife, whom he always ...
3. Then, in summer, she started ...
4. The only thing he really seemed ...
5. Our cabin was ...
6. He ran round and ...
7. The three of us were sitting ...
8. He tied one end ...
9. As if he had never done ...
10. When the dog appeared ....

5 Answer questions

1. How old was Samantha when she brought the dog?
2. What did Samantha try to teach Scraffy?
3. What was the only thing he seemed to understand?
4. Where did they spend their winter holidays?
5. What was the frightening noise they heard?
6. Where was Samantha when the others were having tea?
7. What did Forrester do with the rope?
8. What did Samantha's parents do when the girl was safe at last?
9. What did the dog look like when he appeared in the end?

6 Why-Fragen

1. Why did Mr. Nuttle care so much about hygenie?
2. Why could they skate on the lake?
3. Why was the ice melting?
4. Why could the helicopters not start?
5. Why did the rope tighten?
6. Why did Samantha scream Scraffy's name from inside the ambulance?

TESTS

Englisch ist ein sogenanntes „aufbauendes" Fach. Das heißt, daß du alles, was du lernst, auch noch später beherrschen und anwenden mußt.

Ein * bedeutet „Stoff von früher (1. bis 3. Klasse)" oder „Wiederholung"; (*) bedeutet „zum Teil Wiederholung, zum Teil neu".
Wenn du dir deiner Sache nicht ganz sicher bist oder Zweifel auftreten, sieh in den „Durchstarten in Englisch"-Bänden für die 5., 6. und 7. Schulstufe nach. Du findest dort die nötigen Informationen!

Die Punktewertung ist bei allen *tests* die gleiche:

40–38 = Sehr gut
37–34 = Gut
33–28 = Befriedigend
Unter 28 Punkten = Arbeite die fehlerhaften Stoffgebiete noch einmal durch!

Good luck! You can do it!

1st test

"some" and "any" *
present tense: simple or progressive
prepositions of time (*)
past tense: simple or progressive

1. Fill in *some* or *any*.

10 Punkte

a) Is there . . .thing we can do to help you? – No, thanks.
b) Are you hungry? There's . . . cold chicken in the fridge, if you want . . .
c) Marcia was so angry that she couldn't think of . . .thing to say.
d) Have you seen my basketball shoes? They must be . . .where around here.
e) Does . . .body know when the concert begins? – I'm not sure, but I think . . .time around 8 or 8:30 tomorrow evening.
f) These are really hard times for all of us, but . . .how we'll make it!
g) . . .one I don't know wants to talk to you, Kevin. – What does he want? – I don't know. He didn't say . . .thing.

2. Fill in the most suitable prepositions of time from the box.

10 Punkte

Für jede richtige „Lücke" kannst du dir einen halben Punkt gutschreiben.

in – till – before – on – from . . . to – since – for – after – at – ago

a) Columbus first landed in America . . . October 12 . . . the year 1492. That was more than 500 years . . .
b) My Mum worked for "Benson & Son" . . . 1981 . . . 1988. In other words, she stayed with them . . . almost eight years.
c) The accident at Chernobyl happened . . . April 1986, five years . . . the end of the Soviet Union . . . 1991.
d) Danny usually gets up . . . 7 o'clock . . . the morning, but . . . Saturday and Sunday he stays in bed . . . 9 or 10 o'clock.
e) My grandfather's brother emigrated to Canada . . . the summer of 1947, two years . . . the end of the Second World War.
f) When did you arrive? – . . . Saturday. – How long will you stay? – . . . the end of next week. – Have you been here before? – Yes, three years . . . – How long did you stay then? – . . . March . . . June.

3. Present tense: simple form or progressive form?

10 Punkte

a) Look, there are Bill and Mia. They (come) from their dancing lesson.
b) Where (you, come) from, Mr Clinton? – I'm from Arkansas. I (live) in Little Rock, which is the state capital.
c) Mr Clinton and his wife (stay) at the Mayfair Hotel at the moment.
d) Cuckoos always (lay) their eggs in the nests of other birds.
e) Look, I (understand) your problems and I (really, try) to help you, but you must give me more time!
f) Joe, what (you, do) with my walkman? – Nothing! I (just, look) at it.
g) My grandmother (bake) the world's best chocolate cakes.

4. Past tense: simple form or progressive form?

10 Punkte

a) What (you, do) when I (call) you Sunday morning? – I (record) a "Universum" film about gorillas.
b) From 2 to 4 yesterday afternoon I (wait) for Jenny, but she (not, come).
c) Helen (fall) asleep while she (listen) to some oldies on the radio.
d) We (leave) the house at 7:30 this morning and (walk) to the bus stop. It (take) us 3 to 4 minutes to get there.

2nd test

the article comparison of the adjective *	present perfect tense: simple or progressive prepositions of place (*)

1. Article or no article? Fill in (or don't!): the – a – an.

10 Punkte

Für jede richtige „Lücke" kannst du dir einen halben Punkt gutschreiben.

a) . . . most people enjoy . . . summer more than . . . winter.
b) I remember . . . summer of 1983 very well; it was very hot all . . . time.
c) . . . Tower of London is well-known all over . . . world.
d) Be careful! . . . tea is still very hot. But you can put . . . cold water in it.
e) My brother is going to study at . . . Oxford University next year. He has not yet decided whether he wants to be . . . doctor or . . . lawyer.
f) . . . earrings Jamie was wearing yesterday are made of . . . gold.
g) . . . English proverb (Sprichwort) says: ". . . apple a day keeps . . . doctor away."
h) Uncle Gerald has been . . . teacher for 22 years. Now he has been made . . . headmaster of . . . school in our town.

2. Compare the following people and things. Use the given adjectives and fill in the proper *(passende)* words.

10 Punkte

a) My brother is (strong) . . . . you.
b) I think a good snowboard is (expensive) . . . . good skis.
c) My sister is almost (tall) . . . . my Mum and she walks like her as well.
d) The (bad) . . . thing you can do now is run away.
e) I've never seen (good) . . . films . . . the "Indiana Jones" series.
f) French is not (easy) . . . . . . to learn . . . English, but many people say that German is (difficult) . . . . . .
g) The (near) . . . petrol station is just around the corner, but if it's closed, you'll have to go to the next one, in High Street.

3. Present perfect tense: simple form or progressive form, for or since?

10 Punkte

a) How long (Charlie, be). . . here? – . . . three days.
b) I'm afraid I (leave). . . my workbook at home, sir.
c) Uncle Leo (work). . . for my Dad . . . 1990.
d) It (snow). . . heavily . . . the beginning of this week.
e) How long (you, know). . . Terry? – . . . we went to school together. We (be). . . very good friends all these years.

4. Fill in suitable prepositions of place (from the box).

10 Punkte

Für jede richtige „Lücke“ kannst du dir einen halben Punkt gutschreiben.

between – above – through – during – from – out of – behind – into – on – below – across – in – to – next to – in front of – at – after – by

a) It's cold today! – Yes! The thermometre shows 25° . . . zero.
b) The two men went . . . the building half an hour ago, but they have not come . . . it yet.
c) The castle stands . . . a hill. You have to walk . . . a large park before you get to it, however.
d) You can't see Charlie because he is hiding . . . the tree over there.
e) We can hear the plane but we can't see it because it is flying . . . the clouds.
f) I'll wait for you . . . the corner of Church Street and Station Road. I'll be in the park . . . the supermarket.
g) Fritz, where are you going? – . . . the cinema. And you? – I'm walking home . . . basketball practice.
h) I'm sorry, but my Dad is not . . . home. He is . . . town with Mum.
i) Let's stop for dinner here. There's no restaurant . . . here and where we want to go.
j) Richard ran . . . the man, but he could not catch him.
k) Be careful when you walk . . . the street! There's always a lot of traffic.
l) Grandpa likes to read his paper while he is sitting . . . the window.
m) . . . the winter holidays we often go skiing . . . the mountains.
n) The film was okay, but I only saw half of it. A woman with a giant hat was sitting directly . . . me.

3rd test

relative clauses *
the infinitive
mixed tenses (*)
"The Way to Heaven"

1. Fill in a suitable relative pronoun (who, that, whose, . . .) where it is necessary; don't write one where it is possible. Put commas where they belong. **10 Punkte**

Je ein halber Punkt für „Beistrich oder nicht" und für „richtiges oder gar kein Relativpronomen".

a) I've never met the people . . . moved into the house next to yours.
b) What do you think about the model helicopter . . . I got for Christmas?
c) Charlie often calls Mac "chicken" (= Feigling) . . . isn't very funny.
d) Do you understand . . . I have just said?
e) This picture was painted by Picasso . . . also painted "Guernica".
f) Niki Lauda . . . airline consists of more than 10 planes today often pilots one of these planes himself.
g) I'd like to know . . . you told Marietta about me!
h) Aunt Liz . . . is famous for her Christmas puddings uses only things . . . she produces herself.
i) The biggest river . . . runs into the Gulf of Mexico is the Mississippi.

2. Mixed tenses: Fill in present tense, past tense or present perfect tense, simple or progressive form. **10 Punkte**

a) Columbus (discover) America more than 500 years ago. Since then, millions of people from all over the world (move) to the New World.
b) Charlie, what (you, do) here? – I (wait) for Susi. – How long (you, wait)? – For almost an hour, but she (not come) yet.
c) (you, ever, be) to the United States, Doris? – Yes, twice. I first (go) there three years ago, with my parents, and in the following year I (spend) three weeks there by myself.
d) Listen! Can you hear that funny noise? I think Max (practice) the trumpet again.

3. Translate the following sentences using an infinitive. **5 Punkte**

a) Ich bat John, seinen Eltern nichts von dem Unfall zu erzählen.
b) Wir möchten, daß ihr dieses Lied bei der Feier (= *party*) singt.
c) Du erwartest wirklich, daß ich diesen Unsinn glaube?
d) Sie müssen mir verraten (= *tell*), wie man diesen herrlichen Kuchen macht.
e) Vater beschloß, das Moped selbst zu reparieren.

4. Infinitive with to or without to? Fill in a suitable verb from the box.

8 Punkte

come – go – wash – take – watch – help – stay – hurry

a) I don't want . . . to the theatre tonight. I'd rather . . . at home and . . . TV.
b) Dad agreed . . . me with the maths homework if I promised . . . his car.
c) You needn't . . .! There's enough time left.
d) How long have you been here? I didn't hear you . . . into the room.
e) Mark's mother is very nice. She offered . . . us to the station in her car.

5. "The Way to Heaven" – Finish the following sentences so that you get a "mini version" of the story.

7 Punkte

Hier gibt es natürlich viele „richtige" Antwortmöglichkeiten! Lies ruhig in der Geschichte nach, bevor du diesen Punkt des *test* in Angriff nimmst!

a) Charan lived . . . and Wendy came . . .
b) They met . . . while Wendy's father . . .
c) They soon . . .
d) One day, right after lunch, smoke . . .
e) It was streaming up . . .
f) Wendy and Charan . . .
g) When Wendy was safe again, her Dad . . .

4th test

passive voice *	conjunctions (*)
gerund	gerund or infinitive

1. Make the following active sentences passive!

7 Punkte

a) Careless skiers cause thousands of accidents every winter.
b) (In the western I saw yesterday) the Army attacked an Indian camp.
c) They have not opened the new shopping centre yet.
d) They were playing "God Save the Queen" when we arrived.
e) They would build the new bridge sooner if they had more money.
f) You can't sit on this bench! They have just painted it.
g) This report says that they are shooting "Rocky VIII" at the moment.

2. Fill in a suitable connecter.

7 Punkte

a) Dad promised to buy me the latest version of "Phantasmagoria", . . . then he forgot.
b) I was angry and sad . . . I had really wanted this game for a long time.
c) Now he says . . . I will get it on August 1, . . . is my birthday.
d) Give me back my pocket knife . . . I will tell my parents!
e) Mum and Dad were sleeping, . . . they did not hear us come home.
f) I always read a book or a newspaper . . . I am waiting for the bus.

3. Translate the following sentences into English with the help of a gerund.

12 Punkte

a) Kannst du dir vorstellen, mit Joe zu tanzen?
b) Ich schlage vor, das Training morgen fortzusetzen (= *continue*).
c) Habt ihr daran gedacht, jemand um Hilfe zu bitten?
d) Ich habe es satt, jeden Tag so spät nach Hause zu kommen.
e) Bist du wirklich daran interessiert herauszufinden, wer der Mörder ist?
f) Mike ist stolz darauf, der beste Fußballer seiner Klasse zu sein.
g) Ihr solltet mit dem Rauchen aufhören!
h) Niemand kann mich davon abhalten, am Samstag ins Kino zu gehen.
i) Mr Jackson freut sich darauf, im Sommer nach Schottland zu fahren.
j) Wenn du einen Witz erzählst, muß ich einfach lachen.
k) Es hat keinen Sinn, mit Charlie zu sprechen.
l) Ihr solltet zusammenarbeiten, anstatt zu streiten.

4. Use a gerund to shorten or connect the following sentences. **6 Punkte**

a) After Joe had posted the letter, he went to a café.
b) Before Kelly leaves the house in the morning, she checks all the doors.
c) When Stephanie read the telegram, she began to cry.
d) You can win the "jackpot" if you tick off the correct numbers.
e) The storks (= *Störche*) fly to Africa after they leave Europe.
f) Benny surprised us all. He scored four goals in a single match.

5. Gerund or infinitive? Fill in the correct form. **8 Punkte**

a) I'm very sorry, but I forgot (inform) your parents.
b) We'll never forget (watch) the sun rise over the island.
c) Do you remember (tell) me about Henry's birthday?
d) Please remember (ask) Albert if he wants to play in our group.
e) The tourist stopped (take) a picture of the dancers.
f) Dad, stop (take) pictures! We're hungry.
g) Did you try (speak) with Mrs Trask yesterday?
h) If you can't do it yourself, try (find) somebody to help you.

5th test

indirect speech *	the future
present participle	"The Dog That Knew No Tricks"

1. Put into reported speech. Use different reporting verbs and change as much as you can change. **10 Punkte**

Die Ziffern in Klammer am Satzende sind halbe Punkte!

a) Lisa said, "Nothing grows in my garden. It never gets any sun." (4)
b) "It isn't as foggy today as it was yesterday," Bob remarked. (4)
c) "I've no idea what time it is, but I'll call 1-2-3 to find out," Cal said. (5)
d) "Why don't you take a taxi?" Uncle Alec asked. (3)
e) "Please pay at the desk!" said the assistant. (2)
f) "Don't shout at me!" Dad said. (2)

2. Put the following sentences into the correct "future".

10 Punkte

a) What (you, do) if you win a million Pounds? – I think I (buy) my parents a bigger house.
b) Look at Tim! He (fall) asleep any time now! He must be very tired.
c) Emily's train (arrive) in ten minutes. We (have) to hurry if we want to meet her at the station.
d) Ladies and gentlemen, in a few moments you (see) something you have never seen before!
e) We (go) on a class trip tomorrow. (your class, go) too?
f) When I (see) Ronny next time, I (tell) him about your plans.

3. Shorten or connect the following sentences with the help of a present participle.

12 Punkte

a) As we were hungry, we ate everything that was in the fridge.
b) The tourists looked at the paintings that were hanging on the walls.
c) The man ran after the car. He shouted as loudly as he could. (2)
d) As Bernie had not enough money, he couldn't buy the CD.
e) When Conrad entered the room, he noticed several people who were talking to each other.
f) The little boy was sitting in the grass. He was crying for his mother. (2)
g) As the water was too cold for swimming, we decided to rent a boat.
h) Marcus stood in the rain and tried to open his umbrella. (2)
i) I can hear Jenny. She is singing next door.
j) When Gus came home from school, he found his lunch on the table.

4. "The Dog That Knew No Tricks" – answer the following questions so that you get a "mini version" of the story.

8 Punkte

Hier gibt es natürlich viele „richtige" Antwortmöglichkeiten! Lies ruhig in der Geschichte nach, bevor du diesen Punkt des *test* in Angriff nimmst!

a) How did Samantha's parents react when their daughter came home with Scraffy?
b) Why did they believe that he was "stupid as a stone"?
c) Where did they go the following winter? How did they spend their time?
d) What was the fourth day like? What did they do at first?
e) What did they hear? What had happened?
f) Where was Samantha?
g) Why was it impossible to get to her?
h) How did they manage to save Samantha in the end? What was Scraffy's part in it?

Die Durchstartübungen

DIE LEHRE

Die Übungen beruhen auf der Kinesiologie, der Lehre von der Bewegung. Sie unterstützt alle deine Tätigkeiten – auch dein Lernen. Durch die Anwendung bestimmter Bewegungsmuster kannst du deine Möglichkeiten voll ausschöpfen.

DER AUTOR

Kim da Silva lebt in Berlin und arbeitet als Kinesiologe. Er studierte Chemie, Physik, Botanik, Mikrobiologie und Lebensmittelchemie. Nach fünf Jahren als Assistent an der Freien Universität Berlin und sechsjähriger Forschungsarbeit in der chemischen Industrie arbeitete er viele Jahre in einem pharmazeutischen Weltkonzern.
In seiner Jugend reiste er viel und erwarb sich sein Wissen um die verschiedenen Philosophien und Heiltraditionen.
In den 70er Jahren lernte Kim da Silva die Kinesiologie kennen. Er war einer der ersten, die bei Dr. Paul Dennison eine Ausbildung in Edu-Kinestetik erhielten. Heute zählt er zu den wenigen europäischen Ausbildern für Edu-K-Teacher.
Von Kim da Silva sind bereits einige Bücher erschienen.

DIE AUTORIN

Do-Ri Rydl, geboren 1958, vom Beruf Drogistin, lernt und lehrt seit 1985 mit Kim da Silva. Seit 1988 leitet sie ein Kinesiologie-Zentrum in Mödling und die Edu-K-Teacher-Ausbildung für Österreich.

Kim da Silva & Do-Ri Rydl freuen sich, wenn du ihnen von deinen Übungserfahrungen schreibst. Sie werden dir gerne antworten und auf Wunsch auch mehr Informationsmaterial über ihre Arbeit zusenden.
Schreibe an:

Kinesiologie-Zentrum
Do-Ri Rydl
Wiener Straße 80
A-2500 Baden

Kim da Silva
Türkenstraße 15
D-13 349 Berlin 65

EM·K
ETERNAL MOVEMENT
KINESIOLOGIE ZUR SELBSTHEILUNG

Versetzung gefährdet – was nun?
Rechtlicher Rahmen und Aufgaben der Eltern

Wenn die Versetzung eines Kindes gefährdet ist, sind auch seine Eltern gefordert. Auf jeden Fall ist es sinnvoll, daß Schule und Elternhaus dieses Problem gemeinsam erörtern, nach den Ursachen fragen und nach Abhilfe suchen. Sie als Eltern sollten nicht nur über den rechtlichen Rahmen zur Leistungsbeurteilung und Versetzung informiert sein; Sie sollten auch wissen, was Sie selbst unternehmen können, um das festgefahrene Schiff wieder in besseres Fahrwasser zu lenken.

Rechtlicher Rahmen
Auskunft über die jeweils gültigen Rechtsvorschriften zur Leistungsbeurteilung und Versetzung können Eltern in den Amtsblättern und dem Staatsanzeiger nachlesen, die bei jedem Schulleiter sowie dem Schulamt einzusehen sind.
Da für jedes Bundesland eigene Vorschriften existieren, möchte ich die Ausgestaltung des rechtlichen Rahmens am Beispiel des Hessischen Schulrechtes (Quelle: Dienst- und Schulrecht Hessen, GEW-Handbuch, völlig neubearbeitete Ausgabe, Stand März 1994) erörtern.
Wird eine Leistung im Zeugnis mit schlechter als der Note „ausreichend" bewertet, so entscheidet die einfache Mehrheit der **Versetzungskonferenz** über die Versetzung oder Nichtversetzung der Schülerin oder des Schülers. Zur Teilnahme ist jeder Lehrer, der die Schülerin oder den Schüler im laufenden Schuljahr oder vor einem Lehrerwechsel unterrichtet hat und wer die Schülerin oder den Schüler vor einem Lehrerwechsel im laufenden Schuljahr zuletzt unterrichtet hat und noch der Schule angehört, verpflichtet (a.a.O., Abt. 5, § 12,2):

> *„Die Versetzungsentscheidung wird aus* ***pädagogischer Verantwortung und frei von Schematismus getroffen****. Grundlage sind die Leistungen und die Entwicklung der Schülerin oder des Schülers während des ganzen Schuljahres (a.a.O.; Abt. 5, § 11,2)."*

Verschlechtert sich die Schülerin oder der Schüler in einem Fach von einem auf das nächste Schulhalbjahr, so ist dies von der Fachlehrerin oder dem Fachlehrer in der Versetzungskonferenz zu begründen.
Verlauf und Ergebnisse der Versetzungskonferenz werden im **Protokoll** festgehalten, welches jederzeit von den Eltern eingesehen werden kann.

> *„Eine Note schlechter als ausreichend in einem Fach oder Lernbereich kann nur durch die Note befriedigend oder besser in einem anderen Fach oder Lernbereich ausgeglichen werden (a.a.O., Abt. 5, Anlage 1; 11,2)."*

Zusätzlich gilt für Schülerinnen und Schüler an Gymnasien und Realschulen: Schlechter als mit der Note „ausreichend" beurteilte Leistungen in einem der Fächer Deutsch, erste Fremdsprache (für Gymnasiasten auch die zweite Fremdsprache) und Mathematik hindern eine Versetzung dann nicht, wenn die Schülerin oder der Schüler **besondere Fähigkeiten und starken Arbeitswillen** in einem anderen dieser o.g. Fächer oder in mehreren anderen Unterrichtsfächern erkennen läßt. Dies könnte unter Umständen durch die Note „befriedigend" gegeben sein.
Mehr als zwei mit schlechter als der Note „ausreichend" beurteilte Leistungen in den Fächern Deutsch, erste Fremdsprache (für Gymnasiasten auch die zweite Fremdsprache) und Mathematik können in der Regel nicht ausgeglichen werden (a.a.O., Abt. 5, Anlage 1).
In den Jahrgangsstufen 7 bis 10 ist eine **nachträgliche Versetzung** möglich:

„Wird eine Schülerin oder ein Schüler auf Grund schlechter als ausreichend bewerteter Leistungen im Zeugnis in zwei Fächern oder Lernbereichen nicht versetzt, so kann die Versetzungskonferenz die Schülerin oder den Schüler zu einer ***Nachprüfung*** *in einem der zwei Fächer oder Lernbereiche innerhalb der ersten sechs Unterrichtstage des neuen Schuljahres dann zulassen, wenn bei schlechter als ausreichend bewerteter Leistungen in nur einem Fach oder Lernbereich die Versetzung möglich gewesen wäre (a.a.O., Abt. 5, § 16,3)."*

Aufgaben der Eltern
Einfühlungsvermögen und Kommunikationbereitschaft sind grundlegende Eigenschaften von Eltern, die bereit sind, sich frühzeitig mit schulischen Mißerfolgen ihres Kindes auseinanderzusetzen.
Eltern mit solchen Grundeinstellungen sind eher in der Lage, Warnsignale rechtzeitig zu erkennen, um ihrem Kind in schwierigen Schulsituationen rechtzeitig zu helfen.

Ist die „Fünf" in der Klassenarbeit ein Ausrutscher oder schon ein Warnzeichen?

Suchen Sie dazu das **sachliche Gespräch mit Ihrem Kind**, um gemeinsam über Gründe des Mißerfolges nachzudenken und nach Lösungen zu suchen!
Darüber hinaus kann ein **Gespräch mit der unterrichtenden Lehrerin oder dem unterrichtenden Lehrer** zu wichtigen Erkenntnissen führen. Die Sprechstunden der Lehrerinnen und Lehrer während des Schuljahres werden kaum wahrgenommen. Das Gespräch wird meistens dann gesucht, wenn es bereits „zu spät" ist.

Bei **anhaltenden Mißerfolgen** müssen sich die Eltern fragen:

Ist mein Kind in dieser Klasse mit dem jetzigen Lernstoff überfordert?

Langfristige Überforderungen führen in der Regel zu psychischen Verletzungen des Kindes; ständige Mißerfolge kratzen am Selbstwertgefühl und wirken demotivierend. Die Familienatmosphäre ist zumeist auch in Mitleidenschaft gezogen.
Dabei sollte es das Ziel der Eltern sein, ihrem Kind aus der Zone der Mißerfolge herauszuhelfen, damit es bei Erfolgen wieder Lob und Anerkennung erfahren kann.
Dazu könnte unter Umständen die **Änderung des Schul- und Ausbildungsweges** erforderlich sein. Vielleicht nimmt aber schon ein **rechtzeitiges Zurückgehen** Ihres Kindes in die vorhergehende Jahrgangsstufe den störenden psychischen Druck.

Sollte eine schlechte Note auf kurz- bzw. mittelfristig zu schließende Lücken oder Defizite im lernmethodischen Bereich zurückzuführen sein, können – bei Bereitschaft des Kindes – **außerschulische Förderungsmaßnahmen** (z. B. Lernhilfen, Nachhilfe, Kurse „Das Lernen lernen") sinnvoll bzw. erfolgreich eingesetzt werden.

Hedi Jantsch
Vorsitzende des Schulelternbeirates
am Friedrichsgymnasium Kassel

„Nicht genügend"!
Was können Eltern dagegen tun?
Pädagogische Aspekte und rechtliche Situation in Österreich

Der pädagogische Beurteilungsspielraum

Die Bestimmungen des Schulunterrichtsgesetzes über die Leistungsbeurteilung an den Schulen zielen einmal darauf ab, ein höchstmögliches Ausmaß an Objektivität zu gewährleisten, sind doch oft sehr wesentliche Berechtigungen an das Bestehen oder Nichtbestehen einer Prüfung geknüpft. Andererseits wird auch der Umstand berücksichtigt, daß eine Leistungsbeurteilung in der Schule immer auch eine pädagogische Maßnahme ist. Es würde sich eher ungünstig auf die Motivation der Kinder auswirken, wenn der nachlässige Schüler auf Grund seiner Begabung leicht zu guten Beurteilungen kommen würde, der strebsame Jugendliche aber immer nur eine unerfreuliche Beurteilung erhalten könnte. Jeder würde im Laufe der Zeit seine Bemühungen einstellen, wenn er sähe, daß er das gewünschte Ziel niemals erreichen kann. Oder umgekehrt, warum sollte sich ein begabtes Kind anstrengen, wenn es auch ohne jede Mühe Anerkennung fände. Das Schulunterrichtsgesetz hat daher dem Lehrer in einigen Bereichen einen „pädagogischen Beurteilungsspielraum" eingeräumt.
Ein Lehrer wird diesen vor allem dadurch nützen, daß er die Mitarbeit des Schülers im Unterricht, seine Bemühungen bei der Anfertigung der Hausaufgaben – so wie es im § 3 der Verordnung über die Leistungsbeurteilung festgelegt ist – gleichwertig in die Gesamtbeurteilung einbezieht. Hier hat der Lehrer die Chance, ausgleichend, motivierend, ermutigend die Leistungsbeurteilung mit seinem pädagogischen Auftrag zu verbinden. Es wäre pädagogisch unklug und widerspräche den Bestimmungen des Schulunterrichtsgesetzes, wenn nur die Schularbeiten zur Leistungsbeurteilung herangezogen würden.

Die Informationspflicht des Lehrers

In engem Zusammenhang mit diesen Bestimmungen ist die vorgeschriebene Transparenz zu sehen. Eine pädagogische Maßnahme kann nur dann eine günstige Auswirkung haben, wenn der Schüler Informationen darüber erhält, inwieweit es ihm gelungen ist, Leistungen nachzuweisen, etwa bei der Wiederholung oder Erarbeitung neuer Lehrstoffe. Positive Rückmeldungen in diesem Bereich werden auch den schwachen Schüler veranlassen, sich lebhaft am Unterricht zu beteiligen, was sich im allgemeinen längerfristig auch positiv auf die Ergebnisse der Schularbeiten auswirken wird.
Der Lehrer ist verpflichtet, Aufzeichnungen im erforderlichen Ausmaß anzufertigen, Schüler und Eltern haben ein Recht auf Transparenz.

Was darf geprüft werden?

Grundsätzlich darf nur das geprüft werden, was im Lehrplan steht (Schulbücher gehen oft weit über die Anforderungen des Lehrplans hinaus!) und was bis zum Prüfungszeitpunkt durchgenommen wurde.

Die Benotung

Bei der Festsetzung einer Note für ein gesamtes Schuljahr hat der Lehrer alle im Laufe des Jahres erbrachten mündlichen wie schriftlichen Leistungen (nicht Leistungsbeurteilungen) zu berücksichtigen. Die vielgeübte Praxis, einfach eine Durchschnittsnote zu bilden, entspricht nicht den Bestimmungen des Schulunterrichtsgesetzes, schon gar nicht, wenn dazu nur die Ergebnisse der Schularbeiten herangezogen werden. Es geht vielmehr darum, am Ende des Schuljahres zu beurteilen, ob der Schüler durch seine Leistungen gezeigt hat, daß er das, was im Unterricht durchgenommen wurde (und was auch im Lehrplan vorgesehen ist), wenigstens überwiegend kann. Wie und bei welcher Gelegenheit, ob im Rahmen der mündlichen Mitarbeit, etwa bei der Lösung einer Aufgabe an der Tafel oder bei einer

Schularbeit oder bei einer mündlichen Prüfung, Leistungen nachgewiesen wurden, ist dabei unerheblich. Alle erbrachten Leistungen müssen gleichwertig herangezogen werden.

Ein Lehrer wird eine Leistung mit **„Gut"** oder **„Sehr gut"** beurteilen, wenn ein Schüler über das Wesentliche hinaus oder weit über das Wesentliche hinaus Leistungen erbringt.

Ein Lehrer wird eine Leistung mit **„Befriedigend"** beurteilen, wenn der Schüler den Anforderungen in den „wesentlichen Bereichen" entsprochen hat. Ein **„Genügend"** signalisiert hingegen, daß der Schüler in den „wesentlichen Bereichen" Lücken hat. Er hat den Anforderungen nur überwiegend entsprochen. Gerade in den sogenannten aufbauenden Gegenständen, in denen der neue Lehrstoff auf Vorkenntnissen aufbaut, kann das fatale Folgen haben. Hat zum Beispiel das Kind in der Unterstufe des Gymnasiums in Mathematik nur lückenhafte Kenntnisse erworben, sind Schwierigkeiten in der Oberstufe fast vorprogrammiert. Ein „Genügend" genügt also nicht immer! Der Lehrer wird Auskunft darüber erteilen, wo diese Lücken sind und wie man sie möglichst schnell schließen kann.
Ein **„Nicht genügend"** erhält ein Schüler dann, wenn es ihm nicht gelungen ist, den Anforderungen in den „wesentlichen Bereichen" wenigstens überwiegend zu entsprechen. Was sind nun die sogenannten „wesentlichen Bereiche"? Das Bundesministerium für Unterricht und Kunst vertritt hier die Meinung, daß ein Lehrer dies im Laufe des Unterrichtsjahres selbst zu definieren hat. Es ist jedenfalls nicht zulässig und widerspräche dem Grundsatz der Transparenz, erst nach einer Prüfung zu sagen, was wesentlich und was unwesentlich gewesen wäre. Gegen ein „Nicht genügend" bei einer Schularbeit oder bei einer Prüfung können Eltern keine Berufung einlegen, auch wenn diese Note als ungerecht empfunden wird. Ein Schüler, der sich über eine verpatzte Schularbeit ärgert, hat jedenfalls das Recht, sich einmal im Semester in jedem Gegenstand zu einer mündlichen Prüfung zu melden.

Meinem Kind droht ein „Nicht genügend". Was soll ich tun?
Für Eltern ist es wichtig zu analysieren, worauf ein so umfangreiches Versagen des Kindes zurückzuführen ist. Hat nur das eigene Kind versagt oder der größte Teil der Klasse? Hat das Kind sich mit dem nötigen Fleiß vorbereitet oder nicht? Haben vorübergehende physische oder psychische Probleme zu einem eher einmaligen Versagen geführt? Zu einer objektiven Klärung der Ursachen führt in erster Linie ein Gespräch mit dem zuständigen Lehrer, auch ein Kontakt mit anderen Eltern der Klasse kann hilfreich sein. Führt dies nicht zu einer befriedigenden Antwort, kann die kostenlose Hilfe des schulpsychologischen Dienstes in Anspruch genommen werden. Durch entsprechende Tests kann der Schulpsychologe herausfinden, ob das Kind in einer seiner Begabung entsprechenden Schule ist, oder ob ein Schulwechsel auf Grund der Begabungsrichtung für das Kind nicht besser wäre.
Eltern mögen bedenken, daß sich hinter einem sogenannten „faulen Kind" nur allzuoft ein Schüler verbirgt, der den Anforderungen nicht genügen kann oder dies jedenfalls von sich selbst glaubt. Es ist oft weniger diskriminierend, faul als dumm zu sein. Eine rasche Klärung und eine vernünftige Reaktion der Eltern werden dem Schüler helfen, ein gesundes Selbstwertgefühl aufzubauen. Schulische Erfolge werden sich so viel leichter einstellen. Kein Kind mit einem „Nicht genügend" fühlt sich besonders wohl. Auch ein Schüler, der seine Pflichten versäumt hat, benötigt Hilfe und Informationen, wie die Lücken geschlossen werden können, Hilfe bei der Zeitplanung und bei der Beschaffung von Lernunterlagen, mit denen das Kind selbständig arbeiten kann. Lob und Anerkennung für die ersten kleinen Erfolge helfen dem Kind mehr als Vorhaltungen. Ein Nachhilfelehrer sollte nicht gleich bestellt werden, kurzfristige Erfolge könnten längerfristig dazu führen, daß sich ein Kind an Hilfe gewöhnt und womöglich zu dem Ergenbis kommt, daß es alleine zu guten Leistungen nicht fähig ist.
Sollten alle Schüler einer Klasse mehr oder weniger nur genügende oder nicht genügende Leistungen erbringen, und sollte dies wiederholt geschehen, ist der zuständige

Elternvertreter aufgerufen, mit dem Lehrer und – wenn dies nichts fruchtet – auch mit der Schulaufsicht Kontakt aufzunehmen. Einerseits kann auf Dauer nicht hingenommen werden, daß den Schülern nur lückenhafte Kenntnisse vermittelt werden können, andererseits sind negative Auswirkungen auf die Motivation zu befürchten. Die Schüler könnten „lernen", daß alle Anstrengungen doch nur zu einer schlechten Beurteilung führen, und in ihrem Fleiß nachlassen.

Was soll mein Kind tun?
Meldet sich ein Schüler bei einem drohenden „Nicht genügend" zu einer mündlichen Prüfung, wird ihm der Lehrer die Gelegenheit einräumen, Leistungen in den „wesentlichen Bereichen" nachzuweisen, wo dies dem Schüler bislang nicht möglich war. Eine umgekehrte Vorgangsweise wäre schikanös und anfechtbar. Wenn es dem Schüler gelingt, zu den bisher erbrachten Leistungen, die für ein „Genügend" noch nicht ausreichten, zusätzliche Leistungen nachzuweisen, wodurch die Anforderungen in den „wesentlichen Bereichen" nunmehr überwiegend erfüllt werden, so ist ein „Genügend" zu erteilen.
Bei allzu großen Lücken, die im Laufe eines ganzen Jahres entstanden sind, wird es aber eher aussichtlos sein, im Rahmen einer einzigen mündlichen Prüfung, deren Dauer auf 10 bzw. 15 Minuten begrenzt ist, nachzuweisen, daß alle Lernrückstände aufgeholt wurden. Schüler neigen dazu, allzu große Hoffnungen auf diese letzte Prüfung zu setzen. Nur bei einem geringen Rückstand besteht die Möglichkeit einer Notenkorrektur.

„Nicht genügend". Kann mein Kind trotzdem aufsteigen?
Grundsätzlich sind Schüler mit einem „Nicht genügend" nicht zu einem Aufsteigen in die nächste Klasse berechtigt. Ganz im Sinne seiner pädagogischen Ausrichtung sieht das Schulunterrichtsgesetz jedoch eine wichtige Ausnahme vor.
Hat der Schüler nicht bereits im vorigen Jahr im gleichen Gegenstand ein „Nicht genügend", und ist dieses Fach weiter im Lehrplan vorgesehen, kann die Klassenkonferenz, in der alle Lehrer vertreten sind, die in der Klasse unterrichten, beschließen, den Schüler aufsteigen zu lassen. Voraussetzung für eine positive Entscheidung ist, daß die Leistungen in allen anderen Fächern so gut sind, daß der Schüler aller Voraussicht nach im kommenden Jahr erfolgreich am Unterricht teilnehmen kann.
Der Gesetzgeber geht hier davon aus, daß die Leistungsreserven eines Schülers begrenzt sind. Die Lehrer einer Klasse müssen gemeinsam eine Prognose darüber abgeben, ob ein Schüler die Lücken in einem mit „Nicht genügend" beurteilten Gegenstand bei fortschreitendem Unterricht im folgenden Schuljahr angesichts der Situation in den anderen Fächern wird aufholen können:
Wieviele mit „Genügend" beurteilte Gegenstände enthält das Jahreszeugnis?
Hat ein solches „Genügend" eher eine Tendenz zum „Nicht genügend" oder zum „Befriedigend"?
Reichen die Kenntnisse in einem mit „Genügend" beurteilten Fach aus, oder müssen auch hier erst Lücken geschlossen werden, um dem Unterricht im kommenden Schuljahr folgen zu können. (Ein schwaches „Genügend" steht einem Aufsteigen in die nächste Klasse dann nicht entgegen, wenn zum Beispiel in Geographie Kenntnisse in Gesteinskunde fehlen, im nächsten Jahr aber die Wirtschaftsräume auf dem Programm stehen.)
Hat ein ansonsten zufriedenstellend arbeitender Jugendlicher aus besonderen Gründen (zum Beispiel Scheidung der Eltern, schwere Erkrankung) nur vorübergehend nachgelassen und steht zu erwarten, daß er leistungsstark genug ist, die Defizite aufzuholen?
Die Lehrer werden auf Grund ihrer Erfahrung und ihres Sachverstandes zu einer vertretbaren, sinnvollen Lösung kommen.

Die Berufung
Eltern können gegen die fehlende Berechtigung zum Aufsteigen in die nächste Klasse berufen und dabei das „Nicht genügend" und die Entscheidung der Klassenkonferenz anfechten. Aussichten für eine erfolgreiche Berufung sind dann gegeben, wenn Eltern bei

einem „Nicht genügend" darlegen können, daß sachfremde Gründe, etwa disziplinäre Schwierigkeiten, bei der Beurteilung eine Rolle gespielt haben, die geforderten Kenntnisse aber sehr wohl vorhanden sind. Es ist sicher nicht einzusehen, daß in einem solchen Fall ein Kind nur wegen seines unangenehmen Verhaltens ein ganzes Jahr wiederholen soll. Manchmal können auch reine Formfehler eines Lehrers dazu führen, daß ein „Nicht genügend" aufgehoben wird. Lehrer sind keine Juristen und sollten es wohl auch nicht sein. Ein so erfochtener Erfolg ist in der Regel kein Erfolg für das Kind. Die Lernrückstände des Kindes werden so nicht geschlossen, und ein vertrauensvolles Klima der Zusammenarbeit zwischen Eltern, Lehrern und dem Schüler könnte nachhaltig gestört werden.

Gegen den Beschluß der Klassenkonferenz könnte erfolgreich eingewandt werden:

– daß außergewöhnliche Belastungen des Kindes nicht berücksichtigt wurden, besonders, wenn gegen Ende des Schuljahres wieder eine steigende Tendenz erkennbar war;

– daß die fehlenden Kenntnisse in einem mit „Genügend" beurteilten Fach im folgenden Jahr keine Rolle mehr spielen oder nicht grundlegend für das Verständnis des Lehrstoffes im kommenden Schuljahr sein werden. Nicht erfolgreich sind meistens Berufungen, die sich auf einen Notenvergleich mit anderen Schülern beziehen.

Berufungen sind formlos. Ein einfacher Brief an die Schule genügt, in dem zum Ausdruck gebracht wird, daß man gegen die Nichtberechtigung zum Aufsteigen in die nächste Klasse beruft und das „Nicht genügend" und (oder) den Beschluß der Klassenkonferenz nicht für gerechtfertigt hält. Die Chancen steigen mit einer möglichst sachlichen Begründung. Die Schule leitet die Berufung an den Landesschulrat weiter. Dieser kann entweder auf Grund der vorgelegten Unterlagen entscheiden oder, wenn diese nicht ausreichen, kurzfristig eine kommissionelle Prüfung unter dem Vorsitz eines Schulaufsichtsbeamten durchführen. Der gesamte Jahresstoff kann Gegenstand einer solchen Prüfung sein. An dieser Stelle sei noch einmal darauf hingewiesen, daß das wichtigste Kriterium für eine Berufung die abgesicherte Überzeugung der Eltern sein sollte, daß das Kind über die erforderlichen Kenntnisse verfügt.

Gegen die Entscheidung des Landesschulrates ist eine Berufung beim Bundesministerium für Unterricht und Kunst möglich. Es kann sinnvoll sein, wenn eine auch räumlich weiter entfernte Behörde die Angelegenheit noch einmal prüft. Immerhin werden im Schnitt ca. 25% der dort eingelangten Berufungen positiv entschieden.

Ingrid Buschmann
Pressesprecherin des Bundesverbandes der Elternvereinigungen an Höheren und Mittleren Schulen Österreichs

DURCHSTARTEN

weitere Bände für:

Deutsch
für die 5. Schulstufe
ISBN 3-85303-014-9

für die 6. Schulstufe
ISBN 3-85303-015-7

für die 7. Schulstufe ☆
ISBN 3-85303-044-0

für die 8. Schulstufe ☆
ISBN 3-85303-116-1

Mathematik
für die 5. Schulstufe
ISBN 3-85303-018-1 (Ö)
ISBN 3-85303-081-5 (D)

für die 6. Schulstufe
ISBN 3-85303-046-7 (Ö)
ISBN 3-85303-094-7 (D) ●

für die 7. Schulstufe ☆
ISBN 3-85303-117-X (Ö)

Englisch
für die 5. Schulstufe
ISBN 3-85303-016-5

für die 6. Schulstufe
ISBN 3-85303-017-3

für die 7. Schulstufe
ISBN 3-85303-045-9

für die 8. Schulstufe ●
ISBN 3-85303-110-2

je
ca. 160 Seiten mit Lösungsheft
durchgehend witzig und farbig
illustriert, Paperback
DM 26,80/öS 198,–/sfr 26,80

Französisch
für das 1. Lernjahr
ISBN 3-85303-019-X

für das 2. Lernjahr
Teil A:
Adjektiv, Adverb ●
und Hervorhebung
von Satzteilen
ISBN 3-85303-108-0

Teil B:
Verb, Bindungsgefüge ●
und indirekte Rede
ISBN 3-85303-109-9

● **erscheint im Frühjahr 1996**

☆ **erscheint im Herbst 1996**

Zum Lernen motivieren

Ausgehend von den beliebten „Durchstartübungen" bietet das Buch eine ausführliche Gebrauchsanweisung zu den lerngymnastischen Übungen. **Energietanken pur** sozusagen. Darüber hinaus zeigen die beiden Autoren **Übungen, die mental besonders fit machen** und Lernen als positive Aufgabe erleben lassen:

- **Fit und stabil jeden Tag.** Turnübungen am Morgen für mehr Energie tagsüber.
- **Den inneren Widerstand überwinden.** Cool werden und Lust aufs Lernen bekommen.
- **Die Feuerwehr.** „Dampfablassen-Übungen" gegen schlechte Laune.
- **Kreativ lernen.** Zusammenhänge besser begreifen und nützen.
- **Eine gute Schrift haben.** Übungen zur Feinmotorik.
- **Jetzt geht's los!** Übungen zum Einschalten für den Sport.
- **Kreativ lernen für bestimmte Fächer.** Gezielte Übungen für Deutsch, Englisch, Französisch, Mathematik und Latein.

Einfach ausprobieren – Erfolg garantiert!

zahlreiche Fotos
und Illustrationen,
ca. 120 Seiten, Paperback
ca. DM 26,80/öS 198,–/sfr 26,80
ISBN 3-85303-079-3

KERLE

STICHWORTVERZEICHNIS